Critical Essays

on Education, Modernity, and the
Recovery of the Ecological Imperative

Critical Essays

on Education, Modernity, and the Recovery of the Ecological Imperative

C. A. Bowers

Teachers College, Columbia University
New York and London

Published by Teachers College Press, 1234 Amsterdam Avenue
New York, New York

The painting on the cover of the paperback edition is *Minnow, 1957* (tempera on
paper) by Morris Graves, photographed in black and white by Paul Neevel with
the permission of the University of Oregon Museum of Art.

Library of Congress Cataloging-in-Publication Data

Bowers, C. A.
    Critical essays on education, modernity, and the recovery of the ·
    ecological imperative / C. A. Bowers.
        p.   cm.
    Includes bibliographical references (p.   ) and index.
    ISBN 0-8077-324 (alk. paper).—ISBN 0-8077-3244-3 (pbk: alk. paper)
    1. Education—Social aspects.   2. Educational anthropology.
3. Deep ecology.   4. Computers—Social aspects.   5. Intercultural
education.   6. Education—Philosophy.   I. Title.
LC191.B6736   1993
370.19—dc20   93-18527

ISBN 0-8077-3245-1
ISBN 0-8077-3244-3 (pbk.)

Printed on acid-free paper
Manufactured in the United States of America
99 98 97 96 95 94 93   7 6 5 4 3 2 1

Contents

Acknowledgments

The articles in this collection first appeared in the following publications: "Cultural Literacy in Developed Countries," *Prospects* (1977); "Curriculum as Cultural Reproduction: An Examination of Metaphor as a Carrier of Ideology," *Teachers College Record* (Winter 1980); "Linguistic Roots of Cultural Invasion in Paulo Freire's Pedagogy," *Teachers College Record* (Summer 1983); "The Dialectic of Nihilism and the State: Implications for an Emancipatory Theory of Education," *Educational Theory* (Summer 1986); "Teaching a Nineteenth-Century Pattern of Thinking through a Twentieth-Century Machine," *Educational Theory* (February 1988); "How Computers Contribute to the Ecological Crisis," *The Trumpeter* (Winter 1991); "Ideology, Educational Computing, and the Moral Poverty of the Information Age," *Australian Educational Computing* (May 1992); "A Batesonian Perspective on Education and the Bonds of Language: Cultural Literacy in the Technological Age," *Studies in the Humanities* (December 1988); "Implications of Gregory Bateson's Ideas for a Semiotic of Art Education," *Studies in Art Education* (Winter 1990); "The Anthropocentric Foundations of Educational Liberalism: Some Critical Concerns," *The Trumpeter* (Summer 1991). I wish to thank the editors for their original support and for granting the right to publish the articles here.

Preface

The scope of the environmental/population crisis brings into question the adequacy of Western culture and the assumptions upon which it rests. Of particular concern are the cultural assumptions underlying the belief system of the developed countries whose technologies and patterns of consumer-oriented living are depleting the world's energy resources at an alarming rate.

These opening sentences from the first essay in this collection, published in 1977 and intended as a summary of the main arguments in *Cultural Literacy for Freedom* (1974), introduce the two main concerns that tie together this collection of essays. These two concerns—the danger of actually destroying the life-sustaining ecosystems and the culturally specific assumptions underlying modern consciousness that reframed the spatial and temporal aspects of individualism to fit the current myth of technological progress—have framed my analysis of educational issues over the last 15 years. They also put me at odds both with the mainstream technocratically oriented educators and with radical educational reformers who were promoting, as I saw it, contrary aspects of modern culture. The former equated increased efficiency and predictability of outcome (and now the ability to manipulate data) with progress, while the latter called for structural changes in society and pedagogical reforms that would liberate individuals from myriad forms of social oppression. During the 1970s and 1980s it was fashionable to question the technocrat's vision of educational and social progress, but to suggest that the educational radical's view of progress was equally problematic (albeit for different reasons) seemed beyond the pale of legitimate educational criticism.

It now seems a more propitious time to bring together a collection of essays that clarify how the beliefs and values reinforced through the educational process, as well as those that would result from proposed educational reforms, contribute to deepening the ecological crisis. With the explanatory power of Marxism greatly diminished by the internally borne ennui of a 20-year-old movement, along with recent events in

Eastern Europe, radical educational theorists have turned elsewhere for new ways to frame their vision of an emancipatory form of education. But the recent questioning attitude toward the foundations of modernity and increasing concern with the deeper implications of a multicultural society have helped, more than anything else, to create a more receptive atmosphere for grounding educational and social theory in a deep understanding of the culture/language/thought connection. The near daily media accounts and scholarly books documenting the rapid destruction of the world's ecosystems now add a greater sense of urgency for clarifying the role that education can play in the development of more ecologically sustainable cultural patterns. In effect, the need I identified in 1974 for addressing the educational/cultural aspects of the ecological crisis can no longer be avoided.

The essays in this volume are grouped together in three categories: Rethinking the Foundations of Modernism, Cultural Mediating Characteristics of Educational Computing, and Recovering the Ecological Imperative in Educational and Social Thought. These categories, or what should more properly be called themes, reflect three distinct phases of thought that began with the first attempt to frame the educational/cultural aspects of the ecological crisis in terms of a sociology-of-knowledge account of how the educational process reproduces, as part of the student's taken-for-granted way of knowing, cultural patterns that are environmentally destructive. This part of the analysis still seems essentially correct, but in *Cultural Literacy for Freedom* (Bowers, 1974) there was also a strong emphasis on the importance of the student's existential freedom. The freedom to define the nature and limits of individual responsibility was to be increased by making explicit the otherwise hidden cultural patterns that are ecologically problematic. This collection of essays represents the intellectual path taken after it became clear to me that the existential view of human freedom cannot be defended in terms of a deep understanding of culture or used as a basis for addressing the ecological crisis.

As in any human activity, the effort that goes into serious writing is never entirely an individual activity. The graduate students at the University of Oregon as well as colleagues with whom I have had extended intellectual exchanges—Ron Scollon and Suzanne Wong Scollon, Alan Mandell, Ted D'Urso, Annie Herda, Karen Hamblen, and, more recently, Kathleen Kesson and William Doll, Jr., to cite just a few—have had an important influence on the direction of my thinking. A more immediate source of influence includes the ongoing conversations with my wife, Mary Katharine Bowers. The encouragement of Brian Ellerbeck to publish this collection of essays with Teachers College Press, as well as his insightful editorial judgments, has also been a valued influence.

Critical Essays

on Education, Modernity, and the
Recovery of the Ecological Imperative

Part I

RETHINKING THE FOUNDATIONS OF MODERNISM

With the exception of "Cultural Literacy in Developed Countries," which appeared in the UNESCO journal *Prospects,* the three other essays in this section were published in mainstream educational journals. What is distinctive about these essays is the argument that radical critics of mainstream educational thought and practice were themselves embracing, in formulaic fashion, other aspects of the modern agenda. For several years in the early 1980s, it seemed that with such extreme forms of modernity being advocated, issues relating to how educators could be more responsive to the cultural aspects of the ecological crisis had to be temporarily set aside. For example, the Marxist analysis of how curriculum is part of the social reproduction process that sustains a class society also included a vision of a new social order characterized by individual freedom and equality. The inability of radical educational critics to address the vexing problem of imposing a Marxist interpretation of the Enlightenment vision on non-Western cultural groups seemed to bring into the open the even deeper problem of using a conduit view of language to articulate an emancipatory theory of education. Metaphors like "freedom," "oppression," and "equality" (like the technicist metaphors of "efficiency" and "rationality") were being used as though they had the same meaning to every cultural group. One of the purposes of the essay examining the metaphorical nature of the language/thought connection, and how language encodes the schemata (ideological orientation) of a cultural group, was to clarify for both radical and more mainstream educators the dangers of basing theory and classroom practices on a conduit view of language. Radical educational theorists continued to ignore the problem, but the essay served later as a basis for considering how ecologically disruptive beliefs and values are encoded in the metaphorical language of classroom socialization.

Two other essays in this section, "Linguistic Roots of Cultural Invasion in Paulo Freire's Pedagogy" and "The Dialectic of Nihilism and the State: Implications for an Emancipatory Theory of Education," represent two other challenges to the ideology of modernism being promoted by radical educational thinkers. The main arguments in both essays challenge the ortho-

1

doxy of using the educational process to promote a form of self-determining individualism. The problem in terms of Freire's thinking is not the use of a literacy program to address forms of economic and political oppression, but rather his philosophic anthropology, which leads him to equate the individual autonomy attained through critical reflection with becoming human. The basic criticism of his position is that his fusion of Marxism and the existential view of "man" leads to a form of pedagogy that fosters a Western type of individualism. To put it another way, Freire is an Enlightenment thinker who universalizes the view that rationality is the source of individual empowerment and that change (when directed by critical reflection) is inherently progressive. Armed with the godwords of the Enlightenment, Freire and his followers fail to recognize how their own vision can become a form of domination for non-Western cultural groups. If I were writing a new critique of Freire's ideas it would include the criticism that he continues as an anthropocentric thinker who has taken a generation of largely unquestioning followers into an ideological cul-de-sac that prevents them from addressing ecological concerns.

The essay on "The Dialectic of Nihilism and the State" addresses one of the generally overlooked political implications of making the emancipated individual the primary goal of education; namely, the seeming paradox whereby the emergence of the type of individualism valued by both radical critics and technicists, who actually dominate educational reform at the classroom level, has been accompanied by the extension of the power of the state into more areas of daily life. As the argument goes, the centralization and expansion of state power is facilitated by a society of individuals whose sense of authority (and memory) are not embedded in the patterns of a close-knit cultural group. Individuals who chose their own values and formulate their own ideas (which are two of the more bedrock myths of liberalism) will be more susceptible to manipulation than people whose identity and values are intertwined in what Robert Bellah has called a "community of memory." This essay succeeds in putting into focus one of the more critical, unintended consequences of promoting part of a universalized ideological vision, but it stops short of posing the question of whether it is through the actions of the state or a restored sense of community that we have the best chance of mitigating the destructiveness of our impact on the environment. At this point, my attempts to reframe how the more extreme problems associated with modernization should be addressed through the educational process were still influenced by an anthropocentric way of thinking. I was attempting to understand the "individual" as a cultural and linguistic being; it was not until I understood Gregory Bateson's ecology of mind that I was able to avoid the conceptual limitations of this aspect of modern consciousness.

Chapter 1

Cultural Literacy in Developed Countries

The scope of the environmental/population crisis brings into question the adequacy of Western culture and the assumptions upon which it rests. Of particular concern are the cultural assumptions underlying the belief systems of the developed countries whose technologies and patterns of consumer-oriented living are depleting the world's energy resources at an alarming rate. The core values of this belief system—abstract rational thought, efficiency, individualism, profits—were at one time believed to be the wellspring of individual and social progress. But in societies such as the United States and Canada, where these values have evolved to the point of creating technologically oriented cultures, the sense of progress is being badly eroded.

The elaboration and extension of technology into all spheres of social life has produced disturbing consequences: It has increased the momentum of consumerism by inventing and shaping human needs in accordance with the needs of production and profits; through the ever-increasing use of scientific management, it has increased alienation in work settings by separating the physical from the mental aspects of work, with the latter increasingly being taken over as a function of the managerial class; it has fostered a form of atomistic individualism that has become increasingly powerless to reverse the more detrimental technological developments; and it has fostered the growth of bureaucracy as a means of dealing with the socially disruptive consequences of technology. As these core cultural beliefs are often associated with modernization, the more industrially developed countries find themselves in a tragic double bind: The belief system that contributed to their high material standard of living is also threatening ecological disaster for everybody.

In order to illustrate the cultural roots of the crisis, this chapter will attempt to describe (1) how public education serves as a carrier of the cultural beliefs and values that make up the technological worldview; (2) how the school socialization process transmits social reality in a way that often obscures the underlying cultural assumptions; and (3) how the socialization process could be altered in developed societies in order to transmit the culture at a more explicit level of awareness. This process

3

of demystifying or uncovering the hidden aspects of the cultural belief system is an essential first step in the process of reconstituting those aspects of the culture that are at the root of the current crisis.

SCHOOL AS A CARRIER OF THE TECHNOLOGICAL WORLDVIEW

Because it is one of the most technologically evolved societies, the United States serves as an example of how public schools function as carriers of the values and beliefs characteristic of technological consciousness. Essentially, the values and beliefs that characterize technological consciousness evolved out of the generic liberal values upon which the United States was founded, most notably, the right of the individual to progress through rational effort and hard work. This vision has been transformed under the impact of the technological revolution into a new configuration that often emphasizes efficiency at the expense of human fulfillment, disrupts tradition with incessant change, and diminishes both individual experience and cultural events through the instantaneous availability of the media. A further analysis of how advanced technological consciousness organizes reality reveals a proclivity to think in terms of mechanisticity (seeing the work process tied to a machine process), reproducibility (seeing the work process as reproducible rather than as individually unique), measurability (seeing the areas of human experience as subject to evaluation in quantifiable terms only), componentiality (seeing everything as analyzable into constituent components that are interdependent), problem-solving inventiveness (seeing all areas of individual and social existence as subject to a tinkering attitude and in need of technological solutions), and the self-anonymization of the worker (learning to divide the self into component parts and to accept the human engineering process that organizes the self in terms of technological functions) (P. Berger, Berger, & Kellner, 1974). The continual use of the machine as a model, as represented in systems analysis, for organizing experience in the factory, office, classroom, and home indicates the growing pervasiveness of this mode of consciousness.

Although the recent history of American education is witness to a long series of reforms based on a technological form of consciousness (e.g., behavior modification, competency-based education, mastery teaching, and so forth), we shall focus on how social science textbooks reinforce this mode of thinking. The most traditional and effective carrier of technological consciousness remains the textbook, particularly the social studies textbooks used in the elementary grades. In the earliest grades students learn to see human "wants" in economic-consumer terms; competition as the source of winners in business, politics, and sports; and work as necessary activity that one performs in order to get money. Technology is not simply presented in textbooks; it is celebrated as one of the highest achievements of the nation. As one textbook put it: "The technological revolution is one of the most amazing episodes in the human adventure" (Education Research Council of America, 1972, p. 69). The same textbook gives the value of efficiency an ontological status, thus removing it from the realm of human doubt. To quote: "What makes one method of production replace other methods? The answer to this question is nearly always this: the successful method is more efficient than the others" (p. 65). This same textbook proceeds to dehumanize workers by representing them as part of the "input" that must be valued in terms of being part of the cost of production: "When economists speak of efficiency, they mean the relation of input to output. Input is the amount of labor, capital, raw materials, and managerial skill that goes into production. Output is the amount of goods produced" (p. 65).

While several excellent social studies curricula have recently been developed, the dominant trend is to use textbooks that instill unquestioning acceptance of the technological society. The recent federal policy in the United States to achieve a closer articulation between the classroom and the needs of the workplace symbolizes this trend. Essentially, this work-driven model of education represents the current function and structure of technology as a nonproblematic cornerstone of American life. Curriculum materials are thus designed to foster proper work attitudes in students—commitment to the values of trustworthiness, punctuality, thoroughness, and loyalty—and an understanding of the different work roles available to them when they leave school. They also teach students that one's success as a person is "measured largely by his success in his work," to quote a high school textbook used in California. Traditional class biases are reinforced through textbooks that inaccurately continue the folk myth that a blue-collar worker is a person "who works with his hands or body," while a white-collar worker is a "person who performs mental work." While the curriculum materials teach students to perceive work as a process determined by the economic imperative of profits and the dictates of technology, they remain silent about the sources of alienation in work, the cultural assumptions that underlie the relationship of work and technology, the alternative ways of organizing the process and governance of work that are being tried in other countries, and the relation between our technological-consumer driven form of culture and the ecological crisis.

CURRICULUM AS A PROCESS OF SOCIALIZATION

It is clear that public schools in the United States, as one of the primary carriers of technological consciousness, are not contributing to the solution of the ecological crises. Changes in education are indeed needed in other developed countries as well if these cultures based on resource depletion are to be reconstituted. But the changes must be grounded in an understanding of how the form of socialization carried on by schools shapes consciousness.

All communication that involves the sharing of meanings, assumptions, and definitions of how to think about reality is part of the process of primary socialization. This process goes on continually in classrooms at both implicit and explicit levels. The curriculum is intended to establish in the mind of the student "what is"; this is done at the most basic level by giving students the institutionally legitimated language to describe different aspects of experience. Along with language, which typifies and stabilizes meaning in accordance with other people's shared commonsense reality, the curriculum and teacher also transmit the socially shared interpretational rules and nuances of meaning necessary for relating what has been established as "what is" (e.g., nature of time, work, authority, shame, technology, etc.) to the rest of the individual's belief system. For example, a curriculum unit on "Human Wants" used in the United States typifies "wants" in terms of consumer needs; what one should legitimately "want" is further related to the question of how much money one has. As the student's explanatory framework (vocabulary, theories, and interpretational rules) is built up and sustained through interaction with the teacher and curriculum material, he or she learns to perceive and interpret social reality in a manner that conforms with the dominant society that the school and its personnel reflect.

Not all of the socialization process carried on in the classroom is new. The student comes to school with tacit/contextual knowledge of many aspects of the culture that has been learned through interaction with others. But in many cases students are unable to identify and think about the discrete objects, relationships, and processes that make up the flow of cultural experience they have learned to take for granted. What the school does, in effect, is provide the symbolic tools for thinking about the culture students experience at the contextual level of social interaction. When the school presents the students with the language and explanations that further represent the culture at the taken-for-granted level (e.g., identifying technology with progress, work with money and consumerism, competition with winning, etc.), it legitimizes further the worldview that becomes part of the student's everyday consciousness.

The more the student's worldview is legitimized through the symbolic world presented by the school, the more difficult it becomes to recognize the problematic nature of the assumptions and values upon which it rests.

Much of the socialization process in school concerns ideas and values that students have not tested, and in many cases cannot test, against personal experience. Examples include learning about the history of one's own society and about other cultures and ideas, practices and social conditions that are beyond the realm of the student's own experience. In encountering these areas, students are almost entirely dependent on the representation furnished by the teacher and textbooks. Most textbook descriptions (e.g., of historical figures such as the Founding Fathers, of technological developments such as the automobile, etc.) reflect the typifications that make up the natural attitude of most middle-class teachers. If the teacher typifies the people of another culture as primitive or the ocean as an unlimited resource, it is unlikely students would conceptualize it differently until they encounter a different set of typifications. The crucial point is that the school not only controls how ideas, people, and events are to be represented to students who may be encountering their first formal explanations of these areas of culture, but also the language the student is to use in thinking about them.

Socialization in schools, whether it involves further legitimizing students' commonsense assumptions or exposing them to the symbolic world beyond the realm of individual experiences, can easily lead to mystification. When the teacher communicates his or her own taken-for-granted assumptions and ways of typifying experience, it is likely (for students who share a common cultural background with the teacher) to be experienced at the same level by the students, especially if the students lack the experience from which to make a comparative judgment. Mystification also occurs when the teacher or textbook uses language that objectifies social reality. Such textbook statements as "Healthy cities are like boys and girls; they grow bigger and bigger" and "Programs on radio and television have been designed to assist consumers in getting the most for their money" are typical examples of the objectifying mode of communication that occurs in classrooms. They appear to describe a factual state of affairs, when in fact they are anonymous interpretations that reflect hidden economic interests and questionable cultural assumptions. What the student encounters, however, is an explanation of a social reality that is objectively real, and thus beyond questioning. The objectifying function of language used by teachers and in textbooks obscures in the mind of the student the human authorship of social reality.

Mystification that can easily occur in classroom settings results from the teacher's control of the speech code the student is to use in symbolizing social reality. If the curriculum unit is on "The Nature of Work" and the teacher presents a vocabulary that includes such terms as *reliable, punctual, thorough,* and *loyal,* but not such terms as *alienation* and *exploitation,* the student will be acquiring a restricted speech code that deters him or her from thinking about the contradictions and complexities of the work situation. The speech code acquired in this case limits the student's ability to symbolize work differently from the way it is presented by the teacher. A restricted speech code, with a limited vocabulary and set of explanatory models, has the effect of inducing the student to think in terms of what can be expressed. When the student is not equipped to conceptualize and communicate social experience, silence and distortion become a source of mystification.

Socialization that obscures the human authorship of culture is particularly detrimental in that it reduces the individual's ability to decode his or her own cultural experience. Learning to experience the cultural beliefs, ideas, and underlying assumptions as the natural, commonsense world makes that world deterministic and immutable. Paulo Freire's idea of the "culture of silence" refers to this condition of people in developed as well as Third World countries.

In developed countries the problem extends beyond the need for people to think reflexively about their own individual condition, which within the Western context could simply increase their sense of individual isolation. The environmental/population crisis makes all the assumptions underlying the cultures of developed countries problematic. While schools cannot take on responsibility for the entire problem, they must begin to alter the socialization process in a way that reduces the mystification that has, in the past, accompanied the transmission of cultural values and beliefs. By changing certain dynamics of the socialization process, the schools could provide students with the symbolic tools for rendering relevant aspects of their taken-for-granted culture problematic and for reconstituting it along lines more compatible with the carrying capacity of the ecosystems.

This is essentially the point made in *The Limits to Growth,* by the Club of Rome (1972). A more rational use and distribution of the world's resources is dependent upon the "power of the ideal" (p. 107). In achieving a fairer and more peaceful world, the people of the developed countries must learn to rethink the assumptions upon which their prosperity and technological advancements are based. To put it another way, what is needed is a new level of what Jürgen Habermas called communicative competence and the social conditions that will allow it to be effectively practiced. The schools lack the power to guarantee the essential social conditions, but they can do something about providing the younger members of society with the necessary tools to decode the hidden assumptions of their culture. Such competence implies more than the traditional level of literacy that involves an emphasis on reading the printed word and communication within parameters defined by the technocratic forces in society. In the past, this traditional conception of literacy has led to fuller participation in the dominant social-economic system.

The new level of literacy now needed might be called cultural literacy. That is, the traditional idea of being able to read should be expanded to include the ability and knowledge necessary for making relevant aspects of cultural experience more explicit. This is a necessary first step in demystifying the ecologically nonsustainable aspects of culture and in communicating what is problematic about them.

REFORMING THE CURRICULUM

As pointed out above, the school curriculum in the United States performs the function of distributing and legitimizing the definitions of reality shared by the dominant society. For the student, the curriculum both reinforces experience and provides the approved vocabulary for thinking and communicating about it. By setting the socially sanctioned boundaries for discourse and reflection as well as communicating the myths and assumptions of the dominant worldview, the curriculum performs as important social-control function.

Reform of the curriculum in a manner that serves more as an instrument of liberation than of social control could occur at several levels. The first level of reform would involve attempting to achieve greater accuracy in how societal conditions are represented in curriculum materials. Accuracy in representing the nature of progress, technology, work, or whatever else is the subject of the curriculum, would involve presenting the complexity, contradictions, and actual prospects that are necessary for reflection. This could lead to presenting an expanded speech code and more than one theory for explaining the phenomenon under discussion. For example, in a textbook on Canada that is used in some American classrooms, there is no reference, in the narrative on economic problems facing Canada, to the fact that a substantial proportion of the Canadian economy is controlled by American capital. The omission results in a distorted, romanticized view of Canadian–American relations, and it leaves the student without the necessary concepts and vocabulary for thinking about the complexities and contradictions that characterize the relationship between the two countries. But achieving greater accuracy in representing societal conditions, such as the relationship between the profit motive and the ecological crises (which is never mentioned in textbooks), would expose economic and social interests that in the past have been effectively hidden in the curriculum. This, in turn, raises serious questions about the relation of the curriculum to the politics of education (Bowers, 1974).

The manner in which the curriculum objectifies social reality is also in need of reform. When the human authorship of statements is obscured in order to present them as objective fact (e.g., "Henry Ford wanted to build cheap automobiles" or "The twentieth century is an age marked by the explosion of knowledge"), the student is put in a vulnerable and passive situation. Such statements appear to designate an independent and objective reality; without knowledge of their social origins, the student has little basis for challenging their factuality. Mystification enters into the socialization process when interpretations are represented as objective fact. The student needs to know about the perspective of the author and the cultural assumptions that have shaped it. As much of what becomes objectified in curriculum materials reflects the natural attitudes of the author, attitudes often shared by most members of the society, it would be unrealistic to expect that all objectified social reality could be eliminated. The conscious effort to eliminate sexism and racism from curriculum materials in the United States is slowly succeeding, which suggests that progress could also be made in deobjectifying curricular content that relates to the making of excessive and unsustainable demands on the environment.

A second and more fundamental reform of the curriculum should involve basic structural changes that take into account the way in which taken-for-granted beliefs are acquired. Students come to school with a considerable range of linguistic and social knowledge, to which they add constantly during their time outside the classroom. The teacher should focus on familiar elements of the student's culture, such as work, family, consumerism, technology, time, space, competition, authority, ways of knowing, and so forth. The focus will obviously vary, depending on the particular circumstances.

The content of the curriculum would be related to real-life experience. If the unit was on the nature of time, a topic which is dealt with somewhat differently in the elementary grades, the students would be encouraged to describe how they experience time (or how time enters into and shapes their experience) in a variety of social settings. The student's phenomenological description would reflect some of his or her own prefigured explanations and typifications, but these would prove valuable later in the attempt to understand why (socially, economically, historically) time is perceived and utilized in the way it is. In addition to providing the "data" for the later relational analysis of time and how it relates to other aspects of the society (e.g., an individual's perceptions of success and guilt, technology, work, position in social space, etc.), phenomenological description can provide a model for how to scrutinize surrounding reality.

Following the phenomenological description phase there should be a careful examination (relational analysis) of how the aspects of cultural experience being studied (e.g., time) influence and interact with other aspects of the culture. This part of the curriculum would be intended to help the student to understand how the culture's sense of time enters into the organization of a wide range of social experiences. The analysis might focus on how the cultural sense of time shapes attitudes toward eating, influences the distinctions that are made between work and play, and forms an integral aspect of technology. This part of the curriculum should also provide the student with a historical perspective on the subject, including the early myths and cultural assumptions that surrounded (to stay with the example) the emergence of a linear idea of time, as well as the later development of a mechanical sense of time. The historical perspective provides a genealogy of basic cultural assumptions, and exposes the human origins of the cultural values.

A clearer understanding of the assumptions underlying the student's cultural experience can be gained through the study of a contrasting culture whose worldview and social organization are predicated on a different set of assumptions. If the curriculum unit includes an examination of a culture that does not have a mechanical sense of time, the student would not only learn how a different sense of time influences people's perception of themselves, their social relationships and institutions, and their form of technology; he or she would also have a basis for looking at his or her own cultural experience in a new way. Understanding a different culture would provide a basis for recognizing how such basic assumptions as time, space, and ways of knowing influence the patterns of commonsense reality within the culture.

The last component in a curriculum unit designed to foster cultural literacy should include an opportunity for the student to examine the part of the culture under consideration in terms of futuristic considerations. This would involve looking at the culture's linear and mechanical sense of time and how it has influenced the sense of progress, the development of technology, the way the natural world is perceived, and so forth, in terms of the consequences that would ensue if the cultural sense of time were to be continued unchanged. In this part of the curriculum the

student should be encouraged to look at his or her own culture in relation to the environment/population crises, and to begin thinking about
which aspects of the cultural belief system are part of the problem and
which aspects are part of the solution.

A curriculum that starts with cultural experience of the student as
the subject matter makes it possible for the student to engage in a relational analysis of how different aspects of the culture interact and affect
his or her taken-for-granted reality. This process reduces the student's
vulnerability to textbook explanations that often leave one with a vocabulary and explanatory models that no longer relate to the current situations. The view of progress, technology, and work taught in American
public schools serves as a vivid example.

REFORMING TEACHER EDUCATION

The task of transmitting culture to the youth of developed countries in a
manner that does not exacerbate the environment/population crises will
require a different approach to teacher training education. Currently, the
taken-for-granted culture acquired as part of the teacher's own socialization from youth to adulthood constitutes a substantial portion of the
knowledge base used to teach students in the elementary grades. This
has certainly been the case in the United States and Canada. Traditional
academic courses and educational methods and theory courses represent
special training for teaching, but they seldom deal with such areas of
experience as technology, work, tradition, or the ideologies that frame
how they are interpreted. This lack of articulation between the academic
education of teachers and the culture they are expected to teach students
in the early grade leads teachers to rely upon curriculum materials (most
now produced by subsidiaries of multinational corporations) and on their
own taken-for-granted knowledge. This must change if the culture is to
be transmitted in a manner that helps the student to make it explicit and
to understand its traditions and assumptions.

Changes in teacher training must be directed at increasing teachers'
understanding of the dynamics of the socialization process. Specifically,
they need a theoretical understanding of different forms of communication, how communication constitutes and stabilizes a person's sense of
reality, and how communication can restrict and mystify as well as be a
liberating force. They also need to understand the existential implications
of acquiring cultural beliefs and assumptions as the taken-for-granted
reality. With a theoretical understanding of the sociology of knowledge,
they should be better able to make explicit both whose knowledge is being

transmitted in the classroom and how it is transmitted. This is essential if teachers are to be able to reduce the mystification and powerlessness that result from transmitting culture as objective reality.

A second major change needed in teacher education relates to teachers' knowledge of the culture they transmit in the classroom. As mentioned earlier, teachers have little formal, in-depth critical background knowledge of much of the culture they reinforce in the classroom. Traditional assumptions about work, progress, consumerism, technology, and so forth are communicated and reinforced in the minds of vulnerable students. If teachers are to help students "read" and understand their own cultural experience, then they must acquire a more appropriate knowledge themselves. They must study directly many aspects of the culture that have traditionally been ignored in academic departments. In addition to learning about the role and history of fundamental myths in the culture, they must also study directly the historical-cultural evolution of the society's beliefs about time, space, technology, work, authority, competition, community, ways of knowing, and progress—to identify some of the most basic components of a cultural belief system. Without this background, the teacher will be unable to provide a historical or cross-cultural perspective. Nor is it likely they would be able to engage students in any serious analysis of the relationship between the cultural beliefs and the environmental/population crisis.

These proposals for redirecting public education in developed countries are made with the full awareness that teachers and students lack the real political and economic power wielded by giant corporations and the social forces that they control. Changes in public education must, therefore, be put in the more modest perspective of being seen as part of the process of fundamental cultural change that is needed. But it is an essential part.

Chapter 2

Curriculum as Cultural Reproduction

An Examination of Metaphor as a Carrier of Ideology

The purpose here is to examine how dependent we are in educational analysis and policy formation on the use of metaphorical thinking, and how metaphorical thinking serves as a carrier of historically rooted ideologies. A second purpose is to clarify the conceptual difficulties that arise when we fail to recognize the difference between the world of everyday life and the symbolic world of metaphor. Attempts to translate the metaphors borrowed from industrial engineering into classroom practice and the more recent efforts to organize the administration of schools in accordance with metaphors borrowed from systems theory are two examples. The analysis of metaphor as carrier of ideology could focus on any one of several recent developments in education: the influence of technicism on educational thought and practice, the alternative school movement (now more a study in the history of ideas), or the accountability movement. Each of these reform movements was heavily dependent on metaphorical thinking, with an attempt being made to frame our understanding of educational issues in terms of analogies borrowed from areas of social experience dominated by concerns with profits and increased efficiency. For our purposes, however, the theory of the curriculum as cultural reproduction will be used as a basis for analyzing how the failure to recognize the metaphorical nature of language and thought can lead to new forms of cultural domination—particularly when the legitimating metaphors are represented as universal ideals. The view of curriculum as cultural reproduction is central to the sociology of school knowledge developed by Michael Young, Basil Bernstein, and Pierre Bourdieu. Their analyses of school knowledge have attracted widespread interest in this country and abroad. As the theory, in part, is derived from Marx's sociological model of social class and ideology, it is represented by some educational theorists as fitting into the category of thought that

Marx associated with scientific, distortion-free knowledge. This promise of knowledge about the mechanisms of social repression and revolutionary change that can be generalized, because of its scientific nature, to different cultural contexts is what makes the writings on curriculum as cultural reproduction particularly attractive for an analysis of metaphorical thinking. As the work of Michael Apple represents a nice synthesis and restatement of the main ideas in the sociology of school knowledge, his work will be used as the primary source of reference.

The analysis will begin with a brief restatement of Apple's interpretation of the theory of curriculum as cultural reproduction. This will enable us to identify both the metaphors and the theoretical context in which they are used. We shall then consider the nature of metaphor and the relationship between metaphor and ideology. After this theoretical foundation is established, we can then return to an analysis of the existential/cultural implications of key metaphors used by Apple and others working in the sociology of school knowledge.

CURRICULUM AS CULTURAL REPRODUCTION

What we should understand about the transmission of school knowledge, according to Apple, are the linkages between the form and content of the curriculum, the system of economic production, and the maintenance of class relationships. Apple focuses on the importance of understanding these linkages when he poses the questions: "What are the manifest and latent social functions of the knowledge that is taught in schools? .... How do the principles of selection and organization that are used to plan, order, and evaluate that knowledge function in the cultural and economic reproduction of class relations in an advanced industrial society like our own?" (1978, p. 372). One of Apple's purposes in raising the questions in this way is to attack as indefensible and naive the view that what is taught in school is objective knowledge and that teachers stand above the fray of political interests as nonpartisan public servants. Not only is school knowledge political; it must also be understood as part of the ideology of the dominant social class. The other purpose is to connect his analysis with Marx's idea that the mode of economic production *determines the general character* of the social, political and spiritual processes of life. While he cautions against accepting an oversimplified interpretation of Marx's dictum that social existence determines consciousness, he nevertheless wants to foreground the primacy of economic activity in determining class relationships and the distribution of knowledge in society.

Cultural transmissions, of which school knowledge is an important part, not only are shaped by the mode of economic production but in turn reproduce in the consciousness of the people the ideas, values, and norms that maintain the relations of reproduction. Apple (1979) suggests that we think of culture in terms of the metaphor of distribution:

> One can think about knowledge as being unevenly distributed among social and economic classes, occupational groups, different age groups, and groups of different power. Thus some groups have access to knowledge distributed to them and not distributed to others. . . . The lack of certain kinds of knowledge—where your particular group stands in the complex process of cultural preservation and distribution—is related, no doubt, to the absence in that group of certain kinds of political and economic power in society. (p. 16)

This process of distributing knowledge in a manner that maintains the patterns of unequal social relationships is, according to Apple, one of the primary functions of the school.

Utilizing Pierre Bourdieu's idea that knowledge can be understood as cultural capital, Apple argues that the schools reproduce the class divisions of a hierarchical society through their distribution of cultural capital. As Apple put it, "Schools, therefore, process both knowledge and people" (1978, p. 376). The linkage between the schools' distribution of cultural capital and unequal ownership and control of economic capital in the larger society can be seen in terms of who is given access to what he terms "high-status knowledge."

The constitutive or underlying social and economic rules Apple (1978) writes:

> make it essential that subject-centered curricula be taught, that high status be given to technical knowledge. This is, in large part, due to the selective function of schooling. Though this is more complex than I can go into here, it is easier to stratify individuals according to "academic criteria" when technical knowledge is used. This stratification or grouping is important because not all individuals are seen as having the ability to contribute to the required knowledge form (as well as partly because of the structural requirements of the division of labor, of course). Thus, the cultural content (legitimate or high-status knowledge) is used as a device or filter for economic stratification. (p. 382)

Because of the hegemonic nature of this cultural code, what Apple calls the ideology that legitimates the unequal distribution of power, the teacher's participation in the process of economic and cultural reproduction is characterized by a sense of taken-for-grantedness.

This is, I think, an essentially fair restatement of Apple's interpretation of the theory of the curriculum as cultural reproduction. As Apple shares with a number of other theorists working within this paradigm— Madeleine MacDonald, Geoff Esland, Michael Young, Madan Sarup— the belief that a fundamental transformation of the social order is needed along the lines laid down by Marx, our purpose here is to examine some of the key metaphors used in the analysis (class, inequality, hegemony, and hierarchical social structure) as well as what we can call the background or reference-point metaphors (classless, equality, and terms that imply the elimination of hegemony, ideology, and status differences in knowledge). As the Marxist sociological model makes a distinction between scientific knowledge (which Marx's paradigm provides) and ideology (distorted thinking that reflects the hegemonic influence of capitalism), it is important to ask whether their key metaphors are free of ideological content. To put it more directly, if social and educational reform were based on their metaphors, would a classless society, free of hegemony, emerge? Or do the metaphors themselves serve as a carrier of a culturally and historically based conceptual schema? Are metaphors such as "equality," "freedom," and "classless society" culturally neutral images that can be adopted by any culture without coming under the influence of Western hegemony? Can they be adopted in our culture at the level of social practice and at the same time be reconciled, without an Orwellian distortion of the language, with other metaphors that we also value, such as "cultural pluralism"? Before examining the cultural orientation embedded in the metaphors that are so fundamental to Apple's analysis and prescriptions for social change, it will be necessary to clarify what metaphorical thinking is and how metaphors serve as carriers of ideological orientations.

METAPHORICAL NATURE OF LANGUAGE AND THOUGHT

The problem for the Marxist educational theorist, for the advocate of "free schools," and for the technicist promoting "competency-based education" is not that they use metaphors; rather, it is that they do not understand the metaphorical nature of the "reality" they think they are reporting on. As a number of writers have observed, *all* thinking is metaphorical. As early as 1873, Friedrich Neitzsche described metaphor as basic to the intellectual process we use to establish truth and meaning. "The starting point," he wrote, "begins with a nerve-stimulus, first transcribed [*ubertragen*] into an image [*Bild*]. First metaphor! The image again copied into a sound! Second metaphor! And each time he (the creator of language) leaps completely out of one sphere right into the midst of an entirely different one" (1968, p. 227). Elsewhere he wrote, "In our thought, the essential feature is fitting new material into old schemas, . . . making equal what is new" (p. 273). What he is describing as a fundamental impulse of humans, the impulse toward the formation of metaphors, he later identifies with the "will to power." This drive to name, to give meaning, to categorize, involves the use of metaphor; that is, the establishment of an identity between dissimilar things.

Ernst Cassirer (1953) made a similar observation on how our phenomenological world is transformed through language. "This differentiation and fixation of certain contents by words," he writes, "not only designates a definite intellectual quality through them, but actually endows them with such a quality, by virtue of which they are now raised above the mere immediacy of so-called sensory qualities. . . . Here lies the first beginning of that universal function of separation and association" (1953, pp. 87–88). More recently, Susanne Langer described metaphor as "our most striking evidence of *abstractive seeing*. . . . Every new experience or new idea about things evokes first of all some metaphorical expression. As the idea becomes familiar, this expression 'fades' to a new literal use of the once metaphorical predicate, a more general use than it had before." She goes on to say that "if ritual is the cradle of language, metaphor is the law of its life. It is the force that makes it essentially relational, forever showing up new, abstract able forms in reality, forever laying down a deposit of old, abstracted concepts in an increasing treasure of general words" (1960, p. 140).

Nietzsche, Cassirer, and Langer, in addition to showing that metaphors are essential to the symbolic openness of both thought and language, provide important clues as to how metaphorical thinking occurs. Each of the quotations refers to "thinking" as a process of moving from one sphere to another, making associations and comparisons, and the expansion of meaning through relating one image to another. In order to formalize our discussion of metaphor in a manner that enables us to understand the use of metaphors in the academic world where truth claims are made about our knowledge of society, and to understand the process to which Nietzsche, Cassirer, and Langer allude, it would be useful to draw on Richard H. Brown's analysis of the cognitive status of metaphor. His book *A Poetic for Sociology* makes an important contribution to understanding the nature of metaphorical thinking within the domains of the social sciences, science, and even educational policy and analysis.

Brown (1978) provides several clear descriptions of the mental process involved in the use of metaphors. "In the narrowest sense," he writes, "metaphors can be understood as an illustrative device whereby a term from one level or frame of reference is used within a different level or frame" (p. 78). To use an example drawn from the previous discussion of curriculum, "culture" is to be understood as though it were like "capital." The metaphor of cultural capital derives its power from the expansion of meaning that comes from associating our understanding of culture with all that we know about capital, that is, capital is owned, is unevenly distributed, and underlies the basis of class divisions. Dewey's view of education as growth, to take another example, involves the expansion of the meaning of education by associating it with the image of growth that was derived largely from a biological frame of reference. Brown points out that the use of metaphor "concentrates our attention on what is patently not there in the language, but which emerges in the interplay of juxtaposed associations" (p. 88). Examples taken from different ideological perspectives include competency-based education, open classrooms, and democratic centralism; each shows how meaning is expanded through this process of juxtaposed association.

In addition to the carryover of meaning as terms are used within different frameworks, metaphors also provide the basis for both model building and theoretical thought. Brown suggests that *analogic* metaphors are basic to the theoretical thinking that characterizes the social sciences and science. Like illustrative metaphors, analogic metaphors involve taking an image or sense of meaning from one context and employing it in another in order to expand or clarify some new sense of meaning that we want to have understood. We use analogic metaphors when we think in terms of comparisons, relationships, and how something can be understood "as like" something else. Thinking of the school as a distribution system would be an example, as is thinking of society in terms of structure and function. School and society are understood not in isolation, but in relation to other images. *Iconic* metaphors, according to Brown, provide us with an image or mental picture of what things are, rather than creating a new sense of meaning through comparison (the process of analogic thinking). Iconic metaphors, such as "class," "power," "intelligence," and so forth, were originally constituted in an earlier process of analogic thinking. To use two of those examples, the image of "power" or "intelligence" that becomes taken-for-granted by later generations is the one that survived the political/cultural process of analogic thinking. In effect, these taken-for-granted iconic metaphors should be understood as encoding the earlier process of analogic thinking, and thus as historically and culturally specific.

"*Root* metaphors," Brown (1978) writes, "are those sets of assumptions, usually implicit, about what sort of things make up the world, how they act, how they hang together, and usually, by implication, how they may be known" (p. 125). Root metaphors constitute the basic frames of reference or paradigms for making sense of our world, and they are the starting point for all theory building. Unlike analogic and iconic metaphors, they usually exist below the level of conscious awareness. Thinking of society as an organism is an example of how a root metaphor provides a conceptual grammar that influences our way of thinking. Root metaphors are the basis of worldviews, ideologies, and religions. They also have a way of showing up in the conceptual underpinnings of social science theories that are supposedly free of archetypal thinking. Marx's statement, for example, that "new, higher relations of production never appear before the material conditions of their existence have matured in the womb of the old society" (quoted in Brown, 1978, p. 130) reflects the basic root cultural metaphor that shaped the thinking of Aristotle, Saint Augustine, Comte, and Dewey. Stages of growth that reflect an inner telos, with the latter stages existing in the embryo of earlier stages, is a basic paradigmatic theme underlying the cultural grammar of all these Western thinkers.

Since metaphors represent a mental construct, they must, according to Brown, be consciously understood in terms of suggesting an "as if" set of possibilities. When Apple tells us to think of culture as a "distribution system," of schools as "processing people," and of "how hegemony acts to 'saturate' our very consciousness," it is important to keep in mind that he is inviting us to understand his meaning in a metaphorical sense rather than to interpret "distribution," "processing," and "saturate" in a literal sense. Serious difficulties arise when metaphors are interpreted literally. Brown notes that in the use of "metaphors a logical or empirical absurdity stands in tension with fictive truth, yet this counter factual truth itself depends on a creative confrontation of perspectives that cannot be literalized or disengaged without destroying the insight which metaphor provides." He goes on to what seems to be the crucial point to remember about metaphors, namely that if the "consciously as if" aspect of metaphor is not retained, there is the danger that we will be used by them rather than using them (1978, p. 84).

Nietzsche was also aware of the danger of interpreting metaphors in the literal sense. His view of how we transform metaphors into symbolic constructions that then influence us is very similar to Marx's idea of how we have objectified the labor process in a manner that leaves the workers' contribution out of our thinking about commodity production. Both Nietzsche and Marx were addressing the fundamental problem of reification; Nietzsche was concerned with reification of our symbolic world, and Marx with the reification of our social relations. Metaphorical thinking becomes an example of reified thought when we cease to be aware that language involves a projection of our thought processes onto the world. In the language of Peter Berger and Stanley Pullberg, metaphors become reified "by detaching them from human intentionality and expressivity.... The end result ... is that the dialectical process in its totality is lost, and is replaced by an experience and conception of mechanical causality" (1964–65, p. 207).

The absurd and humanly tragic emerges when we begin to act on metaphors as though they were to be taken in the literal sense, whereby they take on an objective existence of their own. Educational programs based on the "freedom" of the student, decisions that are "data-based," and the desire to eliminate the sources of "inequality" in all aspects of social and individual experience are examples of the kind of reified thinking that characterizes ideological positions prevalent in education today. In the face of a reified symbolic world—of which "freedom," "data," and "inequality" are examples—individuals lose sight of how their own intentionality is part of a metaphorically constituted thought process. This process of becoming alienated from the symbolic world that is constructed and externalized is in Nietzsche's sense the ultimate expression of the will to power, but expressed in a manner that does not involve taking existential responsibility.

If we go back to Brown's description of metaphor as involving a term or image taken from "one level or frame of reference" and "used within a different level or frame," it is easy to make the connection between metaphor and ideology. Another way to understand "frame of reference" is to think of it in Clifford Geertz's sense of a symbolic world or model. Geertz (1973) suggests that we think of symbolic worlds as "culture patterns—religious, philosophical, aesthetic, scientific, ideological . . . [that] provide a template or blueprint for the organization of social and psychological processes" (p. 216). These symbolic worlds can also be viewed as ideologies that serve as mental templates for making sense of everyday experience. Metaphors, as Brown suggests, derive their expanded meaning from the juxtaposition of these mental templates or from the use of an image taken from one mental template and used in a different context. Viewing society as an "organism" and the curriculum as cultural "reproduction" would be two examples. Put succinctly, metaphors always have an ideological basis that gives them their special symbolic power to expand meaning. When they are used, as in talking about equality or freedom, the metaphors carry or lay down, in Susanne Langer's phrase, "a deposit of old, abstracted concepts" (schemata) that reflect the episteme or ideological framework from which they were borrowed. In this sense metaphors are carriers of meaning and images from one context to another. To think metaphorically means, then, the use of historically and culturally specific conceptual frameworks or, as Nietzsche put it, fitting the new into old schemata.

Before examining how the view of curriculum as cultural reproduction can be understood as an example of ideological borrowing, it is necessary to explain what is meant by a "context-free metaphor." This phrase was used by Alvin Gouldner (1976) in his analysis of how Marxist metaphors, such as "socialism," "proletariat," "imperialism," and "class struggle," are used in a variety of contexts that reflect different forms of social development. What allows the Marxist socialists, he asks, to use "socialism" in the context of agrarian as well as industrially advanced societies, or to interchange the term "proletariat" with "peasantry" and "people" (p. 47)? He suggests that this process of metaphorical switching, where one metaphor takes on the equivalencies of other metaphors, results from the context-free nature of the metaphors. That is, the metaphors are used in a manner that separates them from the ideological framework out of which they are derived. In losing the original image or sense of meaning that the originating symbolic framework provided, context-free metaphors can be given any meaning the user wants them to have. Metaphors then can be switched without seeming to involve contradictions or the misuse of image or framework. Thus "peasant" can be used as interchangeable with "proletariat" or "working class," and, to change ideological frameworks as our source of examples, "freedom" can be interchanged with "natural" or "spontaneous," while "competency" can be interchanged with "input and output measures." The tendency to switch metaphors reflects the user's lack of knowledge of what the images originally meant. The metaphor, thus separated from its original historical and cultural context, is used as context-free. The popular usage of "liberalism" and "conservatism" reflects this lack of historical awareness. As I shall develop in the following analysis, the metaphors used by Apple and others looking at the social-political function of curriculum within the Marxist paradigm are being used as context-free metaphors. But even though the metaphors are used in a context-free manner, they continue to carry vestiges of the ideological frameworks from which they are taken.

METAPHORS AS CARRIERS OF IDEOLOGY

The metaphors most important to the development of Apple's analysis of curriculum include "inequality," "class," "hegemony," "high-status knowledge," and "hierarchy" (in all its social and cultural manifestations).

Metaphors that suggest the opposite image, that is, a classless society, equality, and so forth, are fundamental to his Marxist vision of a social-ist society. Our purpose here is to point out how these metaphors serve as carriers of the deep-structure assumptions and categories of thought that characterized the historical mind-set from which they were bor-rowed. This will help to clarify a point that seems to be generally ignored by Apple and other educational theorists using the Marxist paradigm, namely, that metaphors such as "equality" and "classless society" are not culturally neutral terms. Marx himself understood the social-historical origins of language, but many of his followers seem to overlook this obvious yet exceedingly complex issue.

If the metaphors of social liberation are culturally specific, that is, reflect a particular ideological framework, how can they be used as the basis of cultural and social liberation within a different culture without involving a new form of cultural domination? After examining some of the characteristics of the cultural episteme that gave rise to the idea of equality, freedom, and a classless society, I want to raise several ques-tions about how the metaphors used in the Marxist sociological model can be translated into a new social praxis without engaging in another form of cultural imperialism. The dialectical relation between theory and praxis requires that the implication of a new praxis based on culturally specific metaphors be given more careful consideration than has been characteristic of the work of Apple, MacDonald, Young, and others work-ing in this area. Examining characteristics of the mind-set embedded in the metaphors will also help us to see some of the cultural issues that emerge when metaphors such as "equality," "freedom," and "nonhier-archical relations" are translated into social and educational policy in our own country.

The images evoked when we think of equality, a classless society, a people entering into their true consciousness free of hegemony (*hegemony* is the new term that is roughly equivalent to Marx's idea of *ideology*), are meaningful to us because, in Benjamin Lee Whorf's (1968) terms, we are party to categories of thought that are embedded in the language. The language, which includes the metaphors, transmits the episteme of the culture, with the roots of this episteme going back to earlier stages of cultural development. In terms of the metaphors so prominent in Apple's analysis of curriculum, the cultural epistemology that surrounds and gives the metaphors their special meaning can be traced back to the ideology of the Enlightenment in Western Europe. A general mapping of this episteme reveals some unique deep-structure assumptions about how to organize and think about reality. This conceptual template was in part fashioned by the bourgeois intelligentsia in their struggle to overturn the old regime of church and feudal aristocracy; but fundamental characteristics can also be traced back even further to their Judeo-Christian roots. The purpose here is not to engage in a full-scale archeology of Western consciousness, but to identify those characteristics of thinking encoded in the metaphors we are examining.

Apple's use of metaphor within the Marxist paradigm clearly reflects the influence of the mental template characteristic of Western Enlightenment thinking. In order to make clear the pattern of thinking (episteme) he draws on, I shall quote several of his statements. Apple speaks of the schools' role in the "maintenance of an unequal social order," the need to adopt an advocacy model of research "if substantial progress is to be made," the fact that "the unequal social world that educators live in is represented by the reification, the commodification, of the language they use," and the "stratification of knowledge . . . [that] involves the stratification of people." The deep structure of the mental template that underlies his way of thinking, and is carried as part of the symbolic baggage of his metaphors, includes the following characteristics:

1. A linear sense of time helps to organize events on a continuum that leads from a past into a future. This sense of linear time, which goes back to the earliest symbolic foundations of Western thought, underlies the teleology so fundamental to the Marxist idea of dialectical materialism, wherein the conflict of social classes occurs within a linear patterned time frame.

2. Change is seen not only as part of a linear continuum but as progressive in nature. Thus whatever accelerates historical change, even if it involves violent revolutions, is progressive. While change and progress are inevitable, they can be greatly speeded up through the intervention of intellectuals, who possess a special way of knowing and predicting what the future holds for others too burdened with the cares of the present to concern themselves with the future. The fusing of the linear sense of time with the idea of progress can be traced directly back to the Enlightenment (Bury, 1932; Foucault, 1973). That progress is inevitable is implied in Apple's appeal for an advocacy approach to research; it also underlies and legitimates the intentions of his entire theoretical effort as well as those of his Marxist colleagues. That change might lead to greater bureaucratization of life (the case still has to be made that this would be a more progressive stage of social development) or that it might lead to more atavistic forms of political control is not seriously considered. Like the Marxist metaphor of praxis or Dewey's metaphor of growth, change represents progress.

3. The idea of causality is a basic aspect of the Western mind-set that is part of the deep structure of Apple's analysis of the relationship between school knowledge and the "economic reproduction of class relations in an advanced industrial society." The relationships among the distribution function of school, status knowledge, and the patterns of class relations that are grounded in the mode of production are explained in terms of cause and effect. To the Marxist way of thinking, the mode of production causes a particular mode of consciousness to exist. In Apple's analysis an attempt is made to avoid simple economic determinism; this is done by arguing that the mode of consciousness legitimated in schools is causally related to the maintenance of the capitalist mode of production. An important aspect of the Western tendency to think in terms of cause and effect is the concomitant mental habit of thinking categorically, particularly in the categories of true/false, right/wrong, either/or. Marx's contribution to understanding dialectical thinking (which in his formulation retained the element of teleology) holds out the promise of breaking away from this aspect of Western thinking, which is so characteristically represented in Aristotelian logic. While Marx was unable to shed much of the traditional mental template that stamps his work as the product of a particular historical and cultural period, his followers, including Apple, have been even less successful in avoiding a thought process that organizes reality into rigid categories and linear causal relationships. In the writings of Apple, as well as in those of Bowles and Gintis, socialism and capitalism are clearly organized into the rigid categories of right and wrong, truth and falsity, salvation and perdition. Even Harry Braverman, whose analysis is often brilliant, slips back into the categorical and causal pattern of thinking when he asserts that capitalism is the cause of the increasing separation of mental from manual work (1974). Why the phenomenon Braverman investigated continued to exist in Russia, China, and other societies trying to develop their own form of socialism cannot be explained when it is categorically tied to capitalism. But then, categorical thinking does not relate well to the complexity of actual experience, and thus is best left in its context-free status.

4. Abstract-theoretical thought is believed to have the power to represent more accurately the reality of individual and social experience, as well as to provide a blueprint for the progressive unfolding of the future. This "faith" in the power of rational thought, which can be traced directly back to Enlightenment thinkers for its most fundamental legitimation, is not only a uniquely cultural phenomenon, but is, according to Gouldner, class-specific. The ideology of intellectuals, he points out, holds "that an argument must stand on its own legs, must be self-sufficient, that one

must 'consider the speech and not the speaker,' that it must encompass all that is necessary, providing full presentation of the assumptions needed to produce and support the conclusion." Gouldner also points out that "the culture of critical discourse (intellectuals and theorists) is characterized by speech that is relatively more situation free, more context or field 'independent.' This speech culture thus values expressly legislated meanings and devalues tacit, context-limited meanings. It's ideal," he concludes, "is: 'one word, one meaning,' for everyone and forever" (1979, pp. 28–29). What he sees as a class-specific view of the power of rational thought must also be understood in terms of the fact that intellectuals are the primary group who possess the cultural capital necessary to engage in this high-status activity. Neither Apple nor the rest of us who theorize about education and society can operate without incorporating these deep-structure assumptions into our work.

5. Individuals are viewed as potentially free, voluntaristic entities who will take responsibility for creating themselves when freed from societal forms of oppression. This humanistic ideal is expressed in the Marxist idea of praxis as a process of self-transcendence that occurs as individuals freely interact with the natural environment; it is also at the root of the Marxist metaphorical image of alienation. It is a view, as the Yugoslav Marxist Svetozar Stojanovic (1973) pointed out, that is curiously free of any serious anthropological evidence. That we are free to make choices based on what reason discloses to us (a process that seldom discloses the self-interest and will to power of intellectuals who provide the rational basis on which choice should be predicated) is part of the background metaphor of most writings that are intended to elicit action directed toward social change. The purpose in disclosing how the curriculum reproduces the relations of production is to provide a rational basis for action on the part of a free, voluntaristic individual who is expected to seek the good. An interesting aspect of this part of the Western mental template is that this view of the individual is often reified to the point where, in the abstract, the workers are seen as virtuous and exhibiting the self-transcendent qualities of free beings, while at the flesh-and-blood level of daily life (where their conservative values and materialistic tastes are too evident to be denied) they are seen as being in a false state of consciousness (in theological terms, their condition would be identified in terms of a "fallen state").

6. An anthropocentric universe in which the individual is the source of decision making (not bound by tradition), the source of meaning, and the fundamental reference point is used to legitimate any form of interference with the natural environment. In the tradition of the Western myth that gave "man" the power to name, the environment has been seen as

existing essentially for the purpose of serving human needs. The sense of mystery and sanctity, the obligation to restrict the use of technological power or individual desire are not part of the natural attitude of the person who experiences an anthropocentric universe. This part of the Western mind-set emphasizes the right to take direct action, to plan according to a rational process, and to be the ultimate source of moral authority. It is a fundamentally secular and "man"-centered universe.

For most of us, the acquisition of this symbolic world has been a natural process, reinforced through daily conversations with significant others. It is so much a part of our taken-for-granted attitude toward everyday life that to have parts of this mental template identified, as in the previous discussion, is to feel that the identification of such truisms is an unnecessary form of subversion. My point here is not to claim that this is an exhaustive treatment of the deep structure of Western consciousness, or to make value judgments about its being superior or inferior to the symbolic worlds of other cultural traditions. Instead, my purpose is to make the point that the use of metaphors derived from this cultural episteme also involves adopting these particular, historically grounded patterns of thinking. In the following discussion of the metaphors Apple uses as the basis for his analysis of the relationship between curriculum and social classes, I want to identify some of the issues that need to be addressed if we are going to consider seriously using a Marxist analysis as a basis for social reform. I am not taking the position that this should not be considered, but rather that we should acknowledge the epistemic roots of this analysis, and that it involves a peculiarly Western, modernizing, and secularizing frame of mind. When it is stated openly, rather than being part of the hidden cultural agenda embedded in revolutionary metaphors, some people may press Apple and his colleagues to justify the deep-structure categories of Western thought as superior in a moral sense and as a source of human fulfillment to those of other cultures.

Like Louis Althusser's analysis of schools as being part of the "ideological state apparatus," the analysis of curriculum as a form of cultural reproduction is based on such a basic truism that one can only wonder about the excitement it has produced in certain quarters. Althusser (1971) states that "all ideological state apparatuses, whatever they are, [including schools] contribute to the same result: the reproduction of the relations of production, i.e., of capitalist relations of exploitation" (p. 154). That social institutions reproduce the patterns of thought and economic activity of the culture they transmit is a fact of social existence in *all* societies; this may apply even more in Marxist societies, where there is less freedom of inquiry and local influence on schools. The opposite—that schools would be designed to subvert the social order that established and maintains them—is too simple-minded to be seriously entertained. What raises this commonsense observation to the status of serious social criticism in the theories of Althusser and Apple is that their analyses are developed within the context of background metaphors that give expression to a secular vision that is very much in the tradition of what Max Weber called "emissary prophecy." This vision, or what Marx referred to as the beginning of human history, is based in part on the powerful image of equality that is to guarantee social justice and the realization of our human potential. As equality is one of several background metaphors that give Apple's analysis its appealing moral tone, I want to raise some questions about how we are to translate this metaphor into social action, and whether this can be done without establishing a new form of cultural imperialism. I also want to raise similar questions about other taken-for-granted metaphors—"class," "hierarchy," and "hegemony"—that seems so central to Apple's agenda of social reform. These questions, I believe, will disclose some unique assumptions and problems that will be difficult to reconcile with such other values as the democratic right of cultural self-determination.

POLITICAL AND CULTURAL IMPLICATIONS
OF USING CONTEXT-FREE METAPHORS

The curriculum, according to Apple, must be understood as helping to reproduce the social relations of an "unequal" economic structure. This means that social and educational reform should lead to the replacement of the social conditions that create inequality; but this leaves us with problems of interpreting what "equality" should mean. Does the notion of equality have economic implications, meaning that everybody is to receive an equal wage, or that each will give according to ability and receive according to need? Marx himself does not provide a clear-cut explanation of how to achieve economic equality. Equality in the political sense could mean, as in Yugoslavia, that people should be involved in shaping the decisions that affect them. But politics very much depends on the linguistic competence of the participants. In a political environment where the power to define "what is" depends on the possession of a complex and powerful language code, equality would have to mean achieving the same level of linguistic competence and performance. But since language codes vary in their ability to deal with certain phenomena—for example, the black ghetto vernacular is less powerful in defining "what is" in the scientific domain than is the language code of university-trained experts—is equality to be attained by forcing one cultural group to adopt the more powerful language code of another? Whose language code is to be adopted as the basis for establishing linguistic equality? Can linguistic equality be reconciled with cultural pluralism or, for that matter, can it be achieved in a technocratic society where experts utilize their own language code as a means of legitimating both their knowledge and their status? If not, it would seem reasonable to expect the technological infrastructure to be dismantled in order to achieve linguistic equality. The metaphor of equality—that abstract, context-free image of the Enlightenment mind—is equally illusive when we ask how to structure the experience of people in a manner that fosters equality. Are the older members of society to deny that they have learned anything from their longer life in order to achieve the status of equality with youth? The alternative school movement led many adults to adopt a stance that could only be described in terms of Sartre's idea of self-deception in order to be true to the ideological requirements of a society of equals. But, as many participants in the alternative school movement discovered, this stance could not be easily maintained, and many had to acknowledge that the range and depth of their experience had to be recognized if they were not to act in bad faith. How is Apple's interpretation of equality to overcome this form of inequality, or, for that matter, the more existential aspects of inequality where we see people differing in their ability to take responsibility for their lives?

The metaphor of equality also raises some interesting questions about the structure of the family, particularly in cultures where the extended family involves a hierarchy of authority and responsibility. But within our cultural context of the nuclear family, the image of equality poses important questions about how equality is to be attained within the family unit (are children to have the same voice in all matters as parents?) as well as between families. To achieve equality in the sense of compensating for differences in family background is one thing; to achieve equality through state interference with the desire to pass on some sort of inheritance (moral as well as material) to one's children is a more problematic policy that runs counter to a basic human motivation expressed in a variety of cultural ways.

The image of equality was the creation of the Enlightenment mindset that fused romanticism and rationalism. While a progressive mode of thought in its era, it nevertheless lacked an awareness of the multiple realities experienced in different cultures. The discourse of that period was characterized by abstract theories that ignored the influence of culture on language and thought patterns. Indeed, thinking about reason, freedom, equality, and fraternity in the abstract is an archetypal example of the Enlightenment mentality. If we apply the abstract concept of equality to the context of the multiple cultural realities that make up our world, we have to ask whose culture is to become the one that will be adopted as the basis for achieving an equal social/cultural order. The deep structure of Apple's metaphor of equality—the coding of reality into either/or categories, the preeminence given to theoretical/abstract thought over pretheoretical experience, the image of equality that is based on an image of atomistic/voluntaristic individualism, the anthropocentric universe—seems to imply the dominance of the Western cultural episteme.

The attempt to place Apple's use of context-free metaphors within the context of people's cultural experience is not intended to overturn the question of how to achieve social justice, a question that concerns more people than Marxists. Attempts to attain social justice are bound to fail if they do not start with a recognition of cultural differences and a recognition that these cultural differences cannot all be explained in terms of the same economic paradigm and in terms of metaphors that contain deep-structure assumptions that are foreign to the culture to which they are being applied. If the formula for defining social justice—an egalitarian society in terms of Apple's paradigm—ignores the cultural traditions that ground the phenomenology of everyday life, the formula cannot be seen as a source of social justice. Questions of social justice must take account of differences in cultural context, which means that social justice cannot be reduced to a simple formula.

A second metaphor fundamental to Apple and the others looking at curriculum in terms of a Marxist framework is the image of social class. The theory of cultural reproduction is predicated on an image of class relations involving two antagonistic social classes—the capitalists or the bourgeoisie who buy the labor of the working class or proletariat. It is a dichotomous model of class, highly abstracted and highly metaphorical in its image of conflict between the owners of capital and those who, as the real producers, have only their labor to sell. The categorical thinking that underlies the epistemic tradition that Apple operates within includes the vision or metaphorical image of a classless society, where alienation and exploitation cease to exist. The closest Apple comes to spelling out what would be involved in a society free of class antagonism is when he urges the "progressive articulation of a commitment to a social order that has as its very foundation not the accumulation of goals, profits, and credentials, but the maximization of economic, social, and educational equality." The structural relations, he goes on to say, "must be such as to equalize not merely access to but actual control of cultural, social, and especially economic institutions" (1979, pp. 11–12). The equalization of power and cultural capital, as well as control over the means of production, would produce a society free of social class. As there is no empirical referent for such a society, it exists for Apple and his colleagues as a mental image or metaphor. More importantly for our purposes, this metaphor of a classless society serves as a carrier of the Western assumptions about free and self-creative individuals who will introduce the reign of reason (scientific Marxism) into human relationships. Again, the deep structure underlying the metaphor raises the question of a new form of Western cultural hegemony when the metaphor of a classless society is adopted in a non-Western culture. Within our own culture of advanced industrial-social relationships, there is a more fundamental question of how to relate Apple's metaphor of dichotomous classes to everyday experience. Categorical divisions formulated in the abstract (part of the mental template of Western thought) are difficult to relate to the lives of real people.

The metaphor of a classless society, which includes the image of the equal distribution of cultural capital, also raises some rather intriguing questions about what is to happen to the role of the intellectual and the technological expert. Apple clearly sees himself as an example of the former. Yet in his vision of a classless society there is no room for his type of intellectual activity without the emergence of a fundamental contradiction. Historically Marxist revolutions have been guided by intellectuals, and the centralization of power and the extension of bureaucratic control in Marxist societies has extended the influence of intellectuals as a new class (Giddens, 1975; Gouldner, 1979). Unfortunately there has been no attempt on Apple's part to explain the contradiction between the theory of a classless society and actual practices in Marxist societies. Apple's dependence on context-free metaphors serves as a gloss that fails to put the future of intellectuals in a classless society in any kind of perspective that takes account of the role they have played in pre- and postrevolutionary social development. The historical record of Marxist revolutionary movements gives a clear picture of Marxist practice; it would be useful if Apple could illuminate for us the disjuncture between Marxist theory and the historical evidence of Marxist practice, as well as when we might expect to see the "withering away" of the intellectual vanguard. It would also be useful if he would explain how a new educational praxis could be based on his metaphors of "equality" and "classless society." Unless he can relate his metaphorical image to the world of experience, we must either view his thinking as based on a form of historically grounded idealism or begin to ask questions about the hidden ritual/religious function of metaphor in Marxist theory.

A basic problem of the theorists of cultural reproduction who write on schools and curriculum is that they have treated their key and background metaphors—"inequality," "class," "hierarchy," and "hegemony" —in a literal sense, where they become culture-free images that can be generalized to a variety of cultural contexts. This generalization of reified images becomes a new form of cultural imperialism when the historical/cultural epistemology out of which the metaphor is derived is ignored. In developing his theory of metaphor, Brown (1978) observes that

> new metaphors, especially when elaborated into models and theories, are not merely new ways of looking at the facts, nor are they a revelation of what the facts really are. Instead, the metaphor in a fundamental way creates the facts and provides a definition of what the essential quality of an experience must be. And for this new reality to be entered into and comprehended—from the inside as it were—the metaphor must be taken as if it literally were the case. (pp. 84–5)

This shaping of how we think and act, what Gouldner refers to as acquiring a set of conceptual lenses, points to the importance of understanding the genealogy of our language. While we may think we can achieve liberation through the use of a revolutionary-sounding language, we also have to remember that it may be important to liberate ourselves from certain controls embedded in the conceptual schemata of our language. This applies to Marxist educational theorists such as Apple, but also to the educational technocrats and educational humanists who have their own set of metaphors that enable us to "see" certain aspects of experience and to not "see" what the metaphors put out of focus. My own embeddedness in the Western mind-set leads me to think that this ability to decode the hidden patterns in our cultural experience as a complex set of language systems, what I have elsewhere called cultural literacy, is important, but I no longer assume that people will want to do this because they understand its rational nature, or that it will lead to progress. Nor would I necessarily recommend it in societies that do not share the cultural grammar of Western individualism and rationalism. However, in terms of the Western mind-set, it seems that ecological and social events no longer give us a real choice as to whether we want to think about the possibility of cultural literacy.

I know that chapters should end in a nice summary fashion, and usually with an optimistic, uplifting thought. But somehow Nietzsche's observations seem appropriate to concluding my comments on metaphor, curriculum, and social change: "Man can no longer make his misery known to others by means of language; thus he cannot really express himself any-more . . . ; language has gradually become a force that drives humanity where it least wishes to go. . . . The results of this inability to communicate is that the creations of common action all bear the stamp of mutual noncomprehension" (quoted in Strong, 1975, p. 65). Nietzsche did not see progress as an inevitable force that would shield us from our vanities and well-intentioned mistakes.

Chapter 3

Linguistic Roots of Cultural Invasion in Paulo Freire's Pedagogy

Paulo Freire's commitment to using education for the purpose of individual and cultural liberation has made him one of the more dominant, if not charismatic, educational theorists today. His views on furthering social justice are often eloquently expressed, and his pedagogy has been widely used in adult literacy programs in Third World countries. Yet for all of his contributions, which I consider major, fundamental questions persist about whether his pedagogy is free of cultural domination. The most basic questions relate to whether the cultural mind-set underlying his pedagogy leads to a modernizing and Westernizing mode of consciousness. If this is the case, the use of his pedagogy in Third World countries may actually be furthering the influence of Western culture there. As the actual form and degree of cultural invasion introduced by the use of his pedagogy is an issue that can be settled only by careful investigation in the field, I should like to limit myself here to establishing a conceptual framework for putting in clearer focus how activities intended to liberate can become hegemonic. I would also like to identify the policy issues that arise when we take off the cultural lenses that prevent us from seeing our moral orientations and patterns of thinking as culturally specific. An awareness of the policy issues may lead to the same choices that are now made in the name of social progress. But we will have to make our justifications more explicit, and live with the contradictions that cannot be masked by cultural orientations that are given ontological status.

The source of the irony of a pedagogy that liberates by displacing traditional cultural patterns of thought with a distinctly Western mode of thinking can be traced back to the specific cultural underpinnings of Freire's position. More specifically, the problem arises because of his way of viewing the connections between language, thought, and culture. His writings and pedagogical principles demonstrate a deep understanding of the connections between language and thought, particularly the form of political control embedded in the acquisition and use of language.

Freire does not start with the naive assumption about a form of individualism where thought is generated *sui generis*. Language serves as a carrier of cultural codes (cognitive maps that shape the individual's perceptions and way of understanding). For instance, Freire (1971) views language "as an interiorized product which in turn conditions men's subsequent acts" (p. 16). To be a passive recipient of the language of other people leads to internalizing their conceptual maps and to experiencing reality in terms of their categories and assumptions. This part of Freire's understanding of the connections among language, thought, and the conceptual codes that make up the culture is not substantively different from what anthropologists have been telling us about the nature of belief systems and how they are reproduced through language (Black, 1973, pp. 509–517).

But whereas the anthropological literature on belief systems adopts a nonjudgmental attitude toward the multiple realities of different belief systems, Freire sees the connections among language, thought, and culture through lenses that organize the world in terms of the categories of oppressor and oppressed. He also introduces the chiliastic element of liberating people who unconsciously internalize the belief system of others who are characterized as being in a "semi-intransitivity of consciousness," meaning that they are unable to apprehend problems situated outside their sphere of biological neccessity. "Their interests," according to Freire (1973), "center almost totally around survival, and they lack a sense of life on a more historic plane" (p. 17). In terms of education, he designated the passive acceptance of other people's knowledge as the banking approach. Culture reproduced through language in this mode is seen as oppressive, alienating, and inauthentic. Liberation, on the other hand, is achieved by uniting thought and action in a manner that transforms the world. He sees learning to read and write as "an opportunity for men to know what *speaking the word* really means: a human act implying reflection and action. "As such," he continues, "it is a primordial human right and not the privilege of a few. Speaking the word is not a true act if it is not at the same time associated with the right of self-expression and world expression, of creating and recreating, of deciding and choosing and ultimately participating in society's historical process" (1971, p. 12). Freire's philosophical anthropology—the view that to be authentically human means to invest the world with one's own sense of meaning and to transform the world through action—will serve as our starting point for examining how his pedagogy serves as a carrier of a Western mind-set.

An essential element in the Western pattern of thinking is reflected in his view of people as agents of historical change. "When adults learn to read and write," according to Freire, "they begin to take initiative in shaping history in the same way that they begin to make themselves." He goes on to say that "shaping history means being present and not merely *represented*" (1981, p. 29). Though many of Freire's comments must be understood in terms of his interest in the liberation of people from Western forms of colonialism, his comments about the need for people to express their humanity by exercising control over their own historical destiny ("to reinvent society, to make history") reflects the Western Enlightenment attitude toward the historically progressive nature of rational thought. Freire sees critical awareness as the ability to decode the cultural rules that otherwise would unconsciously dictate the patterns of everyday life. He represents this conceptual process as an essential attribute of being human and argues, along with Marx and Dewey, that thought is dialectically related to acting in the world in a manner that transforms it. While his view of critical reflection could be seen, with justification, as reflecting the Western view of individualism, he tempers his anthropocentrism by saying that learning to think must lead to democratic and mutually responsible forms of community (1978).

Freire has written a great deal about the danger of pedagogical practices that place the student in bondage to the teacher's pattern of thinking. The "banking concept of education" is thus criticized for treating the student as a passive recipient of other people's knowledge. His emphasis on the importance of maintaining a dialogical relation between the educator and learner, though highly idealistic and surprisingly naive about the sources of vulnerability and dependency in most interpersonal situations, reflects a genuine concern with the liberating possibilities of education. In a letter to co-workers in Guinea-Bissau, he describes the dangers that educators must avoid in teaching students to read the relation between surface-structure experience and deep-structure cultural codes:

> When we start with this manner of reading, moreover, and then seek to go on to a deeper level of coding, the educator must not press his own position to the point that the learner's position is a mere reflection of his own. At the same time, the educator must not negate, as though from shame, his own insights. (1978, p. 92)

Numerous other statements that identify the unique and difficult role the educator is to play could be cited as evidence of Freire's deep commitment to "avoiding every kind of cultural invasion, whether it be open or cleverly hidden" (1978, p. 15).

Yet this is the very point I want to raise about Freire's pedagogy. In order to identify how his pedagogy serves as a carrier of a Western and modernizing mode of consciousness, I would like to identify the essential elements of the Western episteme underlying his view of human liberation. The Western pattern of thought can be seen as being reproduced through his use of metaphors such as "freedom," "liberation," "critical reflection," and "praxis" as well as the idea that man's historical mission is to create a new society. Though he uses these metaphors to argue against cultural domination, he fails to recognize that his own moral and social orientations are expressed in a language that reflects a historically and culturally specific mind-set. While I may agree with most aspects of his moral, social, and pedagogical position, it would be wrong to misrepresent his position as free of cultural invasion. As we begin to examine the assumptions and pattern of thinking implicit in his statements about the process of liberation and what our human nature requires of us, we see that he takes for granted Western assumptions about the progressive nature of change, the power and legitimacy of critical reflection, the moral authority of individualism, and an anthropocentric view of the universe (which makes his position especially problematic in terms of the ecological crisis).

The basic issue that arises when his culturally specific pattern of thinking is introduced into a non-Western culture relates to whether his pedagogy can succeed only by undermining the traditional cultural belief system. Freire intends his views on liberation to apply in all situations where people's thought and social behavior are controlled by the hidden norms of their culture, not just in overcoming the forms of colonial domination practiced by the Portuguese or the British. One of the strengths of Freire's pedagogical theory is that it uses the life world of the learner as the source of the vocabulary and generative themes. Thus the curriculum is always grounded in the taken-for-granted culture of the learner. Learning to read, according to Freire, should never be a passive or abstract experience for the learner. He sees it, instead, as a way of giving the student the symbolic tools to read or decode the pattern of thought and value that shapes his daily life. As he put it:

> In our method, the codifications initially take the form of a photograph or sketch which represents a real existent, or a real existent constructed by the learners. . . . The aim of decodification is to arrive at the critical level of knowledge, beginning with the learner's experiences of the situation in the "real context." . . . The learners, rather than receive information about this or that fact, analyze aspects of their own existential experience represented in the codifications. (1971, p. 10)

Even the selection of vocabulary to be used as the bases of learning to read is derived from the context of the learner's life world: "One selects not only the words most weighted with existential meaning and thus the greatest emotional content, but also typical sayings, as well as words and expressions linked to the experience of the groups in which the researcher participates" (1973, p. 49). The source of cultural invasion in Freire's pedagogy certainly cannot be traced back to a lack of concern about relating the learning process to the life world of the learner. A major strength of his pedagogy, as indicated earlier, is the way thought is dialectically related to action within a specific cultural setting. Ironically, it is Freire's insistence that the primary purpose of the educational process is to change the culture, as well as to strengthen the learners' capacity to take control of their own lives, that is the source of cultural invasion. This view of the individual as agent of change is clearly expressed in Freire's statement that the "act of knowing involves a dialectical involvement which goes from action to reflection and from reflection upon action to a new action. . . . The literacy process must relate *speaking the word* to *transforming reality*, and to man's role in this transformation" (1971, p. 13).

While Freire is sensitive to the importance of grounding the learning process in the context of the learner's life world, he has never in his writings examined the deep symbolic foundations of different cultural codes. Consequently he fails to recognize that there are "reality sets" that provide different ways of understanding and responding to what Daniel Bell (1977) has referred to as the "core questions that confront all human groups: how one meets death, the meaning of tragedy, the nature of obligation, the character of love," and so on (p. 428). Much of Freire's own work has been in highly charged political situations where colonialism had destroyed much of the indigenous culture, and the immediate task was to develop literacy to a level that would allow the development of a new governmental infrastructure. Yet the special revolutionary context of his own work is not a sufficient excuse for avoiding the question of whether elements of traditional cultural belief systems should be preserved, even when they are based on fundamental assumptions that differ radically from those held by Enlightenment thinkers like Freire.

As a means of clarifying the political implications of Freire's silence on the question of how to justify the use of his pedagogy in non-Western cultural settings, I would like to identify some of the characteristics of the Chipewyan mode of consciousness, as described by Ron and Suzanne Scollon in their ethnographic study *Linguistic Convergence* (1979). The Chipewyan are a native cultural group living in the northern part of Alberta, Canada, who have retained their traditional mode of consciousness even though they have interacted with the English and French for over a hundred years. They have even succeeded, with mixed results, in resisting the efforts of public schools to assimilate them into a Western mode of thinking. As the purpose for discussing their pattern of thinking is to establish comparisons with the cultural episteme that Freire takes for granted, I shall identify only those characteristics that appear irreconcilable with the pattern of thinking embedded in Freire's pedagogy. These include the integrative, nonintervening, and individualistic nature of their way of knowing.

In contrast with the dominant Western pattern of thinking, which places a high value on abstract/theoretical thought (whereby theory is to guide practice), the Chipewyan accept as knowledge only what can be fully assimilated into daily experience. The Scollons' report that the Chipewyan have "an absolute mistrust of hearsay knowledge, written accounts of events, and of history itself. . . . True knowledge is considered to be that which one derives from experience" (1979, p. 185). Events are viewed personally, and knowledge must enable the individual to survive life in the bush. Consequently knowledge that is concrete and pragmatic gives the Chipewyan "a sense of mastery, while the abstract means losing control" (p. 201). An example of how the integrative way of knowing differs from the traditional Western pattern of thinking was demonstrated by a Chipewyan who learned to drive a road grader. In contrast to the Western approach, which would involve reading operating manuals and listening to someone else explain the steps of the operation, the Chipewyan, according to the Scollons, sat on the side of the road watching the operation of the road grader. After watching for several days, the man operated the grader with skill and ease. In interviewing the man, the Scollons found that he could not give an abstract explanation of how he operated the machine. The integrative way of thinking enabled him to learn from direct experience; to be able to explain the operation in the abstract, to have theoretical knowledge in our sense, was useless—particularly in terms of other Chipewyans, who would trust only what they learned from their own experience.

The nonintervening nature of the Chipewyan reality set has led Westerners to view them as "passive," "unresponsive," "withdrawn," and "irresponsible." As they tend to think more holistically, the nonintervening aspect of their way of thinking leads them to avoid the form of analysis that segments experience into component parts or to engage in critical reflection for the purpose of changing things. Nonintervention is also reflected in the Chipewyan attitude toward the activities of others. The Scollons observed that adults taught children to be nonintervening by rarely exercising control over their activities. Children were to learn from their own experience; when adults intervened, it was, according to the Scollons, taken as a serious matter.

The last characteristic of the Chipewyan pattern of thinking to be identified for purposes of comparison with Freire's cultural episteme relates to the Chipewyan way of thinking about individualism. In the social sense, their view of individualism involves freedom from dependence on other people. Living in the bush, totally reliant on one's own skills and knowledge, is where the greatest freedom is felt. On the other hand, being with others, especially in larger social groups, causes feelings of unease and disharmony. The Scollons (1979) point out that where "the value is placed on a highly individualistic and personal view of reality, it is then at least consonant with this value that individuals should avoid contexts in which this personal reality is open to challenge and negotiation. We can see, then, that nonintervention in the affairs of others is extended to include nonnegotiation of personal, individualistic reality" (p. 203).

This is admittedly an incomplete representation of the categories and assumptions that underlie the Chipewyan pattern of thought, but the characteristics identified here help put in focus the issue I am raising about the hegemonic nature of Freire's pedagogy. For those who might say that I have chosen an unusual example for my source of comparison, we could substitute the pattern of thought of the Sherpas of Nepal, with their gods who must be propitiated if the well-being of the people is to be assured. Or we could use the Bangang, who live in the western region of the United Republic of Cameroon. The Bangang mind-set involves a strong sense of village solidarity and kinship that influences how they perceive and deal with the problem of witchcraft, which is understood as the expression of selfishness, personal ambition, and the feeling that one can be above the law. The priests or cult members charged with responsibility for detecting and healing witchcraft serve to strengthen the value of sharing, being hospitable, being kind, and so forth—values essential to their notions about village solidarity (Ortner, 1978; Thompson, 1974). If further examples are needed to demonstrate the point of multiple realities, we have only to look at any of the Islamic cultures to find examples of a worldview that is based on cultural assumptions fundamentally different from those shared by Freire and his followers.

As the characteristics of the Chipewyan mind-set have been elaborated above, the question of whether Freire's consciousness-raising pedagogy could be introduced successfully without engaging in a rather traditional form of cultural domination needs to be asked more directly in terms of the Chipewyan mind-set. Freire's concern with teaching literacy is tied to his belief that being able to read about the world gives individuals greater power to distance themselves from the natural attitude toward everyday life. Critical reflection involves examining the relationship of component parts and abstracting themes from the gestalt of the life world. It assumes a connection between abstract thought and the power of human agency. It is also predicated on culturally specific assumptions about the individual's right to question and even reject the traditions of one's cultural group, and to base future actions on abstract and highly experimental ideas. In contrast with the Chipewyan attitude of not wanting to be in situations that lead to the questioning and renegotiation of beliefs, Freire's view of critical thought assumes that the ability to question and reformulate the most basic aspects of everyday life (except for the culture episteme he takes for granted) is what separates man from animals. As he put it:

> From the point of view of a theory of knowledge, this means that the dynamic between codifications of existential situations and decodifications involves the learner in a constant re-construction of their former "ad-miration" of reality. . . . To "ad-mire" is to objectify the "not-I." It is a dialectical operation which characterizes man as man, differentiating him from the animal. (1971, p. 15)

Rather than fostering an integrative form of knowing, like that of the Chipewyan, Freire's view of the rational process is intended to separate us, to give us distance, from immersion in the ongoing flow of experience. The same pattern of thought, when carried to an extreme, is expressed in the activities of technocrats who reify the power of abstract/ theoretical thought. Freire himself is highly critical of abstract theory because he sees it as nondialectical and authoritarian, but the cultural episteme underlying his pedagogy is based on the same epistemological assumption that can easily lead to the extreme forms of technological culture that he criticizes.

Freire's contrasting assumptions about individualism and intervening in the world are, like the Chipewyan views, interrelated. But they are part of a mind-set that is diametrically opposed to the Chipewyan view of reality. To reiterate the Chipewyan position, individualism means dependence on personal experience as the basis of learning; it also means not intervening in the lives of others for the purpose of uplifting their level of thought or saving them from the oppression of others. On the matter of intervention in the lives of others, Freire's position reflects what Max Weber refers to as the "emissary prophecy" tradition, which is fundamental to Western thought: the belief that one possesses a truth that must be shared with, and even imposed on, others in order to save them. Christian missionaries have been displaced as the chief carriers of this element of Western thought by more secular types who can justify their intervention in the lives of others on equally high-sounding moral

grounds. The point that is pertinent to the problem of whether his pedagogy serves as a carrier of a Western mind-set relates to Freire's natural
attitude about the moral certitude of intervening in the lives of others. If
the ability to engage in reflective thought is what differentiates man "from
the animal," as Freire put it, it would seem we have an unquestionable
moral obligation to intervene in other people's lives in order to teach a
pattern of thinking that will enable them to fully express their human
nature. Freire's cultural bias toward change, progress, social revolution,
and the continual problematizing and renegotiation of the rules that
govern everyday life makes intervention in the lives of others both a
moral and ontological obligation. That it may be justified in some cases,
but not in others, is not mentioned in his writings. If a revolutionary
socialist government were to come to power in Canada and invite Freire
to use his adult literacy program with the Chipewyan, he would undoubtedly welcome the opportunity to emancipate another group from the
oppression of their own cultural traditions. Even if it were possible to
establish dialogue, the pedagogy would involve the most fundamental
forms of cultural domination.

On the question of individualism, Freire's mind-set is equally distant from the Chipewyan position. Freire reflects the existential-humanistic view of individualism. From the existential (and Christian) tradition he has taken the idea that rational thought should govern individual
choice. His cultural episteme also includes the idea that the higher form
of individualism involves continual self-transformation and struggle to
avoid being "submerged in the historical process." The highest state of
being, what Freire (1973) called "critical transitive consciousness," is
"characteristic of authentically democratic regimes and corresponds to
highly permeable, interrogative, restless and dialogical forms of life"
(pp. 18–19). Unlike the Chipewyan's view of individualism, Freire's inter-
ventionist and transformative view of individualism leads to participation in the "cultural circles" where, through dialogue between learners
and coordinators (educators), the cultural codes that shape individual
and social life in the community are problematized and reformulated.
This approach to learning would involve a fundamentally alien (and
Western) experience for the Chipewyan.

Since Freire's pedagogy reproduces the mind-set of a Western and
modern mode of consciousness, it would be quite appropriate to use it
with adult populations who possess language codes based on Western
categories of thought. It may also be the only approach that can be taken
in revolutionary situations such as Guinea-Bissau, where traditional cultures have been overturned or partially assimilated into the culture of
the colonizing power. Whether the pedagogy should be used in an Islamic

culture or one not already partially assimilated to the Western mind-set is problematic. Since I do not have field research available to me, and Freire's categories of thought appear to blind him to the problem, I would like to proceed at a theoretical level by posing several questions for which I do not have a good sense of what the answer should be. The questions arise from both personal uncertainties and the inability to ignore an increasing body of evidence dealing with the degraded state of the earth's ecosystems, the inability to resolve social justice issues through the political process, and the quality of social life that suggests that modernization along the lines of Western cultures represents an experiment in cultural evolution that is not likely to survive in the long run. The questions I want to raise about the wisdom of extending the hegemonic influence of Western patterns of thinking may possibly be interpreted by some as the expression of naive romanticism about the virtues of traditional cultures, or as a more perverse form of reaction to efforts at social reform. Both would be a misreading of the questions and the spirit in which they are being asked. I am as motivated by concerns with social justice as are revolutionary social reformers. But I have learned that the language used to justify reform and revolutionary change often masks the displacement of one form of injustice by another form. Today, political rhetoric succeeds as social policies increasingly fail. The questions are thus not intended to impugn the value of working for social justice, but to challenge the natural attitude that views change and modernization as progressive, critically reflective individualism as an expression of the highest mode of consciousness, and the state as the most progressive form of social and political organization. The issues are far more complicated than our teleological mode of consciousness has allowed us to recognize. Since I cannot entirely escape the Western categories of thought that I share with Freire, my questions are as much a challenge to my own position as they are to his.

Between January 1975 and the spring of 1976, Freire wrote a series of letters to Mario Cabral about the role education should play in the reconstruction of Guinea-Bissau during and following the struggle for liberation from the Portuguese. The letters are a rich mixture of theory and concrete suggestions for educating a society to the values of socialism. Although he addresses problems he sees as associated with capitalistic societies—separation of mental and manual labor, the artificiality and alienation of a commodity/consumer society, the need to free the work process from the profit motive—he does not address other problems that are fundamental to understanding the Westernizing trajectory of Guinea-Bissau culture that is furthered by his pedagogy. These problems include secularization in a modernizing society, the double bind connected with the reflective form of individualism, the rise of the state, and the relationship between socialism and the growth of a commodity/technicist culture.

The connection between modernization and secularization can be understood in terms of the increasing privatization of religious beliefs and the use of utilitarian principles and a purposive mode of rationality to justify the moral basis of social policies. The privatizing of religious belief, as we have experienced it in the West, is, in part, a result of Enlightenment thinking about the separation of church and state. This accommodation, it was thought, would allow reason to guide the destiny of society, with the result that faith and superstition would control only the lives of church members. Whether the limiting of the influence of religion has led to the triumph of reason in settling daily affairs, or has contributed to the emergence of new forms of religion, is a heavily debated issue. Although the literature on secularization includes numerous and often conflicting theories, there are nevertheless powerful arguments being advanced pertaining to the influence of modernization on religious belief (Bellah, 1970; P. Berger, 1967; Luckmann, 1967). I should like to identify several of the issues raised in this literature, and to suggest several questions that arise from the use of Freire's pedagogy in Third World countries.

One of the most persuasive arguments on the secularizing influence of modernization is advanced by Peter Berger. As it is developed in several books, I shall summarize the essential aspects of his analysis. In saying that "there is a tendency toward the secularization of the political order that goes naturally with the development of modern industrialism," Berger is pointing to changes he sees precipitated by the emergence of a technological bureaucratic mode of thinking that he associates with modernization (1967, p. 130). This mode of consciousness involves a purposive rational mode of thought that translates the commonsense world into abstract and theoretical concerns. This mode of consciousness further understands the world by segmenting experiences into component parts that can then be reconstituted into new patterns and systems. The proclivity toward thinking in terms of components and systems underlies, in social practice, the development of separate fields of expertise; it is also the modern epistemological foundation for the separation between mental and manual labor. Technological consciousness also relies on measurement and data to validate its claims. Consequently it discounts other forms of knowledge and ignores what cannot be interpreted in terms of the positivistic framework. This pattern of thinking, according to Berger, leads to segmenting the life world of the individual to the point where the individual operates within many different roles, but becomes "homeless" in the sense that the life world ceases to lack symbolic unity (P. Berger, Berger, & Kellner, 1974). This segmenting of the individual's life world, as well as the dominance of positivistic thinking, leads to secularization and the privatizing of religious belief.

In order to put in focus the political-moral issue that results from the privatizing of religious belief, it would be useful to establish a working definition of how the word *religion* is being used. For this purpose I shall use Clifford Geertz's explanation:

> Religion is: (1) a system of symbols which acts to (2) establish powerful, pervasive, and long lasting moods and motivations in men by (3) formulating conceptions of a general order of existence and (4) clothing these conceptions with such an aura of factuality that (5) the moods and motivations seem uniquely realistic. (1973, p. 90)

Religion can thus be understood as the overarching belief system that provides answers to existential questions pertaining to how life is to be lived and how to interpret the meaning of death; it must also be seen as providing the moral basis of decisions affecting the life of the individual and the community. A functionalist interpretation of religion would further emphasize how religious beliefs bond the individual and the community and the collective life of the community to tradition. The issue that arises in terms of the modernizing and Westernizing influence of Freire's pedagogy relates to the shift in the mode of moral legitimation that occurs as the members of a society adopt the Western view of rational individualism. Manfred Stanley analyzed this shift in Western consciousness from a medieval to a modern form of consciousness and has noted that from "the Reformation onward theological individualism followed by political, economic, and social individualism became part of the Modernist attack upon all received traditions of corporate authority, even as modern materialism in scientific philosophy gradually eroded the ontological foundations of divine revelation as a source of guidance for social control" (1972, p. 288). Stanley also observed that one of the fundamental cultural changes that followed in the wake of secularization was the increasing dependence on the use of utilitarianism for determining the moral legitimacy of social policy. Jürgen Habermas, viewing the rise of purposive rationality from a critical-theory perspective, also warned of a "legitimation crisis" as the state extends its epistemological orthodoxy into domains of social and individual life that were previously guided by belief systems that addressed deeper existential needs. Although the adherents of the positivist position generally acknowledge that their epistemology is not equipped to deal with moral questions, both

Stanley and Habermas saw it as the epistemological orthodoxy of the technocratic society. As a consequence, other modes of knowing, including religion, have become delegitimated as sources for justifying the moral principles that underly political decisions.

Although this discussion covers complex issues that deserve far more extended treatment, the issues that need to be addressed by people using Freire's pedagogy are nevertheless quite clear. The first issue relates to the tension between the form of individualism to which his form of critical reflection leads and the legitimacy of traditional religious beliefs that bond the individual to the community and the traditional moral codes—including the codes regulating relationships within the larger biotic community. The second issue relates to whether secularization (the disenfranchisement of religion from the public sector) contributes to the rise of a new class of intellectuals and expert technocrats who will provide a new symbolic foundation for directing the community and the state. The third issue relates to how democratic and collective decision making can be sustained when the purposive rational mode of thought is seen as the only legitimate basis for public discourse and values clarification. If we take Geertz's definition of religion seriously, we can identify a fourth implication of the modernization process: namely, the displacement of traditional religious control by the ideology of the state. Bell points to the possible emergence of political religions when he asks, "Is it an accident that the modern world, having delimited the authority of religion in the public sphere, has been the first to create 'total power' in the political realm—the fusion of beliefs and institutions into a monolithic entity that claims the power of a new faith?" (1977, p. 447).

Freire's own position on the role religion is to play in the reconstruction process is unclear. During the time he worked as a consultant to the government of Guinea-Bissau, he was associated with the World Council of Churches in Geneva. But his major writings do not contain the word *religion*, which is surprising because of the influence religion has had on the lives of the people Freire's pedagogy is designed to liberate. Does he see it in some social contexts as a conservative force that must be overturned, and in other social settings as a liberating force? Is a primitive religion that has no creed or separate church organization, and that involves its members in a fluid relationship between the world of myth and the actual world, inferior to rationally based religions as we know them in the West? Are all forms of religion to be replaced by rationality, as Marx and other followers of the Enlightenment tradition thought? As religious belief provides for both constraint and release, one can only assume from reading Freire that religion must be dealt with in the terms of the Western formula that requires that it become a matter of personal belief or, hopefully, displaced entirely by rational thought. The constraining aspect of religion, which occurs at both psychic and social levels, would seem to be in conflict with Freire's view of individuals as engaged in the "constant problematizing of their existential situation" (1971, p. 17). Freire's view of liberation appears to involve an important paradox in that it can be achieved in a non-Western setting only by giving up one's traditional worldview and adopting the segmented world of Western thought—including the natural attitude toward a secularized world that fosters the growth of individualism

This brings me to the second area of concern about the Westernizing influence of Freire's pedagogy. His view of individualism encompasses the most deeply embedded cliches of the Western mind-set: knowledge is power, change is progressive, man is (ought to be) the master of his fate, and so forth. Although a student of social linguistics would raise serious questions about the ontological status of Freire's existential-humanistic image of the individual who is perpetually engaged in both social and self-transformation, another set of questions can be asked about the potential conflict between his view of critically reflective individualism and the eschatological aspects of his ideological orientation. The view of individualism that he adopts is, according to Lucian Goldmann, part of the worldview created during the Enlightenment to serve the interests of the bourgeois. A concomitant of their view of the rational, self-determining individual was a view of the state that served essentially as an impartial referee; its function was not to plan, rationalize, or control the lives of people, but to ensure that contracts were fulfilled and the law upheld. Freire is attempting to accommodate the liberal bourgeois view of the critically reflective individual with the idea of the state that has the obligation to plan the future development of society and to intervene in the lives of people to ensure that their behavior and expectations are consistent with the goals of the state. One source of the double bind inherent in his view of individualism relates to the difficulty of reconciling a planned society with his view of the existentially responsible, critically rational individual. Even if he assumes that the planning can be done democratically (he is highly critical of "rigid bureaucracy"), there is always the possibility that critical reflection will lead the individual to act more like Dostoevsky's "underground man," who deliberately falls out of step with the rationally planned society.

The other source of the double bind connected with Freire's view of individualism relates to the fact that an increased emphasis on individualism can lead to subjectivism, whereby traditional knowledge and moral codes are increasingly seen either as a constraint or as irrelevant (and probably both). Although Freire urges the students in Guinea-Bissau to learn their own history, his view of history as a source of control is particularly nondialectical, which is surprising given his commitment to dialectical thought. Unlike the cultural conservative who recognizes the dialectical tension among the past, present, and future, Freire aligns himself with the modernizing ethos that glorifies the individual's right (Freire makes it an ontological necessity) to overturn tradition. His references to recognizing the context and history of the learner are always made with the understanding that the purpose of literacy is to enable the learner to "make history." This emphasis on change pits the individual against the authority of tradition. As the authority of tradition is eroded, subjective feeling and critical reflection (also grounded in the subjectivity of the individual) become the new source of authority. Irving Howe (1967) observed that subjectivity is an essential characteristic of the modern way of thinking. How to think about tradition, according to Howe, is an unresolved problem for the modern mode of consciousness—as he put it, "the dilemma that modernism must always struggle but never quite triumph, and then, after a time, must struggle in order not to triumph" (p. 13). By recognizing critical reflection as the only source of knowledge and legitimation of moral values, Freire introduces a new dialectic that he hopes will lead to corporate forms of responsibility but is more likely to contribute to the growth of subjective individualism.

The third area where Freire's theory, if carried out, represents a form of cultural invasion has to do with the rise of the state as a source of total political power. Since we do not yet have good cross-cultural studies of the rise of the state, it would be inappropriate to identify the emergence of the state as a uniquely Western political phenomenon. But there has been more attention given to the social, political, and cultural changes that accompany the rise of the state as the preeminent source of political power. Like my own view of the state until fairly recently, Freire sees the authority of the state as a natural aspect of social existence. Thus he can write about education in Guinea-Bissau: "The definition of what to know—without which it is not possible to organize the programmatic content of educational activity—is also intimately related to the overall plan for the society, to the priorities this plan requires, and to the concrete conditions for its realization" (1978, p. 101). An "overall plan for society" implies the existence of the state as the center of political power for the organization of daily life. The "creation of a new society" that is to follow in the wake of a literacy program also yields other benefits that ensure that the new society has the characteristics of the modern state. Freire establishes this connection between the learning activities that go on in the "cultural circles" and the need of the state to regulate the activities of its citizens:

Another important aspect is the active role that the participants in the Cultural Circle must play from the beginning of the discussions, including the pre-program presentations as a work project. Individuals and groups should have, if the project is accepted, an active role in the collection of local data, basic to various parts of the program. All kinds of data must be assembled locally—about the area of rice cultivation, the way this cultivation takes place, the number of cultivatable acres and the number actually under cultivation, the difficulties the peasants meet in their daily work, the number of inhabitants of the area, distribution, the means of communication work instruments, health, education, etc. This investigative activity is itself highly educational, and also increases the information of the educators or offers them entirely new information. What is more, the results offer a source of information of inestimable value to the government. (1978, pp. 118–119)

This rather lengthy quotation finally gets to the real purpose of literacy—the need to have a literate population that can provide data on their activities to governmental authorities, and to be able to follow the policies that the government dictates.

The connection between literacy and the rise of the state is a central theme in Ivan Illich's *Shadow Work*. Before reading Illich, I shared the conventional wisdom that connected literacy with the self-determining individual, and viewed it as essential to overcoming reactionary social elements. Freire also seems to share this Western view of literacy, with all of its romantic yearnings about social progress and individual uplift. Illich's analysis of the development of literacy in the West exposes the political fact that the state needs a literate population if it is to communicate with them. The state also needs, as Illich has shown, a universal form of education that ensures that literacy involves a common language if it is to exercise effective control over all regions of the country. Before the emergence of the state, people spoke vernacular languages and lived in small, self-sufficient cultural groups where life was governed by traditional beliefs. Illich notes that at one time the crown respected the autonomy of cultural traditions that existed within the realm, but that the emergence of the modern state required a common language in order to ensure central control. Thus universal education became a way of undermining the influence of local cultural traditions, just as secularization and the rise of rational individualism eroded other sources of constraint that interfered with the power of the state. As Illich states:

The new state takes from people the words on which they subsist, and transforms them into a standardized language which henceforth they

are compelled to use. . . . The switch from the vernacular to an offi-
cially taught mother tongue is perhaps the most significant—and, therefore, least researched—event in the coming of a commodity-intensive
society. (1980, p. 44)

The self-sufficiency of vernacular groups that Illich considers as a
positive form of social organization is, for Freire, a hindrance to the
growth and planning of the state. In "Letter 11" addressed to co-workers
in Guinea-Bissau, Freire discussed the possibility of what he termed
"regressive illiteracy." Where the principles of socialist production were
being implemented, the danger of people's returning to traditional cultural patterns was, in his view, being minimized. But where conditions
for change do not exist, he warned, "the possibility of failure accompa-
nies the literacy struggle from the beginning; the chances of regressive
illiteracy are enormous." He goes on to recommend:

> It is for this reason that it appears to us that a campaign of adult lit-
> eracy in Guinea-Bissau, even if it is national in scope, ought to begin
> in the areas where the process of transformation is underway, and,
> possibly, in those places where, following the plan of the government
> and of the Party, certain changes will take place within a short time.
> In this hypothesis, literacy education could even stimulate some of the
> changes. (1978, pp. 113–114)

How this decidedly Western view of the role of the state, with its emphasis on change, growth, and centralized planning, could be reconciled with
the "re-Africanization of mentality" Freire does not say. His liberation
rhetoric appears to blind him to the fact that when it is used in a non-
Western cultural context, it could legitimately be viewed as a continua-
tion of Western domination. Although Freire understands that language
cannot be viewed as apolitical, he does not recognize that it reproduces
conceptual frameworks that are culturally and historically specific.

    This brings me to the last area of concern about the Westernizing
influence of Freire's pedagogy, namely, the relationship between socialism and the growth of a commodity/technicist culture. Again, Freire
makes morally appealing statements but fails to recognize that the
epistemic tradition embedded in his pedagogy has historically led to the
very cultural conditions he warns against. For instance, he writes his
co-workers that "a society becomes totally ambiguous when, while
attempting to follow socialism, it allows itself to become fascinated by
the myth of consumerism" (1978, p. 108). Socialism, by its very nature,
should enable people to avoid the materialism of capitalism. For a person who stresses the vital connection between theory and practice (rheto-

ric and reality), it is surprising that he does not look at the historical record of societies organized in accordance with Marxist principles. If socialism should lead to a form of society that avoids the excessive materialism of a consumer/technicist culture, why has the dream not been realized? That Marxism is built on the same deep epistemic codes that produced capitalist forms of society is a possibility that does not occur to Freire. On the surface the differences between the two forms of society—Marxist society emphasizing centralized planning and utilitarianism as the basis of its moral principles and capitalist society emphasizing the free market of supply and demand, and profitability—appear fundamental. But when one gets beyond these surface differences—surface because capitalist societies must engage in more planning, while Marxist principles are now being abandoned for free-market conditions—there is, as the bedrock of both systems, a common pattern of thought that explains why the two systems have evolved substantially the same forms of a consumer/technicist culture. Both systems are built on a teleological view of reality that equates change with progress. They also share a common view of rationality that elevates abstract-theoretical thinking over other ways of knowing, which contributes to both the separation of mental and manual labor and the rise of a class of intellectual experts. Other aspects of a shared epistemic tradition include a bias toward positivistic forms of knowledge, an obsession with using efficiency as the basis for determining worth and effectiveness, using utilitarian principles as a moral source of legitimation for policy decisions, and upholding a secular-anthropocentric view of the world that has ravaged the environment. The connections between these epistemic orientations and what others have called a technological mode of consciousness should be, by now, so much a part of the conventional wisdom that it comes as a particular surprise when a person as thoughtful and informed as Freire suggests that socialism can avoid the materialism of capitalistic societies.

If space permitted, I could pursue two other lines of analysis that would help explain why socialism cannot lead to any form other than a consumer society that degrades the environment. One line of analysis would take us into the Marxist tendency to emphasize "man" as producer. The other line of analysis would involve examining the traditional cultures that are viewed as backward, primitive, and unenlightened by Westerners in order to determine how their belief system enables them to maintain cultural patterns that do not reduce the individual to the role of consumer-producer and the environment to a "natural resource." I suspect that one of the differences between self-sufficient, traditionally directed cultures and the modernizing cultural model that Freire wants to further in Guinea-Bissau relates to the role that religion plays in regulating the individual's relations with others and the natural environment. A comparative study would lead, I suspect, to recognizing that the reflective individual, educated to see the emptiness of myth and ritual, not only stands at the center of the universe, but stands alone. Not able to experience the sacred or participate fully in the communal, the individual's primary avenue of expression will be that of a consumer and producer who is programmed by the dominant cultural code to expect change.

Fortunately, the lived world is quite different from that represented by Western theorists. The anomic tendencies I identified with reflective individualism must be understood as only a cultural orientation. The life world of the individual includes dimensions of experience that may even be explicitly rejected in terms of ideological commitment: Radicals conserve cultural traditions through their language, rationalists possess a cosmology with characteristics that are surprisingly similar to those of religious belief, advocates of revolutionary change often live ordered lives and possess bourgeois tastes, and so forth. The inability to adapt the patterns of thought and action of daily life to the contours of Western ideology, no matter how attractive and messianic the ideology, will also characterize the Third World persons' encounter with "re-inventing" their society. Freire's bias toward change might cause them to view cultural atavisms as examples of "regressive illiteracy," but there will be cultural continuities—at least for those who are not forced, in the name of "overall planning," to give up their vernacular language. But the nature of his pedagogy carries a powerful and seductive message, and it will undoubtedly have a modernizing effect. The degree of Westernization that it introduces and the degree to which "society becomes totally ambiguous" are questions that require careful attention on the part of Freire and his followers. As I said at the outset, I find much about this pedagogy attractive and usable—but only in an already Westernized cultural context. Whether it should be used in a non-Western setting is problematic. The justification will have to be framed in arguments that go beyond the Marxist/humanist framework Freire uses, since that framework underlies older, more easily recognizable forms of cultural imperialism.

Chapter 4

The Dialectic of Nihilism and the State

*Implications for an
Emancipatory Theory of Education*

The argument that an emancipatory form of education that liberates the individual contributes both to the nihilism of modern culture and to strengthening the authority of the state requires thinking against the grain of conventional wisdom. But if we do not think against the grain of the liberal orthodoxy that connects emancipation with political empowerment of the individual, we may fail to recognize the irony that characterizes the relationship between emancipation and nihilism, and the ways in which the state is dependent upon the growth of nihilism. In contrast to the conventional argument, what is being suggested here is that emancipation, when based on the liberal view of the atomistic individual, leads to a decline of individual authority and to an increase in the ability of the state to claim the forms of authority essential to legitimating its exercise of power. How the state is strengthened by the nihilistic tendencies within the modernizing process can be more fully clarified by identifying the epistemological differences between a modernizing culture and traditional cultures. The suggestion that there is a modernizing culture and a great many expressions of traditional culture is predicated on the argument that modernization involves a pattern of thought that is essentially Western in origin; it also recognizes important similarities in the patterns of thought that characterize traditional cultures.

At the epistemological level, which involves conceptual categories and assumptions used to organize reality into coherent and meaningful patterns, it is possible to recognize fundamental differences between the modernizing culture and the conceptual patterns of traditional cultures. Although the distinctions deserve more extended analysis, I shall identify only the differences particularly relevant to understanding how the state, in promoting the modernizing process, gains by undermining the symbolic underpinnings of traditional cultures. A basic distinction between modern and traditional cultures relates to the forms of knowledge that are recognized as legitimate. What Robin Horton (1982) terms "cognitive 'modernism' " tends to value explicit forms of knowledge that can be expressed in the form of theory and treated as context-free (thus allowing for generalization) (p. 243). Alvin Gouldner (1979) points out how this form of knowledge is essential to the discourse of intellectuals and technocrats, who reject traditional sources of authority by assuming that assertions must be justified on the basis of evidence within a competitive intellectual arena. Michael Oakeshott (1962), in arguing that all human activities involve both practical (tacit) and technical forms of knowledge, makes the same point by stating that the modern form of rationalism devalues tacit knowledge by promoting only the technical (explicit) forms of knowledge that can be formulated into rules, principles, directives, and maxims that can be communicated in the abstract. Traditional cultures depend more on tacit, implicit forms of knowledge, which are context-dependent and shared as people participate in routines of everyday life, rather than explicit and technical forms of knowledge (Douglas, 1975). As context becomes an important source of meaning, the forms of knowledge tend to be more communal and consensual in orientation. The epistemic difference can be seen in the relationship among explicit forms of knowledge, literacy (which involves abstract, decontextualized forms of knowledge), and the growth of individualism. A greater emphasis on tacit, implicit forms of knowledge involves, on the other hand, oral patterns of knowledge transmission and communal rather than individualistic forms of relationship (Goody, 1977).

Other differences that separate modern from traditional cultures include the assumption that change is inherently progressive and can be rationally controlled. This assumption, which represents a teleological pattern of conceptual organization, underpins the natural attitude of modern consciousness. By way of contrast, members of traditional cultures tend to see a continuity between the present and the past, use human memory as a repository of traditional forms of knowledge that have survived over time, and view change as a threat to the more certain path of "tradition handed down by instruction, example and commentary" (J. Berger, 1979, p. 203). Another basic difference between modern and traditional forms of cognition relates to the nature and locus of authority. Modern consciousness tends to locate authority in the judgment of the individual, even as real power is increasingly centralized in the bureacracy of the state and the epistemic traditions of elite social groups. In its earlier phase of development, the emphasis was placed on rationality as the source of individual authority; more recently, the rationalistic foundations of authority have been challenged as being overly technicist by those who want to use authentic inner feelings as the basis for recognizing the ultimate authority of individual judgment. In contrast, traditional cultures tend to recognize a variety of sources of authority— community, tradition, sacred texts, myths, and so forth. The key point of difference is that authority is not located in the critically reflective process of the individual, in the purposive and rational mode of thought of experts, or in emotive judgments.

The last difference that I want to identify relates to the secularizing tendencies of modern culture. The emphasis on individualism and the rational process, as well as the belief that people are in control of their own destinies, undermine both the conceptual unity and sources of legitimation that characterize religion within tradition cultures. Unlike modern culture, where religion is segmented and treated as a matter of personal preference, religion in traditional cultures cannot be separated from the shared symbolic and aesthetic sense of order. The point to be made about the secularism of modern culture relates to the use of utilitarian principles and, more recently, technicist forms of knowledge, as a substitute basis for legitimating moral decisions within the public domain. Measurement rather than the "authoritative conception of the overall shape of reality" (Geertz, 1973, p. 104) becomes the new basis of authority.

If we accept Max Weber's view of the state as the self-expanding center of bureaucratic control and administrative efficiency, or Foucault's notion of the modern state as taking over the traditional pastoral power of the church and increasing its control through the development of new forms of technical knowledge, we come back to the basic political issue of how the authority for the exercise of power is to be legitimated. But before we examine how the problem of legitimation influences the actions and ideological orientation of the state, particularly in relation to traditional cultures, it is necessary to elaborate more fully Foucault's view of the pastoral function of the modern state. Pastoral power, as previously exercised by the church, involved intervention in people's lives for the purpose of salvation. The achievement of this goal, in turn, required the acquisition of information not only about the community's life in general, but also about the thoughts and activities of each individual member—over the span of their entire life. The purpose of pastoral power was to obtain information about the individual and to bring into play the political technologies necessary for aligning the life of the individual with the definition of truth that provided the basis of authority for the exercise of pastoral power. According to Foucault (1982), the modern state secularized the idea of "leading people to salvation in the next world" by "ensuring it in this world" (pp. 213–216). This new form of pastoral power thus is concerned with health, education, security, protection, economic well-being, and so forth. To fulfill its secular pastoral responsibility, the modern state has expanded the apparatus for acquiring information (which involves greater surveillance and information storage), crisis mediation, and police control. It also developed a globalizing ideology to justify the centralization of power as well as its ever-expanding penetration into the activities of everyday life. Foucault makes the point that the modern state, given its expanding pastoral function and control over the use of political technologies, requires a particular form of individualism. In his dialectical view of power, which involves "an action upon an action," there is a particular "type of individualization which is linked to the state" (1982, p. 216). To put it in a way that illuminates the state's vested interest in a modernizing ideology, the state requires a modern form of individuality—one that is educated to think in terms of the progressive nature of change, the authority of expert knowledge, the primacy of self-interest, the relativity of all values and ideas, and the myth of the autonomous individual.

A second reason for the promotion of modernization by the state is that it must control the symbolic foundations of the legitimation process. That is, it must be able to establish the form of knowledge that will be perceived as authoritative. The existence of alternative sources of authority, as found in traditional cultures, would not only diminish the administrative efficiency of the state, but continually threaten its basis of legitimacy. In his discussion of the state's expanding role in managing economic crisis, Jürgen Habermas identified the problem of legitimation as crucial to the changing relationship between the state and individuals still rooted in traditional cultures. Not only did he view the state's use of purposive rationality as undermining traditional modes of consciousness (and thus displacing the moral foundations of authority with more technicist-oriented criteria); he also viewed the extension of administrative planning as a process that disrupts taken-for-granted beliefs by politicizing "areas of life previously assigned to the private sphere" (1975, p. 72). This process of politicizing tacit forms of knowledge essential to the bonding processes in traditional cultures creates liminal spaces in thought and social practice. In experiencing the liminality of being "betwixt and between" established definitions that previously served as the basis of social experience, the individual who is under the influence of a modernizing institution like the public school will encounter the systematic relativizing of traditional beliefs and behavioral norms. But the restoration of meaning, as well as the symbolic foundations upon which it must be grounded, is now to be governed by the cognitive rules of modern consciousness. These include the assumption that the new definitions of how to think and act will be determined through a form of discourse that uses evidence to support assertions and assumes that in a competitive environment the most powerful and truthful ideas will emerge and that no area of experience should be immune from being problematized through critical inquiry. In effect, the politicizing process that Habermas puts in focus leads to adopting the cognitive rules that characterize the modernizing speech code of intellectuals and technicists—the very groups who possess the cultural capital necessary for communicative competence and for controlling the definition of what constitutes relevant evidence.

This brings us back to the question of how public schools strengthen the process of nihilism in modern cultures and, in the process, contribute to the pastoral power of the state. In *Shadow Work*, Ivan Illich made the point that the modern state "requires a standard language understood by all those subject to its laws" (1981, pp. 47–48). Although the ideology used to justify public education, and thus universal literacy, emphasized empowerment in the many activities connected with citizenship, public schools undermined the conceptual authority of vernacular languages by teaching in the language prescribed by the state. This insured that subjects would adopt a mode of consciousness and thus a set of taken-for-granted attitudes essential for conceptual subjugation to the interests of the state. The use of the schools by the state to undermine the authority of traditional cultures resulted in important variations and challenges that cannot be taken up in this chapter. What can be dealt with, however, is how the schools in North America serve as carriers of a modernizing and nihilistic mode of consciousness that strengthens the authority of the state. Elements of this analysis may also be relevant to other modernizing cultures.

Educators do not consciously promote modernization, as very few of them have even thought about the cognitive differences between modern and traditional cultures. Nor have many educators thought about the nature of nihilism. Their concerns are more with subject matter, teaching techniques, and managing the social relationships essential to the ecology of schools. The rationale they give for schooling, when they are asked, is that education strengthens the self-development of individuals and empowers them in an economic and political sense. Although this ideology is not entirely naive, it hides the relationship between schools and the problematic aspects of modern consciousness that they reinforce.

More specifically, this ideology serves to obscure the contradiction between the claims made on behalf of individualism and democracy, and the political and cultural processes actually going on.

To state the argument in its most succinct form, schools reproduce in the consciousness of students the conceptual categories and assumptions essential to modernization. When one examines the characteristics of modern consciousness, it becomes quite clear that schools are not conservative institutions, unless one wants to argue that schools conserve a pattern of thought that takes for granted that the future can be controlled only as the past is destroyed The chief elements of modern consciousness reinforced through schooling include a taken-for-granted attitude toward the idea that individuals are autonomous beings who have feelings, make rational judgments, choose their own values, and are responsible for their own success or failure. A second element of modern consciousness reinforced in schools is that the rational process, expressed either as critical reflection or as theory buttressed by data, is the primary source of power and authority. Other elements include a taken-for-granted attitude toward the progressive nature of change, the legitimacy of technological innovation, and the authority of expert knowledge. These elements of modern consciousness are not taught directly or made explicit; rather, they are transmitted as part of the conceptual framework within which the facts and explanations provided by teachers and textbooks must be interpreted.

In terms of the argument that schools foster nihilism and, in the process, enhance the power of the state, it is essential that the connection between the chief characteristics of modern consciousness and nihilism be established. Nihilism involves the loss of meaning and the sense that nothing has authority in one's life. It is the relativization of all ideas, values, and cultural norms (Dreyfus, 1981). When "inner experience" becomes the ultimate concern, there is no reason to have commitments shared by others; in effect, everything is equal in value to everything else. Nietzsche viewed the Western approach to rationalism as contributing to "the *advent of nihilism*" (1968, p. 3). The process of critical inquiry involves, as he viewed it, a double bind wherein the continual search for truth is based on the assumption that truth could never be found. But the search, when considered as evidence of progress, has the effect of relativizing the foundations of belief by making authority contingent upon the emotive or reflective judgment of the individual. Johan Goudsblom (1980), the Dutch sociologist, extended Nietzsche's analysis of nihilism to take account of how a culturally specific language code, with its epistemological categories, not only reproduces in successive generations a relativizing mode of thinking but also provides the ideological justification, that is, the idea of progress, moral integrity, and the discovery of a higher truth.

Nihilism is also fostered by those aspects of technological consciousness that emphasize instrumental control of the present and future either by the actual destruction of the past (in the name of efficiency and cost-effectiveness) or by omission from the socialization process. Traditions that are not sustained as part of the symbolic world adults share with youth will cease to be part of individual memory and thus will not represent an alternative source of authority for assessing the political and cultural significance of new ideas and technologies. Endless cultural experimentation, expressed in the willingness to incorporate every form of innovation into daily life, requires, as part of individual's natural attitude, the acceptance of the relativity of all cultural norms, ideas, and values.

In socializing students to the pattern of thought and the language codes that underpin modern consciousness, the schools contribute to the growth of nihilism and, to use a much older sociological category, the alienation of the individual. For the loss of meaning, shared commitments, and sense of authority outside of subjective experience leave the individual feeling alone and alienated. This is one of the great ironies of the modern ideology, which represents the remissive/hedonistic personality as the most progressive expression of freedom; as John Carroll (1977) observed, the promise of the remissive life of pleasure and freedom has undermined the symbolic foundations of individual authority.

Traditional cultures—which recognize the individual as an integral part of the larger whole; the importance of implicit and tacit forms of knowledge; the manner in which everyday life is grounded in living traditions; the connection between context, technical forms of knowledge, and practical experience; and shared sources of authority not contingent upon individual judgment—do not exhibit the cognitive and personality traits associated with nihilism and alienation. They may not be as technologically advanced, but the individual members do not experience the sense of meaninglessness and relativism associated with nihilism. This fact should not be used as a basis for arguing that modernization should be reversed. But it can be used for arguing that people concerned with the process of cultural transmission and renewal should be concerned with mitigating the most extreme and destructive elements of modern consciousness. For educators, this means understanding the pattern of consciousness reinforced in the classroom and asking whether the form of individualism that results from this form of consciousness empowers the state or contributes to what Peter Berger and Richard Neuhaus call "mediating social structures" that stand between the private life of the individual and the mega structures of the state (1977, p. 2).

Schools cannot entirely escape transmitting the ideological orientation of the larger society, but it is possible, in the case of modernizing societies, to reformulate traditional educational goals in a manner that modifies significantly the ideology that underlies the advent of nihilism. By not reinforcing the nihilistic tendencies within society, the schools will also be contributing to a different form of individualism, one that is not linked to the expanding pastoral power of the state. Emancipatory theories of education, with the exception of those propounded by John Dewey, have been based on the assumption that greater self-direction (autonomy) of the individual could be attained if the educational process fostered critical reflection. This particular interpretation of individual empowerment rests on Enlightenment assumptions about the nature of the atomistic individual, the culture-free nature of the rational process, and the progressive nature of change—assumptions that also underlie modern consciousness. Given these assumptions, emancipation is interpreted as escaping not from specific forms of social injustice, but more generally from the authority of tradition and the norms of community. As Paulo Freire (1971), a leading educational theorist of liberation, puts it: "To exist humanly is to name the world, to change it" (p. 76). Through critical reflection, the individual is transformed from being an object to being a subject of history; or, as Freire (1985) stated: "As active participants and real subjects, we can make history only when we are continually critical of our very lives" (p. 199). Although the merits of Freire's pedagogy can be justified on other grounds, Freire's philosophical anthropology, and thus his view of emancipation, can be criticized as contributing to the spread of nihilism and, indirectly, to the growing authority of the state (see Chapter 3 of this volume). The emphasis on the authority of reflective thought, the power of theory to guide action, and the view that the future can only be controlled as the past is destroyed represents, to reiterate, the relativizing of all forms of authority except the reflective judgment of the individual.

The educational goal of empowerment, what I would refer to as communicative competence, needs to be understood in terms of a set of assumptions different from those derived from the Enlightenment. It must also take into account the dangers of cultural nihilism and the malaise of individual alienation. Instead of assuming that atomistic individuals think, communicate, and transform the world in terms of their subjective intentionality, we need to recognize the individual as a social-cultural being; that is, in terms of an intersubjective self formed by social and linguistic characteristics of the culture. The idea of empowerment also needs to take account of tacit forms of knowledge that bind individuals together into a community, as well as the authority and complexity of living traditions—linguistic, behavioral, moral, technological, institutional, and so forth. The metaphorical image of tradition as the "dead weight" of the past has led to a grossly oversimplified way of thinking about the nature of tradition—which involves, according to Edward Shils, "anything which is transmitted or handed down from the past to the present" (1981, p. 12)—and to an obscuring of the distinction between tradition, which always involves the element of human agency, and traditionalism, which is reactionary in the sense of attempting to go back to traditions outgrown by society.

By using a conceptual framework different from that given to us by classical liberal and Enlightenment thinkers, it is possible to formulate a theory of education that addresses the crises of modernization—which include the relativizing of norms and beliefs as well as the growing authority of the state to organize social life according to the canons of purposive rationality. Education that empowers the individual must balance the transmission of tacitly shared knowledge essential to the bonding process of community life with providing the more explicit form of socialization that provides the student with the symbolic foundations essential for communicative competence. Although the means of achieving this balance between transmitting certain aspects of the culture at a taken-for-granted level and providing students with the language frameworks necessary for making explicit and thinking theoretically about certain aspects of the culture need closer attention, I will devote the remaining discussion to the dynamics of providing the conceptual foundations necessary for communicative competence.

Today, communicative competence takes on greater political significance because of modern society's penchant for relativizing the authority of traditional beliefs, practices, and norms. The relativizing process creates the liminal space where communicative competence becomes a political factor in determining whether the new definitions that will become the basis of social action are to be negotiated democratically or imposed. The problem for the educator is to determine the areas of social life that are likely to involve, as a result of a relativizing process (i.e., caused by technological innovation, critical reflection, etc.), the liminal spaces where basic assumptions, social practices, and beliefs will be redefined, and thus the areas of social life within which the student must be able to exercise communicative competence. This sensitivity to the politicization of social life becomes, then, a factor in determining both the content of the curriculum and the areas of the curriculum that will involve the more explicit process of socialization necessary for developing the conceptual basis for communicative competence. Changes in the areas of work, technology, social relationships, and the nature of authority (i.e., the growing dominance of a technicist-purposive rational mode of thought) suggest some of the areas that should become part of the school curriculum.

In the remaining space I would like to identify some of the characteristics of an empowering form of education. As the relationship between classroom socialization and communicative competence has been explored more fully in *The Promise of Theory* (1984), I shall identify only the elements pertinent to the previous discussion of nihilism and the growth of the state's pastoral power. A basic characteristic of cultural transmission in schools is the teacher's control over the words, concepts, and theory frameworks that will be made available to students for thinking about the culture. Without these symbolic tools, it is difficult for the individual to make explicit the tacit cultural knowledge that is experienced as taken-for-granted; and without this symbolic means of representation, the individual lacks the means to communicate and thus to participate in the political process. The crucial issue here is the teacher's control over the language acquisition process that determines whether the student acquires the symbolic basis for reflection or has the already acquired, taken-for-granted beliefs reinforced.

In what I call the language game of socialization, the teacher needs to ensure that, in terms of the topic under discussion (e.g., the nature of work), the student acquires the words, concepts, and theoretical frameworks necessary for thinking about the complexity of that aspect of the life world. In giving the student the more elaborated language code, the teacher should also help the student recognize the powerful role that language plays in influencing thought: its metaphorical nature, the influence of its deep epistemological structures on the pattern of thought, and the political nature of language (i.e., the connection of language and power.) By attending both to providing the symbolic basis for a more complex understanding of the topics of the curriculum and to helping students understand how language binds them to the conceptual patterns of a language community, the teacher is helping to overcome the cultural myth of the autonomous individual who must interpret political issues in terms of self-interest. Political issues are cultural and collective, and the individual (understood as linked linguistically to culturally shared traditions of thought) must conceptualize them in terms of balancing individual with communal interests.

In addition to controlling the words and concepts made available to students during the process of primary socialization (the first naive encounter with a part of the culture one has not learned about before), the teacher also controls whether the student will be given an explanation characterized by a sense of objectivity and factuality or an explanation that takes account of historical continuities and the conceptual framework that shape the interpretation in a particular way. Socialization in the classroom that leaves students without a sense of history often results in reified forms of knowledge that leave them with a sense of powerlessness to question or reconceptualize. The lack of historical perspective also prevents students from acquiring the knowledge necessary for making judgments about historical continuities that are worth preserving or for judging changes in terms of a historically informed perspective. In effect, this part of the socialization process is crucial to whether memory includes the historical perspective that enables the individual to place issues in a broader context and to exercise a form of critical judgment that can hold accountable those who misrepresent the past in order to gain political advantage.

The conceptual foundations of communicative competence must help students situate themselves as members of a language community, a culture, and the mediating structures that Berger and Neuhaus identified—family, neighborhood, and voluntary associations. They should also enable them to understand their interdependence with the larger biotic community. Substantive traditions as well as supporting forms of authority essential to communal existence (including the moral norms that regulate interspecies relationships) are increasingly threatened by the relativizing process of modernization. It is only as students learn about the traditions essential to the patterns of communal (and sustainable) existence, as well as face the continual challenge to renew traditions under changing social circumstances, that they will represent an alternative center of power to that of the state. If these traditions cease to be meaningful, students will not feel committed either to their preservation or renewal and will more likely seek meaning in privatized experiences while accepting the anonymous status conferred by the state as it attempts to manage its various populations.

Part II

CULTURAL MEDIATING CHARACTERISTICS OF EDUCATIONAL COMPUTING

My longstanding interest in the cultural and political nature of technology was revived and more sharply focused in 1985, when colleagues began to push the idea that computers should be an integral aspect of every classroom. When my department offered more than a dozen courses on different computer applications in the classroom, it suddenly occurred to me that computers were being used to teach a particular cultural way of knowing and communicating, but that all the references to data and the need to prepare students for the Information Age seemed to make this an irrelevant issue. Before we could discuss intelligently the educational uses of this technology, it seemed that we must first understand its cultural mediating characteristics. This led me to write *The Cultural Dimensions of Educational Computing: Understanding the Non-Neutrality of Technology* (1988).

The three essays in this collection go beyond the book in several important ways. The first essay, "Teaching a Nineteenth Century Pattern of Thinking through a Twentieth-Century Machine," explores how the epistemological orientation built into the technology (i.e., the positivistic tradition whose immediate roots were in the nineteenth century, but whose deeper roots go back to the thinking of René Descartes) puts out of focus the more significant forms of knowledge that constitute the cultural life world of students: for example, the myriad forms of tacit knowledge and the shared schemata encoded in the metaphorical language of their cultural group. The second essay, "How Computers Contribute to the Ecological Crisis," challenges the conventional wisdom that computer simulations and the amassing of data on changes occurring in natural systems provide the most effective basis for dealing with the problem. This essay is used to lay out the argument that the cultural aspects of the ecological crisis (i.e., the cultural assumptions relating to how we think about progress, individualism, an anthropocentric universe, and so forth) are ignored by the emphasis on data as the basis for understanding the changing characteristics of natural systems. In effect, the computer helps us to understand the changes occurring in complex systems ranging from the carbon cycle to the habitat of the spotted owl, but it distorts the way we understand our own relationship to the environment by not being able to deal with the patterns of consciousness that are part of people's taken-for-granted culture. Unless the deeper cultural levels of consciousness are addressed, computer-based ways of understanding the ecological crisis, while contributing to more legislation relating to the more blatant aspects of environmental abuse, will have little effect on the double bind that now characterizes our present situation. The essay ends with a preliminary exploration of issues that developers of educational software should consider—that is, if they are to attempt to make cultural patterns of thought a more explicit and comparative aspect of educational software.

The last essay in this section, "Ideology, Educational Computing, and the Moral Poverty of the Information Age," examines the ideological orientation of the experts who want to expand the use of computers in the educational process. The primary concern of this essay is the consequence of fusing the mainstream liberal assumptions about the nature of the individual and the rational empowerment/social progress connection with the more technicist liberal concerns with privileging reductionist forms of knowledge. In addition to explaining how different forms of conservatism represent a more adequate way of understanding the challenges of education in a multicultural society, the essay also focuses on how more ecologically sensitive cultures have developed languages that represent relationships between humans and other members of the biotic community as participatory in nature. Computers, so the argument goes, amplify the tendency in the English language to maintain the "man/nature" dichotomy by representing human/environmental relationships as essentially instrumental in nature. The expert's use of the image of the Information Age as justification for expanding the educational use of computers is questioned on the grounds that it misrepresents the real challenges that humanity will face in the decades ahead. Being overwhelmed by massive amounts of data is not nearly as critical as the need to recognize the moral and spiritual aspects of the ecological crisis. How we understand ourselves, and our moral relationships with the rest of the biotic community, is more essential to long-term survival.

Chapter 5

Teaching a Nineteenth-Century Pattern of Thinking through a Twentieth-Century Machine

The use of microcomputers in the classroom involves a profound irony that has escaped the attention of those who write the educational software programs and the articles that attempt to explain the uses and limitations of the new technology. The irony is that the software programs for these twentieth-century machines reinforce a nineteenth-century view of knowledge and the individual (a strong case can be made that the roots of this epistemology go back to the Cartesianism of the seventeenth century). A probable explanation for this oversight, which can hardly be viewed as insignificant, is that the people who produce the programs and the literature on the educational uses of microcomputers have unquestionably accepted an interacting set of myths about the nature of technology, knowledge, and the individual. Since these myths underlie the taken-for-granted assumptions that guide most educational thought and practice, it is not being suggested here that the advocates of educational computing are more controlled by these cultural myths than are others. The basic problem, aside from the personal one facing program writers who do not recognize how their own thought process is culturally conditioned, is that the unique power and versatility of the microcomputer will further bind students to a nineteenth-century pattern of thinking and set of assumptions that are now being questioned in many areas of the academic world.

In order to put the problem in clearer focus, it is necessary to recognize that there are three general areas of expertise regarding the development and use of microcomputers in education. These include the development of the computer languages that run the software programs, the writing of the software programs that perform specific educational tasks, and what can, for lack of a better phrase, be referred to as the nontechnical aspects of educational computing. In terms of this tripartite division of the territory, the latter area includes understanding how the educational uses of microcomputers interact with and influence the cultural patterns that constitute the environment of the classroom. These include the patterns of social interaction, the legitimation of what constitutes knowledge, the political ideology reinforced by the content of the educational experience, and how educational computing in the classroom mediates and transforms the cultural transmission process. This third area of expertise (which really has to do with the cultural, educational, gender, and political implications of microcomputers) is the most complex and difficult one of the three. It is, interestingly enough, nearly totally ignored in the professional journals dealing with educational computing. But that is the subject of another article. Our purpose here is to stress the point that the following analysis of how current educational software reinforces a nineteenth-century mode of thinking is only part of an area of inquiry that should be an integral part of computer literacy.

The argument that the use of the microcomputer shapes the student's way of thinking, as opposed simply to facilitating it, is contingent upon settling the issue of whether technology is a neutral tool. The familiar aphorism "garbage in, garbage out" that one encounters in discussions about the influence of microcomputers succinctly represents the orthodox view held by most educators that microcomputers are a neutral technology. The microcomputer, according to this view, simply facilitates and expands our capacity for manipulating symbols and does so with a degree of speed and reliability that we cannot match. As we program these machines, we control them in much the same way we control how the pencil is used (an analogy that educators like to make). This is a totally erroneous view of microcomputers and, for that matter, of the neutral nature of pencils; in explaining why this view does not hold up, we can begin to see how the educational uses of microcomputers reinforce a particular pattern of thought—one that is based on the Cartesian worldview that is now being challenged by people working in the sociology of knowledge and critical hermeneutics (Winograd & Flores, 1986).

The easiest way to understand the non-neutrality of a technology is to follow Don Ihde's (1979) suggestion that we consider how experience is mediated by the technologies we use. Simply put, he asks us to consider the technology (i.e., microcomputers) as part of the field of our experience and to pay close attention to what aspects of experience are selected, amplified, and reduced through interaction with various forms of technology. How the use of a particular technology mediates and transforms the nature of experience can be understood, to start with the simplest example, by looking at what aspects of experience are amplified and reduced when we use a pencil. For example, the use of a pencil amplifies the ability to express our thoughts in written form, and because of the characteristics of this technology, we have the time to reformulate our thoughts in the process of writing them down. By facilitating written expression, the pencil amplifies a whole series of characteristics that have social, cultural, and political consequences: a privatized form of communication, a decontextualized form of thought, creation of a text that takes on an independent existence and thus allows for critical analysis, and communication with an anonymous public (Ong, 1982). At the same time, the use of the pencil reduces (selects out) those aspects of experience connected with sensory awareness and tacit forms of understanding. In the larger scheme of things, the pencil amplifies those aspects of experience that foster individualism, analytic thought, and reification of the word; but it reduces the human capacities that are expressed in oral traditions: context-specific sources of meaning, the full use of all the senses, and the spoken word in an ongoing process of negotiating meanings with others.

To take another example, we can ask what the use of the telephone amplifies and what it reduces. It is a powerful technology for communicating voice over great distances; and since it reduces other aspects of the communication process, it sharpens our tendency to listen carefully. But it reduces our ability to use context and body language (including facial expression) as part of the message system. In learning to think of how different technologies—automobile, fork, book, calculator, flute, and so forth—amplify certain aspects of experience while reducing others, it becomes less strange to ask what a microcomputer, given the current state of software, amplifies and reduces. In order to understand the educational significance of this line of questioning, we need to put in focus a more complex view of experience, one that takes account of the cultural aspects. Thus, before we can examine what the use of microcomputers amplifies and reduces, we need to situate this technology in terms of how culture is transmitted and experienced in the classroom. This will enable us to see what is being amplified and reduced and how this selection process (which involves the microcomputer acting on the student) reinforces a nineteenth-century mode of thought.

Briefly, all aspects of human experience are influenced and sustained by culture: technologies, customs and norms, political and economic institutions, and so forth. But the aspect of culture most pertinent to understanding the amplification/reduction characteristics of microcomputers is the symbolic. And the aspects most important to our discussion have to do with the language systems—verbal and nonverbal—that provide the information codes for thinking and acting (Goodenough, 1981, p. 66). In learning to speak we acquire the conceptual categories and assumptions of our language community, and through the ongoing conversations with others the culturally derived patterns that govern interactions, purposes, and achievement are continually reinforced and modified in minor ways. The key point here is that language, as Claus Mueller (1973) put it, "is a repository of cultural traditions" (p. 15). It provides the conceptual basis for our interpretations, reflective thought, imagination, and thus choices and behaviors. There are three implications of this statement that need to be made explicit: first, knowledge is an interpretation based on the conceptual categories we unconsciously acquire when we become members of our language community; second, most of our knowledge of how to think and act is based on tacit understandings, where performance and context are more critical than our ability to make explicit the knowledge we possess (Gadamer, 1976); third, language provides the symbolic (metaphorical) framework or schema that influences human thought and actions—including the creation of institutions and material objects (Schön, 1979). The implication of this last point is that everything that is humanly created has a history and that it embodies in the present elements of the symbolic order out of which it originated.

By emphasizing the symbolic aspects of culture, we can more easily view the classroom as a complex language environment and thus see more clearly that what goes on in this environment is the transmission of the conceptual patterns and information codes of the dominant culture. The transmission is exceedingly complex and includes talk, reading, use of space and time as an information code, regulation of patterns of social interaction, and use of body language. Part of the transmission process is explicit (the lesson, textbooks, the point the teacher wants to make, the issues that are argued, etc.), but much of the culture is learned and reinforced at the tacit level, where neither teacher nor students are fully aware of the cultural patterns and assumptions that are being learned.

By considering the classroom in terms of a complex language environment, we avoid the mythic starting point that the classroom is made up of autonomous, self-directing, and rational individuals, some of whom find their way over to the microcomputer for the purpose of using the database as a source of objective information or the word processor to express their individual thoughts. In the classroom both teacher and students operate within the limits of language; that is, imagination, reflection, intuition, and interpretation are constrained by the conceptual categories of language. But these limits are also the basis for new possibilities.

Having situated the student and the microcomputer within the context of the complex language environment that characterizes a classroom, we can now turn to the question of how the microcomputer mediates and shapes what goes on in the cultural transmission process. We could discuss the amplification/reduction characteristics of word processing or of LOGO, but the use of a database such as *NewsWorks* will serve as a better example of how knowledge is structured through the characteristics of the technology and, in turn, how the computer technology reinforces a particular pattern of thinking.

What the software amplifies is clearly stated by the creators of *NewsWorks* (1985):

> By using data bases in the classroom, students develop critical thinking skills and improve their ability to use information retrieval systems. Using data base samples encourages students to:
> —compare and construct data
> —determine cause and effect relationships over time
> —make inferences from data
> —form and test hypotheses made from data analysis
> —predict historical and economic trends from data
> —develop inductive and deductive logic by using data
> —improve research skills. (p. 1)

This is indeed an impressive set of claims, and because the assumptions about the nature of knowledge and how we think are embedded in this statement so widely shared by software program writers and teachers, few are likely to see critically how the use of this technology will shape the student's way of thinking.

At this point in the argument, some readers are likely to object that it is unfair to criticize either the content of an instructional program or the promises made on its behalf without taking account of the classroom context in which it is used. Although a few teachers may understand the hermeneutic idea of interpretation, that language is not a "conduit" for transmitting objective information and that learning is not an individually centered activity, most teachers will bring a taken-for-granted schema of understanding to educational computing that corresponds to the Cartesian tradition of rationalism that still, according to Terry Winograd and Fernando Flores, dominates the field of computing (1986). The literature on educational computing, it should be noted, further reinforces the Cartesian view of knowledge by providing mostly articles that deal with the procedural problems of using instructional software programs in the classroom. Readers will not find there a discussion of the metaphorical nature of thought, how educational computing reinforces a masculine mode of thinking, or the difference between analog and digital knowledge. Instead, the cultural myth that reduces knowledge to information is continually reinforced.

When *NewsWorks*, or any other database, is used in a classroom where the teacher is uninformed about the relevant epistemological issues, the software program will reinforce the epistemological orientation of the people who write it. In the case of *NewsWorks*, the selection and amplification process represents knowledge as discrete bits of information (facts) in a manner that leads to objective conclusions (truth). The database will also amplify the ability to collect, store, and retrieve data that can be observed and measured. The database presents a decontextualized and thus abstracted representation of what the words on the monitor signify. Thus the technology further strengthens a longstanding cultural tradition of accepting the printed word (and measurable data) as an accurate presentation of reality and language as a neutral conduit for the transmitting of information.

We should now turn to the aspects of experience that do not get transmitted as the students sit in front of the microcomputer manipulating the data files. As algorithmic system, it is incapable of being programmed for forms of knowledge that cannot be made explicit and organized into discrete components or that have operational rules that cannot be formally represented (Dreyfus & Dreyfus, 1986). Thus the machine in front of the student cuts out of the communication process (the reduction phenomenon) tacit/heuristic forms of knowledge that underlie commonsense experience, the awareness that knowledge is an interpretation influenced by the conceptual categories embedded in the language of the person who discovered or established the knowledge as fact, the recognition that language and thus the foundations of knowledge itself are metaphorical, and finally that the "data" have a history. The binary logic that so strongly amplifies the sense of objective facts and data-based thinking serves, at the same time, to reduce the importance of meaning, ambiguity, and perspective. The sense of history and the cultural relativism of the student's interpretative framework are also put out of focus.

In effect, the use of the computer database mediates the cultural transmission processes that go on between the student and the social world. This can, of course, be said of all technologies. For example, eyeglasses mediate our relationship to the environment in a manner that amplifies our ability to see more clearly but does not strengthen our acuity in areas of taste, smell, and sound. But what is important for educators to consider is the pattern of thought, and image of individualism, that is reinforced by what the microcomputer amplifies and reduces in the cultural transmission process. The claims made in behalf of *NewsWorks*, which are also used to justify other software programs, involve assumptions about the nature of knowledge that are given further legitimacy as part of the positivistic tradition of thinking that had its roots in the nineteenth century. At that time, Auguste Comte and Émile Durkheim (two French sociologists) were helping to broaden the acceptance of the positivistic form of knowledge already entrenched in the scientific community. The scientific method provided them a powerful model for how to think about the social world, hence the concern with reducing social experience to the observable and measurable and with examining the variable relationships. The emphasis on objective knowledge, as well as the tendency to interpret cultural differences within an evolutionary framework, led to a view of knowledge that is essentially identical to the position contained in the quotation from *NewsWorks*.

By amplifying a nineteenth-century view of knowledge, the database reduces (selects out) the elements of understanding that are associated with developments in the twentieth century. These include an understanding that what is experienced as "real" is socially constructed (P. Berger & Luckmann, 1967) and that our interpretations are influenced by the conceptual categories embedded in our natural language. This view of language forces a recognition of the relativism of the interpretative framework used to explain what the "data" mean. In recent years there has also been a growing recognition that the problem of meaning has been put out of focus by the emphasis on an objective world. The problem of meaning (i.e., how the individual interprets and gives meaning to daily life) is fundamental to whether students can make generalizations about other cultures, even when the generalizations are based on "objective data." Generalizations about other cultural groups ignore the taken-for-granted interpretative frameworks of the student, the data collector (often hidden from consideration), as well as the people who are the objects of the generalizations. Lastly, there have been important developments in understanding the difference between explicit and implicit forms of knowledge. Recent advances in anthropology, philosophy, and the sociology of knowledge have provided us a way of recognizing the knowledge we have difficulty making explicit because of its taken-for-granted nature (Douglas, 1975). This is knowledge that we learn from others in context and is basic to successful cultural performances (when it is appropriate to tell a joke, how to adjust our sense of space in accordance with changes in context, and so forth). It also provides a secure taken-for-granted world of shared patterns that allows us to make explicit and reflect upon specific areas of cultural activity.

The nineteenth-century view of knowledge that is amplified in the *NewsWorks* database, as well as in other educational software programs that provide factual information for reasoning, creates a number of educational problems that are related to the mythic view of objective knowledge. One problem relates to the view of individualism reinforced by the nineteenth-century convention that separated the knower from the known (which had its origins in the epistemology of the seventeenth-century thinker René Descartes). The view of thinking as information processing

seems to fit nicely with the liberal view of the individual as an autonomous, self-directing being. To insure that self-direction is based on a
reflective process, it is essential, according to this view, that the individual
be given access to all the facts. Thus the capacity of the microcomputer
to store, manipulate, and retrieve data makes it the ideal educational tool
for facilitating the individual's rational capacity for self-direction. The
only problem with this view of the individual is that it is based on a
number of misconceptions that go far back into Western thought. For our
purposes, we can simply point out that if people speak a language, they
will think within the conceptual categories and assumptions that underlie the culture's worldview and thus cannot be considered as autonomous
or entirely self-directing. But more important than these problems, which
have to do with reinforcing a mythic view of the individual, is the civic
issue of how to educate in a manner that strengthens students' abilities
to recognize that they are members of a larger social group (indeed, biotic
community) and that this membership will provide the cultural resources
that will be individualized as part of their own personal growth. This
recognition also carries with it definite shared responsibilities for strengthening the cultural resource base. Learning about self as part of a "community of memory," to use Robert Bellah's phrase (Bellah, Madsen,
Sullivan, Swidler, & Tipton, 1985, p. 153), is undermined by the view of
the autonomous individual who only needs objective information in order
to be rational.

Another major educational problem raised by the use of the microcomputer in the classroom has to do with the role of the teacher. The
database, for example, far exceeds the teacher's capacity to provide relevant and accurate information. The use of other software programs, which
rely upon a degree of expertise that few teachers can match, makes the
teacher's role even more ambiguous. As educational computing becomes
more widespread, the question of what the teacher can contribute to the
educational process, beyond providing guidance in the use of the technology, becomes a more paramount concern. If we stay with the objective form of knowledge that fits a computer-based system of instruction,
the teacher's role will be that of a monitor of student behavior and a
technical advisor. But if we take seriously a twentieth-century view of
knowledge—that facts represent the objectification of somebody's interpretation, that interpretations are influenced by the conceptual guidance
system of a culture, that objective knowledge is about a world of events
and objects that become more fully understood as we trace their historical development, that language and thus thought are metaphorical in
nature, that explicit/calculating forms of knowledge are quite different
from the tacit/heuristic forms of understanding and problem solving, and

that the structure of knowledge and individual understanding is shared and filtered by what individuals take for granted—then it becomes possible to recognize the unique contribution that only the teacher can make to the educational process.

The teacher cannot match the machine when it comes to the tireless reproduction of factual information or the knowledge base that can be made available through the microcomputer. But only the teacher can amplify those aspects of the cultural transmission process that are reduced by the selective characteristics of the microcomputer. This involves restoring to teachers responsibility for recognizing when to intervene in the educational process by clarifying the conceptual problems that arise from the process of metaphorical thinking, by pointing out that the objective knowledge reflects somebody's interpretative framework and that this framework must be understood in terms of the underlying cultural assumptions, by making explicit the student's taken-for-granted assumptions and how these assumptions influence understanding, by guiding the student to think in terms of historical continuities and transformations, and, finally, by urging students to check the more abstract and context-free forms of knowledge (data, generalizations, etc.) against their own commonsense forms of understanding. This is the aspect of the cultural transmission process that cannot be programmed, because it involves paying attention to what the student and program writer are imposing upon the data, noting the context within which learning occurs, and making the conceptual connections between what is being learned and other parts of the curriculum.

In effect, a twentieth-century view of knowledge involves using the microcomputer as a powerful and legitimate tool of the teacher and students. But it means subordinating the machine to the complexity of the human/cultural experience rather than amplifying only those aspects of experience that fit the logic of the machine.

Chapter 6

How Computers Contribute
to the Ecological Crisis

Recent reports on global changes in life-sustaining ecosystems, such as the annual *State of the World* published by the Worldwatch Institute and a special single-topic issue of *Scientific American* entitled "Managing Planet Earth," support the conventional thinking that computers are one of the most important technologies we have available for understanding the extent of the crisis and the steps that must be taken to mitigate it. Processing scientific data and modeling how natural systems will react to further changes caused by human activity suggest that the computer is essential to a data-based approach to understanding the dynamic and interactive nature of the earth's ecosystems. Having recognized the genuine contributions that computers make to addressing the ecological crisis, I also want to argue that computers help reinforce the mind-set that has contributed to the disproportionate impact that Western societies have had on degrading the habitat. Put simply, computers represent a Cartesian epistemology (an argument that has also been made by Hubert Dreyfus, Terry Winograd, and Theodore Roszak), and the use of this technology reinforces the Cartesian orientations of our culture—which includes the critically important aspect of consciousness, wherein the self is experienced as separate from the natural world.

This Cartesian way of thinking can be seen in how the lead article in *Scientific American*, "Managing Planet Earth" (Clark, 1989), frames the nature of the ecological crisis as a problem of achieving a more rational management of the planet. As the author, William C. Clark, puts it, "Managing Planet Earth will require answers to two questions: What kind of planet do *we* want? What kind of planet can *we* get?" (p. 47). The italics were added here to bring out how a Cartesian way of thinking, with its emphasis on instrumental problem solving, also strengthens the cultural myth, which has roots much deeper in Western consciousness, of an anthropocentric universe (that is, "man" is the central figure and must treat the biosphere as a resource for achieving his purposes). The Cartesian mind-set shows up in the special issue of *Scientific American* and the annual reports of the Worldwatch Institute in another way that is critically important to any discussion of how computers relate to the deepening ecological crisis. Although both publications provide a wealth of data, which, according to one of the canons of the Cartesian position, is supposed to be the basis of rational thought, they largely ignore the fact that culture is part of the problem. In fact, culture is seldom even mentioned in these data-based representations of the ecological crisis.

This is particularly surprising because culture, understood here as encompassing the deep layers of a symbolic world as well as the whole range of human activities given distinctive form by the shared symbolic sense of order, is an aspect of every humanly caused change in the ecosystems now viewed as endangered. Beliefs, values, uses of technology, economic practices, political processes, and so forth, while varying from culture to culture, relate directly to population growth, loss of forest cover, destruction of habitats that threaten species with extinction, warming of the atmosphere, spread of toxic waste in the water supply and topsoil, and so forth. The irony is that the researchers who provide useful data and computer simulations of how natural systems will react under further stress, also contribute to putting out of focus the contributing role that cultural beliefs and practices play in the ecological crisis.

The phrase *ecological crisis* should be represented as the *ecological/ cultural crisis*. When viewed in this way, we can then begin to consider more fully the cultural orientation reinforced not only by the epistemology embedded in the computer, but also by how the computer is represented to the public and to students. We can then also open a discussion of whether it is possible, particularly in educational settings, to create software programs that take into account the deep levels of culture (including differences in cultures) that give form to human thought and behavior. This latter possibility, which may well be beyond the capacity of this Cartesian machine, is important to whether the computer can be used to help illuminate the cultural patterns that are degrading the habitat. But first we need to identify other aspects of the Cartesian cultural orientation reinforced by the computer, which has become the dominant icon for representing the authority of a particular form of knowledge.

The Cartesian mind-set has distinctive characteristics that set it apart from other cultures that, in a variety of ways, evolved along paths that have been more ecologically sustainable, some for many thousands of years. This is mentioned here not for the purpose of romanticizing these cultures but, instead, to bring out that one test of a viable culture is its ability to live in balance with its habitat. This test is perhaps too pragmatically simple for a culture where the abstract theories of philosophers have been given, in certain powerful circles, more legitimacy than the contextualized forms of knowledge that have evolved in habitats lacking a margin of surplus that allowed for experimentation with abstract ideas. But it is the test that all cultures must now meet as we recognize that our surplus is increasingly illusory.

The Cartesian mind-set, in addition to ignoring the nature of culture (and its influence on thought) and furthering the view of a human-centered universe, has other distinctive elements reinforced through the use of computers. These include what has become in modern Western consciousness the basis for objectifying the world (i.e., Descartes distinction between *res extensa* and *res cogitans*, which also served to naturalize the cosmos), a view of the rational process whereby data become the basis of procedural and constructionist thinking, and an instrumental and explicit problem-solving approach to a world that is posited as mechanistic in nature.

The dimensions of human life ignored by the Cartesian mind-set correspond to the weakness in computers. Contrary to the myths constructed by Descartes, Bacon, Locke, and other thinkers of this period, a strong case can be made that most of our knowledge is tacit in nature, learned as analogs that serve as templates for future experiences, encoded in a metaphorical language that provides a shared schema for thinking, and representing a collective interpretation framed by the epic narratives that constitute the basis of the culture's episteme. As we obtain better accounts of other worldviews—Hopi, Dogan, Koyukon, Confucian cultures in the Far East, and so forth—it becomes increasingly difficult to maintain the popularized rendering of Descartes' legacy: the image of a tradition-free individual, objective data, and a conduit view of language. The sociology of knowledge (within our own tradition) and cognitive anthropology point to the cultural basis of thought and behavioral patterns, and to the way in which each cultural group experiences these patterns as part of their natural attitude—this also applies to the members of our Cartesian culture whose schemata cannot take into account tacit and culturally constituted forms of knowledge.

If we turn to the writings of Gregory Bateson, instead of the findings of cognitive anthropology, we find an account of human existence expressed in the language of science that challenges the conceptual foundations of the Cartesian mind-set and, at the same time, points to the possibility that primary cultures (such as the Hopi, Koyukon, aborigines of Australia, etc.) may have taken developmental paths that are more ecologically sustainable. Unlike the modern Cartesian approach to viewing the rational process as something that occurs in the head of an autonomous, culture-free individual, Bateson emphasizes the patterns that connect, the information exchanges that constitute the life of an entire natural/social system of which the individual is a participating member, and the dangers facing humans when their conceptual mapping processes (what he calls "determinative memory") are unable to take into account the information exchanges that signal changes in the condition of the ecology upon which they are dependent. As Bateson put it, "in no system which shows mental characteristics can any part have unilateral control over the whole. In other words, the mental characteristics of system are immanent, not in some part, but in the system as a whole" (1972, p. 316). His statement that "the unit of evolutionary survival turns out to be identical with the unit of mind" (1972, p. 483) has a strong echo in the cultures of primal people, where human practices and the natural world are understood as morally interdependent.

Although it is tempting to dwell further on how a consideration of ecologically sustainable cultures enables us to recognize those aspects of our own belief system that are contributing to the destruction of our habitat, it is necessary to turn our attention more directly to the question of whether the use of computers is really helping us understand the ecological crisis in a way that does not perpetuate the very mind-set that has been such an important contributing factor to it. At some point, accumulating more data on the extent of environmental damage and producing better computer models of changes in ecosystems becomes a distraction from addressing the real challenge, which is to begin the exceedingly difficult task of changing the conceptual and moral foundations of our own cultural practices. We already know that the trend line reflecting the demands of cultures on the habitat is upward, and that the trend line reflecting the sustaining capacity of natural systems is downward. More computer-processed data may enable us to predict with greater accuracy when we will cross certain irreversible thresholds. But that will be of little use if we cannot reverse the demands made by cultures whose belief systems represent the environment as a natural resource and human choices as limited only by a lack of data and economic resources. The challenge now is to become aware of our own taken-for-granted culture, and to evolve new narrative traditions that represent humans as interdependent members of the larger information and food chains that make up the ecosystems.

The use of computers in educational settings seems to be where the question of relevance can be most clearly raised. Since educational software ranging from databases to simulation programs have been written by people who are embedded in the Cartesian/liberal mindset (objective data, autonomous individuals who construct their own ideas, progressive nature of rationally directed change and technological innovations, a conduit view of language, etc.), it may be premature to reach the conclusion that the educational uses of computers can only reinforce the Cartesian mind-set that has, paradoxically, helped to create a form of technological empowerment that contributes to the possibility of our own extinction. As Theodore Roszak (1986) points out, the basic relationship in the educational use of computers involves the mind of the student meeting the mind of the person who wrote the program, and the mental processes that establish what constitutes the "data." If the mind encountered by students, mediated by the amplification characteristics of computer technology, has never considered the aspects of human/cultural experience ignored by Cartesianism, it would be difficult for the students to recognize the deeper levels of culture. Nor would students likely be able to recognize that language and thought are influenced by the episteme of a cultural group.

The close connection between computers and the form of consciousness associated with print technology make it impossible to represent the thought processes of other cultural groups in a way in which students could enter into its epistemic patterns at a taken-for-granted level. As Eric Havelock (1986) and Walter Ong (1982) argue, print makes what is represented appear as data—abstract, decontextualized, and rationally apprehended. But it should be possible to move some distance away from the more stultifying aspects of the Cartesian mind-set reinforced through print-based discourse. Software programs that help illuminate the nature of culture would seem to be a step in the right direction, both in terms of understanding the symbolic foundations upon which thought and social practices rest, and in terms of recognizing that culture is part of the ecological crisis. One aspect of culture that needs to be illuminated, which would be a prelude to considering comparative belief and value systems, is the metaphorical nature of language. Particularly important would be understanding how the root metaphors of a cultural group (for us, a mechanistic image of nature) influence the process of analogic thinking (i.e., choice of generative metaphors) and lead to the existence of iconic metaphors that encode the earlier process of analogic thinking. Iconic metaphors, such as "data," "artificial intelligence," and "computer memory," are examples of this process of encoding earlier processes of analogic thinking, which in turn was influenced by the root metaphors taken for granted at that time. How the metaphorical nature of language provides the schemata for thinking becomes especially critical to the process of recognizing how current thinking about the ecological crisis is largely framed by the metaphors central to Cartesianism. Viewing language as encoding the process of analogic thinking also brings other aspects of culture into consideration: how people in our own past as well as members of other cultural groups have different views of reality, how the past can influence the present at a taken-for-granted level, and how the individual is, in actuality, giving individualized expression to shared cultural patterns. Becoming aware of culture, it should be kept in mind, is just the first step in a process that must eventually engage the more politically difficult problem of sorting out the cultural patterns that are ecologically sustainable over the long term.

There is another line of development in educational software that may be fruitful to explore. This could involve the use of problem-solving simulations framed in terms of the patterns of thinking of other cultural groups who have lived within the limits of their habitats (this would help students recognize the assumptions of our culture that ignore the problem of long term interdependency) and the use of simulations that consider the future ecological impact of our assumptions about human life, material and technological progress, and rational control of the environment.

With the cultures of the world placing increasing demands on biosystems that are showing signs of disruption and decline, the most critical aspect of the problem—at least in terms of the human/cultural roots of the crisis—is to change the root metaphors that underlie the foundation of our Western value system. Serious consideration, for example, should be given to Aldo Leopold's (1970) argument that a land ethic should replace the anthropocentrism of the value orientation that now guides individual decisions—including our uses of technology. Very succinctly, he argues that an ethical consideration of our interdependency with the environment, if taken seriously, should lead to "a limitation on freedom of action in the struggle for existence" (p. 262). Restriction of self for the sake of others, where "others" is understood as including the entire "biotic community," now is paramount to human survival, given the size of the world's human population and the scale of its technological capacities.

What this will mean for how we use computers is not entirely clear at this time, but one seemingly irrefutable point is that the future has a moral dimension to it that is ignored by the image of an Information Age. The moral dimensions of the ecological crisis bring us back to a central theme of this discussion: namely, that "data" and simulation models tend to hide the deeper levels of culture. The transmission of culture, which occurs whenever a language system is used as part of a computing process, points to a need to consider the cultural orientations that are being reinforced by this technology, and to asking whether it is part of the solution or part of the problem. The consequences of taking these concerns seriously are so important that they need to be given a more central place in future considerations of the educational use of computers and in understanding the influence of this technology on social change.

Chapter 7

Ideology, Educational Computing, and the Moral Poverty of the Information Age

Alan C. Kay's *Scientific American* article, "Computers, Networks and Education" (1991), will be used here as the basis for examining the ideological orientation of the experts who develop and promote the educational use of this technology. Insofar as computers embody the conceptual framework (and thus ideology) of the experts who create them, the technology itself can be viewed as reproducing a specific ideological orientation. But here the primary reference point will be on the ideology embedded in how computer experts think about the educational uses of this technology. Kay was chosen as an exemplary figure in this field because of the breadth of issues he addresses and because of his leadership role within the field. The nature and implications of this ideology can be made explicit through the analysis of the following three propositions: (1) The justifications and educational uses of computers reinforce a historically and culturally specific ideological orientation; (2) this ideology is based on fundamental misconceptions about the nature of the individual, what is involved in the processes of knowing (i.e., the nature of intelligence), and how individual empowerment relates to social progress; and (3) the metaphor of an "Information Age," which is the most recent expression of this ideological orientation, serves to hide the moral/spiritual nature of the ecological crisis.

1. *The justifications and educational uses of computers reinforce a historically and culturally specific ideological orientation.* Kay's article presents compelling reasons for embracing computers as the primary technology through which all classroom learning should be mediated. Indeed, the advantages of computers make an impressive list: "interactivity" that takes a variety of forms, including allowing the student to experience interactive processes from within the phenomenon being studied; the ability of computers to "become any and all existing media" (e.g., books, musical instruments, etc.); providing for learning from many different perspectives; building a dynamic model of an idea through simulation;

exhibiting different patterns of reflective thought; and, finally, networking resources that become, in effect, a universal library (pp. 147–148). Like
the introduction of the printing press, Kay views computers as a truly
revolutionary technology that will serve as "powerful amplifiers, extending the reach and depth of the learners" (p. 146). The promised versatility of computers is what is likely to capture the attention of most readers, but the fulcrum that sustains Kay's vision of technologically based
educational empowerment is a core set of assumptions that are so widely
taken for granted they will go largely unnoticed. Since the efficacy of
computer-mediated learning is dependent upon these core assumptions,
we must bring them into clearer focus. These assumptions, as we shall
see, are also basic to the liberal ideology that has been responsible for
the development of the more problematic aspects of modern consciousness.

Although Kay argues that the current state of computer technology
marks a fundamental transition in human development (as great as that
of the Industrial Revolution), he is unable to deviate from the basic pre-
suppositions of modern liberalism. For example, Kay's way of understanding the nature of the individual as a self-constituting being is
reflected in his statement that "each of us has to construct our own version of reality by main force. Literally, to make ourselves. And we are
quite capable of devising new mental bricks, new ways of thinking, that
can enormously expand the understanding we attain. The bricks we
develop become new technologies for thinking" (p. 140). This statement,
along with his argument that different classroom computer applications
simply facilitate the students "who come up with the ideas . . . to
develop knowledge of their own collaboratively" (p. 145), reveals another
assumption that Kay takes for granted as a modern, enlightened thinker.
Namely, that the highest purpose and most essential aspect of human
fulfillment is continually to create new ideas that take account of the
information continually made available by advances in science and technology. This second assumption, to put it more succinctly, is that information is the basis of thinking. Kay's third assumption is essential to
establishing the moral legitimacy of his vision of conceptually autonomous individuals. It also serves to place the process of self-creation within
a temporal framework that represents change as progressive in nature.
Kay writes:

> Humans are predisposed by biology to live in the barbarism of the
> deep past. Only by an effort of will and through the use of our in-
> vented representations can we bring ourselves into the present and peek
> into the future. . . . In other words, each generation must be able to

quickly learn new paradigms, or ways of viewing the world; the old ways do not remain useable for long. (p. 140)

Like other proponents of educational computing, Kay manages to bring all the essential elements of the liberal canon into his "the future is now" argument: the autonomy of the individual, the dependence of rational empowerment upon data, the idea that change is linear and progressive, anthropocentrism, and the universalizing of the tenets of liberalism by equating them with modernization. That this ideology only goes back 17 or so generations, and encodes the metaphorical constructions of European cultures struggling to make the transition from an organic to a mechanistic root metaphor, is made irrelevant by the hubris of his position. Nor does it occur to Kay that there are other ideologies that must be taken into account, particularly when a technology is being represented as possessing the capability of networking everybody into a global information and learning environment. As space is limited here, I will identify different ideological traditions that bring into focus aspects of human experience that are not taken into account by the liberal ideology that guides Kay's thinking. But the suggestion that they represent a different conceptual mapping process, and thus a different political order, does not mean that they are necessarily free of distortions. Rather, they are being identified because they help bring into focus aspects of the human/cultural/habitat relationship ignored by the universalizing and essentializing characteristics of liberalism.

While the categories are not meant to be exhaustive, it makes sense to identify at least three different forms of conservatism that, in their respective ways, challenge the liberal mind-set that justifies both the worldwide use of computers and what is reproduced through their use. The first can be called temperamental conservatism. Basically, it represents the psychological/cultural tendency within human experience to feel comfortable with taken-for-granted patterns and routines, which include the patterns in the multiple languages that enable a person to participate in the larger mental ecology we refer to as "culture." Contrary to the heroic image of liberalism, where autonomous individuals "make contents visible . . . explicitly reshapable and inventable" (p. 140) and thus are always experimenting with conditions of existence, most individuals—even ideologues like Marx, Dewey, and Freire—find personal meaning in taken-for-granted patterns. Although we may find many of the taken-for-granted patterns morally and ecologically problematic, embeddedness in them is probably a more fundamental characteristic of human experience than the images of human existence projected by liberalism.

Philosophical conservatism, which shares with liberalism nearly the same time span and cultural geography, is far more complex than temperamental conservatism, which seems to cut across cultural boundaries and ideological genres. The insight of philosophically conservative thinkers that represents the greatest challenge to Kay's fusing an uncritical view of technologically based cultural experimentation (e.g., computers) with an equally uncritical view of progress is their tendency to frame issues in terms of a dialectical tension—and to continually challenge formulaic political thinking by problematizing the side of the dialectic relationship being overwhelmed by the rush of events. The dialectical tension usually revolves around the specific relationships of individual/community, progress/tradition, and rational, theoretical thought/experience. Philosophic conservatives also have a more complex view of what is metaphorically known as "human nature"; that is, they take into account the historical record of the many ways individuals have used the various sources of empowerment for both positive and destructive ends. While on this point, it is interesting to note that Kay adopts the liberal view of human nature, wherein the tools of reason will always be used for progressive and humanitarian ends. The evidence, as philosophic conservatives would point out, is that computers are also being used to serve the interests of specific groups, such as centralizing economic and political power by making the panopticon society a closer reality and by turning many work settings into "electronic sweatshops" (Garson, 1988). The multidimensional view of human nature central to philosophic conservative thinking led James Madison to argue for a system of political checks and balances. Unfortunately, there is no way of providing for checks and balances in Kay's vision of "massively interconnected intimate computers" (p. 146).

By returning to the relevance of the philosophic conservatives' dialectical concerns, we can see more clearly the limitations of Kay's liberalism. Kay, as well as such other leading advocates of educational computing as Seymour Papert, Alfred Bork, and David Moursund, view the rational process as empowered through the use of data, and they recognize only explicit forms of knowledge. Philosophic conservatives would agree that this is indeed one category of knowledge, but they would also want to take into account both the complexity of tacit knowledge and forms of cultural storage where the messages get communicated through multiple semiotic pathways. Similarly, philosophic conservatives would agree that the scientific method/technology connection worked out over the last three and a half centuries indeed represents a record of progressive achievement, but they would also want to give serious consideration both to the complex nature of tradition (which the scientific/

technology juggernaut seems bent on simplifying and treating as something to be totally emancipated from) and to specific traditions that have been lost as a result of scientific/technological advances. Is mono-agriculture an actual advance over previous agriculture traditions? What traditions were overturned by Frederick W. Taylor's utilization of scientific principles in the management of the workplace? How has television affected people's sense of family and community? What will be the impact of computer-mediated communication on oral traditions? Kay expresses his understanding of the past (tradition can be thought of as anything from the past that is handed down to the present) through the use of such phrases as the "barbarism of the deep past" and "naive reality"; he also views as nonproblematic the statement attributed to Susan Sontag that "all understanding begins with our not accepting the world as it appears" (p. 141). The liberal bias toward emancipation from tradition is such a prominent part of Kay's thinking that he is unable to recognize that every experiment (that is, the introduction of a new idea, value, technology) creates a moment of cultural liminality that should require both an awareness of the traditions that are being altered or lost and a thoughtful consideration of whether the new is a genuine advance over the old. Just as tradition yields to his progressive view of change, Kay is equally silent on the tension between the empowerment of the individual and the forms of interdependency that characterize membership within a community, which is another area of concern to philosophical conservatives (who may come down on the side of more individual empowerment and freedom when the patterns of community existence become too rigid and oppressive).

Philosophic conservatives argue that an individual's self-identity and thought/communication patterns are dependent upon membership in a community. Participation in this cultural ecology involves multiple dimensions of learning and communicating, including analog knowledge that, by its very nature, cannot be made explicit and re-encoded to fit the digital technology required for computer-mediated communication. There is also another aspect of the individual/community relationship that does not fit the form of consciousness amplified by a literacy-based technology, such as computers. Community, as Alasdair MacIntyre (1984) observes, provides the basis for answering basic existential questions. "I can only answer the question 'what am I to do?' if I can answer the prior question 'of what story or stories do I find myself a part?'" (p. 216). MacIntyre is pointing to constitutive forms of knowledge that are not reducible to data or information—which seems to be the only form of knowledge recognized by Kay's narrow commitment to the scientific/technological paradigm. As MacIntyre puts it: "I am not only accountable, I am one who can always ask others for an account, who can put others to the question, I am part of their story, as they are part of mine. The narrative of any one life is part of an interlocking set of narratives" (p. 218). This ongoing process of narrativizing also involves learning, and validating within the context of one's own life, the moral analogs that represent the community's way of understanding good and evil. Not all of a community's analogs of morally responsible behavior will stand the test of critical reflection. Whether the moral templates of a community can really be kept separate from the data flowing through computers and into the heads of students is a question that Kay ignores, just as he ignores the fact that communities are moral ecologies; that is, the life of a community involves ongoing relationships and commitments. These relationships are based on some conception of how a good person acts within a specific context. Later, we shall address what is problematic about philosophic conservatives' view of community, and in the process bring into sharper focus why the liberalism that Kay uses to explain the educational computing/progress connection represents a reactionary position.

The third form of conservatism, what can be generally termed cultural conservatism, provides a different vocabulary, and thus it helps illuminate a different set of issues ignored by the liberal devotees of educational computing. Cultural conservatism complicates all attempts to make ideological distinctions, such as the attempts being made here. Basically, any cultural group that reproduces through its patterns of semiosis the templates or blueprints "for the organization of social and psychological processes," to use Clifford Geertz's way of explaining cultural patterns (1973, p. 216), represents an example of cultural conservatism. In terms of most cultural groups, who reproduce (conserve) their collective patterns through the language systems they privilege, cultural conservatism can be viewed as less reflective than philosophical conservatism. But even the achievements of philosophic conservatives—such as our Constitution, Bill of Rights, and tripartite system of government—can, at this more basic level of political categories, be viewed as the expression of cultural conservatism. Even the cultural artifacts and thought patterns that are the legacy of liberalism, technologies, and conventions that reflect the liberal view of the rights and freedom of the individual as well as the contradictory patterns that evolved out of the classical liberal's concern with profits and the forces of competition, can be viewed as a cultural ecology that reproduces itself through time—and thus can be included in the category of cultural conservatism. That liberalism attempts to conserve the patterns of thought and social practices that accelerate the rate of change and continually relativize the shared moral norms that guide relationships (what Edward Shils [1981] calls an "anti-tradition tradition") is not the critical issue here. But a case can be made that a way of thinking that does not recognize the nihilism in its sanctioned approaches to progress is in deep trouble.

The recognition of cultural conservatism is important to our discussion of Kay's liberalism for two reasons. First, it helps bring into focus that not all cultural groups view change as the dominant characteristic of everyday life. Rather, for them, the reenactment of traditional patterns is the most pervasive aspect of human/cultural existence. Change (reinterpretations, technological innovations, creative leaps, etc.) involves reworking traditions that connect the present to the past. Contrary to Kay's notion of rational empowerment in the quest to determine and control the future, traditions are a source both of empowerment and limitation. He might compare the ontology of liberalism with the practices in the two most antitradition arenas in modern society (science and technology) to see if "advances" involve building upon and reworking the existing knowledge base.

The other reason for bringing cultural conservatism into a discussion of the ideological orientation of educational computing has to do with Kay's failure to recognize that there are many other cultural groups (even within our society) whose symbolic worlds are based on root metaphors that are fundamentally different from the ones underlying Kay's liberal/technocratic view of reality. The forms of knowledge that have authority, approaches to technology, ways of understanding the "individual," and moral and conceptual categories for understanding the human/environment relationship vary widely. Most of these cultural groups do not share Kay's liberal view of the autonomous individual, the epistemology that gives primacy to "objective" data as the basis of thought, or his escalator view of progressive change. The critical issue that Kay sets aside by universalizing his ideological orientation has to do with how a technology that reproduces a specific ideological (including cultural/epistemological) orientation can be used by other cultural groups without subverting their traditions. To put it more succinctly: Is the computer, particularly when used to mediate the complex cultural transmission processes that characterize "education," the liberal's latest means of cultural imperialism? The issue can be made concrete by asking whether the following statement by Kay represents a characterization of the human condition that could be accepted by Native American cultural groups who are attempting to recover their own ontologies: "Each generation must be able to quickly learn new paradigms, or ways of viewing the world; the old ways do not remain usable for long" (p. 140). Native American ways of understanding time, authority, and the fundamental relationships that must be respected if life is to continue, simply cannot be reconciled with Kay's relativistic and experimental approach to existence. The introduction of cultural conservatism into the discussion, in effect, challenges the advocates of liberalism to face up to whether they really believe in a tenet they often identify themselves with: namely, the right to cultural self-determination. Reconciling this tenet with the liberal's tendency to universalize the characteristics of the modern individual represents a double bind within liberal ideology that Kay fails to recognize.

2. *The ideology used to justify educational computing is based on fundamental misconceptions about the nature of the individual, what is involved in the processes of knowing (i.e., the nature of intelligence), and how individual empowerment relates to social progress.* Kay's view of individual intelligence reflects the current orthodoxy that learning occurs through multiple pathways —"doing, seeing, and manipulating symbols" (p. 140). He also subscribes to the key tenet of this orthodoxy: namely, that individuals construct their "own version of reality." "It was the children who came up with the ideas" (p. 140), to recall another statement he made. To put it another way, thinking is an individual activity that is facilitated by acquiring data through all the senses. This modified Cartesian view of intelligence thus continues to buttress the liberal view of the autonomous individual, turning pedagogy into a quest for techniques that will match learning environments with the student's learning style. Computers, as Kay views them, offer unexplored curricular opportunities as "information carriers" that can be articulated to each student's style of learning.

While I am not suggesting that Kay's optimism about the computer's ability to facilitate certain forms of learning is totally unfounded, I am claiming that his ideological orientation, including the Cartesian epistemology that is an integral part of this ideology, leads him to adopt a view of individual intelligence that is no longer defensible. Kay can rely upon Piaget and Bruner (and such other translators of the constructivist position in the field of artificial intelligence as Papert and Minsky) as legitimating authorities for his position, thus making challenges to his position appear to go against the grain of the modern mind-set, with its emphasis on individual self-direction and empowerment. But what current authorities and the sheltering *Zeitgeist* fail to take into account is the growing body of evidence that thought and linguistic patterns are rooted in the epistemic patterns of a cultural group. To put this another way, what Kay identifies as individual thought largely involves the thought patterns of the cultural group—with individualistic variations in interpretation and degrees of reflexiveness.

Briefly, three sources of evidence can be identified as justifying a more culturally based way of understanding human intelligence. Each involves a very complex set of issues and the ability to address the issues (and supporting anthropological and linguistic evidence) through a different interpretive framework from that which liberalism makes available. The first challenge to Kay's constructivist position can be made from the growing recognition that the language/thought connection is metaphorical in nature. As I have discussed this topic elsewhere (1984, 1990), including the role of metaphorical thinking in educational software (1988), I will reiterate only the most salient points—by using examples of how metaphors organize Kay's own patterns of thinking as he explains to the reader the educational potential of globally networked computers. But first a brief explanation of the dynamics of metaphorical thinking may be essential for the reader who is encountering this argument for the first time.

The most important point that attention to the metaphorical nature of thinking helps us to recognize is that a totally new experience cannot be understood on its own terms. We gain an initial basis of understanding through the process of analogic thinking, whereby the already familiar patterns and schemata are, so to speak, mapped onto the new territory. Understanding "artificial intelligence," "virtual reality," "social evolution," "individual," and "data" were (and still are, as the images in the iconic metaphors continue to change) dependent upon thinking of the new in terms of the familiar. The choice of generative metaphor (metaphorical representation of some familiar area of experience or conceptual understanding) is influenced by the prevailing root metaphors of the cultural group. In other words, the root metaphor of viewing the world and all life processes as machinelike made it conceptually coherent to think of the mind as a data-processing device, and to use this image as the generative metaphor for making sense of the first computers. Root metaphors, in effect, provide the master templates or conceptual frameworks that influence the process of analogic thinking and become encoded in the iconic metaphors that survive the politics of analogic thinking. When we recognize that root metaphors are culturally and historically specific, it then becomes easier to recognize that the schemata of understanding involve, in the act of knowing, the forms of intelligence that over time have become encoded in the language that thinks us, as we think within the language. To put it another way, intelligence is both cultural and individualistic.

The culturally specific root metaphor that organizes Kay's view of reality (i.e., his way of understanding how things hang together) is a composite of the mechanistic view of the universe, the view of time and change as moving in a linear/progressive direction, and the view of the individual as the primary social unit—all worked out in the processes of analogic thinking that occurred during the sixteenth- and seventeenth-century transition from the root metaphors of the medieval period to the modern/scientific/liberal form of consciousness. His entire article can be viewed as a series of analogic thought processes, but each liminal possibility—how we might understand "intelligence," "computers" (the computer, he writes, "is like the greatest 'piano' ever invented" [p. 138]), "benefits of this technology," and "change"—is framed by the root metaphors that we identified as central to liberal ideology.

When he uses iconic metaphors such as "change," "experiment," "individual," and "ideas," the schemata encoded from earlier processes of analogic thinking reproduce the already established patterns of thinking. For example, his use (which now becomes a misleading phrase) of the iconic metaphor "change" reproduces the conceptual pattern that represents change as progressive in nature. Similarly, new ideas, more information, new technologies, and the transformation of modern culture itself, are all represented as progressive steps—as he puts it, "great numbers of people will not avail themselves of the opportunity for growth and will be left behind" (p. 148). The principal question here is: Is this statement an example of an individual thought process that is based on data, or is it an example of thought being organized in accordance with the master schemata of a cultural group? If language thinks us as we think within the language, then the liberal notion of autonomous individuals constructing their "own version of reality" goes out the window.

The second kind of evidence that undermines Kay's epistemology can be related to the argument on the metaphorical nature of the language/thought connection, which I have framed here in terms of how past forms of metaphorical thinking within Kay's own cultural traditions continue to influence the present. But it can also stand alone. Literature in the fields of anthropology and social linguistics now provides massive documentation of profound differences in the worldviews of different cultural groups. I shall identify here only a few examples of cultural groups whose root metaphors differ radically from Kay's taken-for-granted symbolic world. The examples were also chosen because they represent cultural groups who understand empowerment in terms of learning the traditional practices that are more attuned to living in ecological balance—which is profoundly different from the view of the form of empowerment and social progress Kay takes for granted.

The root metaphor that helps to frame time as linear and progressive in Kay's thinking is not present in N. Scott Momaday's primary cultural group (Kiowa). Momaday (1987) writes:

> I want to indicate as best I can an American Indian attitude (for want of a better word) toward the world as a whole. . . . I am talking about a spiritual sense so ancient as to be primordial, so pervasive as to be definitive—not an idea, but a perception on the far side of ideas, an act of understanding as original and originative as the Word. . . . For the Indian there is something like an extended present. Time as motion is an illusion; indeed, time itself is an illusion. In the deepest sense, according to the native perception, there is only the dimension of timelessness, and in that all things happen. (p. 158)

Within this way of experiencing time, empowerment would be associated more with the reenactment of proven patterns that help sustain relationships with other forms of life that participate in this ecology of time. Furthermore, the sense of connectedness is grounded in a form of spiritual awareness that is totally absent from the secularizing and anthropocentric way of thinking that characterizes Kay's world of information processing.

The Wintu Indians of Northern California are an example of a cultural group whose view of individualism differs profoundly from the form of individualism and thought patterns that Kay wants to treat as a universal, culture-free being. A study of their language/thought patterns, as Dorothy Lee observes, reveals how the Wintu represent the self in a fundamentally different way than we do in English. For speakers of English, the self is represented as clearly autonomous and in a controlling relationship with the outside world, "a study of the grammatical expression of identity, relationship and otherness," shows that the Wintu conceive of the self not as strictly delimited or defined, but as a concentration, at most, which gives place to the other. "Most of what is other for us, is for the Wintu completely or partially or upon occasion, identified with the self" (Lee, 1959, p. 134). Furthermore, the understanding of self in contextual, relational, and mutually participatory terms with the other, which may involve a person–person relationship or a person–plant or person–animal relationship, involves a different form of knowledge and, by extension, what would be regarded as intelligence. As Lee notes, the Wintu language (and thus thought patterns) does not represent the world in abstract and universal terms—where an ontology of thingness and shared essences exist. Nor is there an understanding of knowledge as encoded in "data" that has unknown origins, and whose validity is separate from contextual considerations. Rather, intelligent behavior (if they were to use such a term) is contextual, participatory, and, in Gregory Bateson's terms, part of a mental ecology that includes the larger biotic community.

If the followers of Kay's ideology think I have chosen an obscure tribal group to buttress my argument that cultural groups have different root metaphors for understanding the patterns and forms of empowerment Kay wants to treat as universals, they might consider the cognitive/language differences associated with the predominant use of count nouns in the English language and the use of mass nouns in Chinese. The works of Chad Hansen (1985) and Ron and Suzanne Scollon (1991) are especially useful in clarifying how fundamentally different ways of knowing, and thus ontologies, are reproduced through the linguistic patterns of a cultural group. Examples from American Indian cultural groups, rather than the Chinese, were used because their language/ thought patterns demonstrate a sensitivity to environmental relationships in a manner that is absent in Chinese thinking. As the ecological crisis is likely to displace the Information Age as the dominant concern in the decades ahead, I chose examples that illuminate the problems with Kay's vision of the future—including his approach to using computers to teach students how to understand ecological systems. The "barbarism of the deep past," to recall Kay's statement, reflects a basic misunderstanding of the achievements of many primal cultures. When judged against the yardstick of technological achievements, they may appear backward. But when they are judged against the more important yardstick of achieving long-term sustainability in a limited habitat, and in developing the patterns that encoded their moral/spiritual knowledge for living within the larger biotic community, it might make more sense to pin the label of "barbarism" on the morally impoverished approach to technology that characterizes Kay's position.

3. *The metaphor of an "Information Age," which is the most recent expression of liberal ideology, serves to hide the moral/spiritual nature of the ecological crisis.* Kay's article provides clear evidence that he considers the ecological crisis an important classroom challenge. "We particularly wanted to investigate," he writes, "how children can be helped to understand that animals, people and situations are parts of larger systems that influence one another" (p. 142). The educational use of computers would allow students to simulate the patterns and consequences that would emerge from different ways of understanding and designing solutions to different human/habitat relationships. The different capacities of the computer would provide the data and simulation models that would empower students to "come up with the ideas," and to "develop knowledge of their own collaborativity" (p. 143)—to recall Kay's way of representing the primacy of the autonomous individual's reflective pro-

cess. However, Kay's sensitivity to the importance of helping students understand the interactive patterns of existence within larger ecological systems is undermined by the ideology that frames his way of understanding the empowerment/social progress relationship. The metaphor of the "Information Age" is emblematic of the double bind that characterizes his position.

Just as the metaphor of the "Industrial Revolution" served to illuminate the special form of technological achievement of the early phase of liberal/modern society, the metaphor of the "Information Age" is supposed to signal a profound change in the direction of technological progress. And just as the earlier metaphor both illuminated and hid at the same time, the new metaphor also creates areas of silence. The way of understanding the moral implications of different kinds of relationships in the era of the Industrial Revolution was dependent upon reifying the arguments of theorists on the nature of individualism, competition, and progress in a way that made them appear to be universal norms. The nonhuman aspects of the world were understood as either a "natural resource" or as part of the wild and predatory world that had to be brought under human control. The underlying schemata for understanding the moral dimensions of relationships have changed with the transition to more information-intensive technologies: Now we include more aspects of the planet's ecosystems in the category of "natural resource." But the essential aspects of liberal ideology that formed moral sensitivities during the Industrial Revolution continue on as the conceptual underpinnings of the new age of progress being ushered in by developments in computer technology.

To superficial thinkers, the progressive development of our moral condition appears guaranteed by the liberal ontology that underlies the dawning of the Information Age. The evidence supporting this optimism, which Kay fully shares, includes the continual increase in technological innovations (evidence of human progress), ever more massive amounts of data (the source of rational empowerment), and the increasing development of a modern form of monoculture as computer networks lead to the wider adoption of English as the preferred language of computer-mediated discourse (evidence of movement toward a unified world order). These developments appear to support the optimism that pervades all areas of the computer-technology community, including the advocates of computer-mediated education. But there is other evidence that is generally ignored by the people who have embraced the Information Age as the logo for the twenty-first century. The continued degradation of natural systems and the alarming increase in human population with only a marginal awareness of environmental consequences

—particularly in areas of the world where local ecosystems are already seriously stressed, reflecting the continued expansion of a wasteful form of consumerism—point to a future scenario for humanity very much at odds with the computer devotee's vision of progress. Elsewhere (see Chapter 7 of this volume) I have argued that the epistemology embedded in computers, in spite of the technology's capacities to collect and process vast amounts of data relating to changes in the earth's ecosystems, contributes to deepening the ecological crisis. Thus I want to focus here more specifically on how the educational uses of computers reinforce the nihilistic tendencies in liberalism—which must also be understood as having devastating consequences for the rest of the biotic community.

Nihilism has generally been understood as the relativizing of belief and values, the loss of shared cultural norms, and the personal experience of meaninglessness. It may take the form of self-absorption to the point where nothing outside the self has value or meaning; it may also take the form of the person who uses the rational process to continually deauthorize all forms of cultural authority (Dreyfus, 1981). Both expressions of nihilism have been associated primarily with humans. But the relativizing process can also be associated with technology, as well as be extended to a discussion of the human/habitat relationship. Computers, which are part of the tradition of print technology and also reinforce the Cartesian epistemology, can be understood as a technology that amplifies the cultural patterns contributing to the more traditional view of nihilism, and to the forms of nihilism expressed in the relationship many individuals have with the environment.

Eugene Provenzo's examination of the moral ecology that students are immersed in as they play video games, particularly Nintendo, clearly illuminates how the messages, simulations, and reinforcement patterns are expressions of nihilism, albeit masked as fun, excitement, and the challenge of problem solving. As Provenzo (1991) notes, "violence is the main operative function in all these games" (p. 89). The immediate excitement of a particular game, which conditions the participant to interact with the fast pace of electronically mediated representations of reality, can be exchanged for other equally segmenting experiences. Supposedly students maintain control over the length and content of their interaction with computer games. This experience of discontinuity from the more reciprocal patterns that characterize everyday life, most of which are governed by shared moral norms, as well as the distinctive moral messages in the games themselves, contributes to nihilism.

But understanding how computers contribute to a nihilistic relationship between the individual and the environment requires that we adopt a more cross-cultural approach. That is, in order to recognize how taken-for-granted cultural patterns amplified by computer-mediated communication and thought processes contribute to the desensitizing of students to interactive, life-sustaining relationships with the "natural" environment, we need to consider the contrasting patterns of cultural groups who understand that their long-term existence depends upon not destroying their habitat. A basic difference that appears to separate primal, ecologically sustainable cultures from the modern culture (including what is envisaged as the culture of the Information Age) is that their languages are attuned to representing the human/environment relationship as collaborative and interdependent. Unlike the grammar of our language, which represents the "I" as separate from the object being acted upon (i.e., the subject, "I," is in control, and the object is separate, passive, subject to "my" control), the grammar of the Koyukon, according to Ron and Suzanne Scollon, represents the person/environment relationship as mutually collaborative. As human relationships are framed by the patterns of moral sensitivities of the cultural group, any discussion of language (which, according to the Scollons, is always about relationships) is also a discussion of the deepest levels of a cultural group's moral codes—including moral codes that are nihilistic. The collaborative nature of relationships in Koyukon can be seen in the sentence "twenty-two aahaa biyil k'iltltul," which the Scollons (1985) translate as "using the twenty-two, along with the lynx as my co-actor, I shot (a gun)" (p. 16). Similarly, the language of the Wintu, according to Dorothy Lee (1959), frames relationships as a "coordinate togetherness, with, at most, a stressed point of view" (p. 137).

The distinction Jim Cheney (1989) makes between a "colonizing discourse" and "contextual discourse" (I would suggest calling it an "ecological discourse") brings out the fundamental moral and political differences between English and the languages of cultural groups that understand humans as interdependent members of a larger biotic community. The colonizing discourse represents the speaker as the actor and the rest of the world as the recipient of the actor's emotive or rational intentions. The ideal of this discourse, as Alvin Gouldner (1979) points out, is "'one word, one meaning,' for everyone and forever" (p. 28). This discourse—and this is where the English language and liberal/Cartesian epistemology come together—is also based on a view of the rational process that involves "objectifying" what is known, making it "explicit" (in fact, recognizing only explicit forms of knowledge), treating the object of knowledge as context-free, understanding the object of knowledge in terms of component parts that can be (at a theoretical level) reconceptualized into a new system, and understanding the object of knowledge from the perspective of the rational subject (Dreyfus, 1981). Knowledge thus becomes context-independent, universal, and objective. It serves as the basis of a colonizing discourse because it conditions the speakers/thinkers to experience themselves as separate from the world that is known and acted upon. Furthermore, the cultural/ecological context is not important, as the discourse (and data) can be used to think and communicate about how to make what is going on in any context more amenable to rational control. If we keep in mind the Scollons' observation that language also helps to frame the moral nature of relationships, we can see that the colonizing discourse frames relationships in instrumental terms. Any possibility of a moral relationship between the human/nonhuman world is eclipsed by economic and political considerations. And what does not have instrumental value (as a "natural resource") falls into the catch-all categories of the useless, material, and nonintelligent—in a word, that which is meaningless from a human point of view. When humans relate to contextual relationships and the nonhuman aspects of the biotic community as meaningless or, at best, as temporarily lacking in instrumental value, they are expressing nihilistic attitudes.

Jim Cheney's observations on the nature of contextual discourse brings into sharper focus the nihilistic elements in the colonizing discourse underlying the scientific/technological culture that Kay identifies with the Information Age. Cheney (1989) writes:

> Contextual discourse . . . assimilates language to the situation, bends it, shapes it to fit. Contextual discourse is not fundamentally concerned with issues of overall coherence. Or, rather, the kind of overall coherence for which it strives is different: a mosaic of language which serves as a tool of many purposes at once. (p. 120)

Whereas the colonizing discourse, with its Cartesian expression of the man/nature dichotomy, frames relationships in instrumental terms, the contextual discourse foregrounds the moral nature of relationships—even when it involves the killing of an animal as the source of food or the use of technologies that help insure human survival. This is brought out in Cheney's (1989) observation that

> in the life of a tribal community . . . [contextual discourse] must articulate a sense of those processes which bind the community together and to the land; and it must do this in a language which functions effectively to call forth appropriate responses. It must provide a means whereby individuals can come into their own in nonrepressive ways; yet, individual identities must be articulated in a language that makes

these individuals intelligible to the community. . . . The language must also articulate a process of human interaction with the land which insures the health both of the land and community. Contextualized language is tuned to quite specific situations and forgoes the kind of totalizing coherence with which we have been preoccupied in the modern world. (p. 121)

To put it another way, contextualized language foregrounds the cultural group's way of understanding the moral responsibility in all the relationships that are part of daily life. The metaphorical content of the vocabulary will be derived from the animal, plant, and physical characteristics of the bioregion. Metaphors that encode the cultural group's schemata for understanding moral responsibility will not be derived from a mechanistic root metaphor, as is the case with the colonizing discourse of the Information Age. Rather, it will draw upon patterns perceived in the life cycle of the biotic community, and these patterns—the cycles of the salmon, the habits of the wolf, the patterns of the seasons—will serve as the analogs that help humans understand their moral responsibilities. Contextual languages, as Cheney describes them, also serve to frame the person's relationship to community in a way profoundly different from the colonizing discourse of individual empowerment within a world community of computer networks. Understanding human actions in terms of the temporal aspects of relationships, where insuring "the health both of the land and community" takes simultaneous account of past traditions that enabled the cultural group to survive and future prospects, adds yet another dimension to their way of understanding moral relationships. For Kay, and others conditioned to think that progress is guaranteed through continued technological innovation, there is no reason to limit the self by bringing our embeddedness in a larger mental ecology (as Bateson calls it) into the foreground or to complicate our view of language and thought by suggesting that the epistemology underlying the promise of the Information Age has closed off the multiple ways of knowing and communicating that may be essential to our long-term survival. The ecological crisis, for Kay, does not suggest the need to understand the moral and spiritual roots of the double bind that now characterizes modern society; rather it suggests the need for more computer simulations, more data, and more individually generated ideas. This failure to understand that the relationships and patterns that make up an ecology should involve, for humans, a sensitivity to the moral dimension of all relationships seems to be a tragic flaw in Kay's thinking. The real crisis is not the lack of data or computer literacy, but the lack of moral and spiritual development that takes account of the interconnectedness of life.

Part III

RECOVERING THE ECOLOGICAL IMPERATIVE IN EDUCATIONAL AND SOCIAL THOUGHT

This group of essays represents a shift away from the earlier efforts to bring into question the more problematic aspects of modernity that gave much of recent educational criticism a formulaic quality, and also away from the focus on the cultural mind-set reinforced through educational computing. These essays also represent a major shift in my own way of understanding the embeddedness of the individual. Whereas the earlier essays gave primacy to the constitutive role of culture (especially language) in shaping consciousness, this last group of essays, in drawing upon the ideas of Gregory Bateson and Aldo Leopold, situate culture within the information and energy networks essential for survival—namely, the environment.

Bateson makes the more fundamental contribution to putting educational theory and practices on a new path. His explanation of why we should give up the old view of the individual as an autonomous observer who may be moved by internal events (thoughts, feelings, sense of self-interest, etc.) to act upon the external world, and focus instead upon the individual as part of a larger interactive system, appears on the surface to be similar to John Dewey's understanding of "transaction" as a way of overcoming the individual/environment dichotomy. But other aspects of Bateson's ideas go well beyond the cultural nihilism of Dewey's last years (I am referring here to Chapter 5 in *Knowing and the Known*, a book he co-authored with Arthur Bentley). Bateson's distinction between "map" (the culture's way of knowing, or schemata) and "territory" (the domain of interactions and information pathways that characterize natural environments) brings back into focus the role metaphor plays in illuminating and hiding important features of the territory—to stay with Bateson's metaphor.

The map/territory distinction becomes even more critical for educational theorists and practitioners to understand when we take account of Bateson's argument that the reification of the individual as an autonomous entity has helped foster the myth that the survival of individuals (or society) can be separated from the fate of the larger system in which the individuals are participants. Bateson, along with Aldo Leopold (who articulated this relationship in terms of a "land ethic"), argues instead that the primary unit of survival is the system as a whole: that is, the "unit of mind" represents the aggregate of information exchanges within the system, including air, water, rocks, plants, animals, humans, and everything else that is part of a living system.

The six essays in this section were influenced by Bateson's ideas, as well as by ecoconservative thinkers who share his nonanthropocentric way of understanding the culture/habitat relationship. These essays should not be viewed, however, as representing Bateson's own ideas on education, but rather as my use of Bateson's ideas for the purpose of elaborating and deepening a theory that has its roots in a number of traditions sensitive to the culture/language/thought connection. Bateson's understanding of a mental ecology helped me work out the conceptual underpinnings of a nonanthropocentric approach to the analysis of what teachers should understand about the relationship between metaphorical thinking and the problem of passing on conceptual maps that represent the nature of the territory (natural systems) in dangerously outdated ways. Bateson's ideas have also been useful in reconstituting how we think about art education: from the traditional view of art as a form of self-expression and the creation of art objects that can be admired and traded as a commodity to viewing artistic expression as a way of communicating about relationships. Bateson's understanding of the system (an ecology of mind), rather than the individual, as the unit of mental activity was also basic to the critique of liberal educational reformers (Paulo Freire, Maxine Greene, and Henry Giroux) and Richard Rorty (one of this country's most important philosophers) as reactionary thinkers still rooted in the least defensible aspects of modern liberalism.

The last two essays represent an attempt to identify the conceptual foundations of an approach to the education of teachers that takes account both of a culturally and ecologically responsive classroom. The knowledge essential to teachers in the years ahead is framed in terms of a series of double binds that now characterize the conceptual underpinnings of mainstream teacher-education programs. In effect, these double binds result in thinking about the present and future in terms of conceptual schemata that evolved in response to historical and culturally specific situations that no longer exist. This essay presents alternative ways of understanding fundamental processes in the culture/teacher/student relationship, along with suggestions for sustaining what will be a long and difficult process of changing the deepest foundations of modern consciousness. The final essay examines the characteristics of traditional cultures that have evolved along more sustainable pathways, and explores what modern teachers can learn from them about living more ecologically centered lives.

In effect, the essays in the last section move beyond the critique of modernism in "radical" theories of education by suggesting positive steps that can be taken in the areas of teacher education and curriculum development to help insure that classrooms become sites for reintegrating culture back into the natural systems on a sustainable basis.

Chapter 8

A Batesonian Perspective on Education and the Bonds of Language

Cultural Literacy in the Technological Age

The anthropologist A. F. C. Wallace gives us a way of understanding how, in periods of extreme stress and distortion within a culture, prophets arise who reformulate the traditional pathway for the people to follow. In our case the revitalization movement, like the ghost dance of the Plains Indians, is currently headed by Allan Bloom, who urges a return to the pathway of following those few exemplary individuals capable of being nourished and directed by reason. In suggesting that our understanding of the process of educational empowerment will shift, according to the metaphorical framework within which the rational process is embedded, I am confronting head-on Bloom's desire to reverse the growth of moral and intellectual relativism by restoring the transcendental authority of rational thought. The recognition of the metaphorical nature of language and thought does, indeed, contribute to the relativizing of cultural belief systems that so deeply concerns Bloom, as well as others who share his desire to insure the survival of an elite "community of those who seek the truth" (1987, p. 381). Recognizing the deeper implications of the metaphorical foundations of our symbolic world is essential if we are to rediscover ancient pathways that enabled human beings to live in ecological balance over a time frame that makes the classical tradition of Greek philosophy that Bloom reveres appear as a rather brief and ecologically disruptive cultural experiment that has almost played itself out. A case will be made that Bloom's view of the rational process contributes to the very relativism and sense of disconnectedness that so concern him. But the main purpose here is not to deconstruct Bloom; it is, instead, to identify how the formal educational process can contribute to a form of empowerment that takes seriously Gregory Bateson's understanding that the basic unit of survival is not the rational individual, but the form of intelligence immanent in an ecosystem.

People conditioned to thinking of rationality as an attribute of the individual may not, at first, take Bateson's radical position seriously. As the subsequent discussion is an attempt to work out the educational implications of decentering the individual as an autonomous rational agent, it is first necessary to elaborate on Bateson's argument that the individual must be understood as being situated in a context, and that the aggregate of interacting parts that make up the context (of which the individual is only a part) is the unit of mind. As Bateson (1972) put it, "when you separate mind from the structure in which it is immanent, such as a human relationship, the human society, or the ecosystem, you thereby embark, I believe, on a fundamental error, which in the end will hurt you" (p. 484). Unlike the Cartesian view of thinking, which Heidegger (1977) criticized for introducing the objectifying "picture character of the world" (p. 132), Bateson views the basic unit of mental activity as information exchanges triggered by differences in relationships that occur between the aggregate parts of a system.

His classic explanation of how information exchanges occur can be seen in the circuit of relationships (information exchanges) involved in the act of cutting down a tree:

> Consider a man felling a tree with an axe. Each stroke of the axe is modified or corrected, according to the shape of the cut face of the tree left by the previous stroke. This self corrective (i.e., mental) process is brought about by a total system, tree-eyes-brain-muscles-axe-stroke-tree; and it is this total system that has the characteristics of immanent mind.
>
> More correctly, we should spell the matter out as: (differences in tree)-(differences in retina)-(differences in brain)-(differences in muscles)-(differences in movement of axe)-(differences in tree), etc. What is transmitted around the circuit is transforms of differences. And, as noted above, a difference which makes a difference is an *idea* or unit of information. (1972, pp. 317–318)

Although Bateson notes that the individual, as a component within a larger message-exchange system, may process some of the information in a more complicated (i.e., symbolic) manner, he nevertheless avoids the Cartesian dualism that separates mind from nature (context). Two other points about Bateson's view of mind need to be introduced. In contrast to the Cartesian view of knowledge as being explicit in nature, Bateson states that "most of the mental process is unconscious" (1972, p. 463). He also challenges the view that human intelligence is of a higher order and thus should be used to bring the natural environment under rational control. "In no system which shows mental characteristics," he writes, "can any part have unilateral control over the whole. In other words, the mental characteristics of the system are immanent, not in some part, but in the system as a whole" (1972, p. 317). The poet Gary Snyder makes a similar observation about the problem of the anthropocentric universe by noting that the information stored in the cells and genes of the life-biomass has been flowing for millions of years. "In this total information context," he cautions, "man may not be necessarily the highest and most interesting product" (1974, p. 108).

If we keep in mind that Bateson regards the language/thought connection as basically metaphorical—"the main characteristic and organizing glue of this world of mental process" (1980, p. 11)—it will help avoid a basic misinterpretation of his position: namely, that he equates all thought with information processing. It will also help us return to the main issue: how to work through the double bind whereby the epistemic codes embedded in the language determine the limits and direction that educational empowerment will take. A form of educational empowerment that strengthens the dominant cultural orientation of viewing self as an autonomous and rational being, a reflective spectator of a world that is distinct, will not contribute to the evolution of a sustainable culture that is "in harmony with the natural systems and rhythms, constrained by natural limits and capacities and developed according to the natural configurations of the earth and its inherent life forms" (Sale, 1985, p. 24). Nor is it likely to reverse the current trend toward greater reliance on technology as the source of power in dealing with relationships—interpersonal, environmental, temporal—that are becoming increasingly stressful.

Educational empowerment, like the rest of our lexicon, must be understood metaphorically. Therefore, what it means in terms of curriculum, the responsibility of the teacher, and the abilities it is supposed to foster will depend upon the coding process that is part of metaphorical thinking. In working out how educational empowerment takes on a different set of meanings, depending upon the metaphorical framework that is used, we will also be clarifying how "language already hides in itself a developed way of conceiving," as Heidegger put it (1962, p. 199). Or, to reframe Heidegger's famous aphorism, "language speaks" us in a manner that supports Bateson's argument that mental processes are part of the field of relationships, and not limited exclusively to an autonomously acting individual. In effect, we need to understand how words, as metaphors, encode past schemata of understanding. The intelligence of the individual is, in part, dependent upon the schema of understanding encoded in the language used to formulate thought and communicate with others. This means that intelligence or mind, to use Bateson's phrase, also

exists outside the individual. As the understanding of language is broad-
ened to include all forms of communication—the whole range of semiotic
systems that make up human culture—we can also see more clearly the
importance of his statement that "most of the mental process is unconscious" (p. 463).

How the thought process is dependent upon the use of metaphor
was explained long ago by Aristotle and, more recently, by Nietzsche,
who put this idea in its most succinct terms: "In our thought the essential feature is fitting new material to old schemas . . . making equal what
is new" (1968, p. 273). The new, in not being conceptualized on its own
terms, is understood in terms of its similarities with familiar domains of
experience of understanding. Thinking of something as if it were like
something else involves carrying over the interpretative schema (encoding process) from one area of experience to another. In presenting a new
explanation of the multiple timing processes that regulate human life, for
example, Jeremy Campbell (1986) suggests that thinking of the clocks of
the body as ticking to a single measure would provide an incorrect
understanding; more appropriate would be the image of an orchestra,
where the different rhythms are integrated into the harmony and complexity of the whole. Recent references to the president as the quarter-
back, and to not changing the economic game plan in the fourth quarter,
are more prosaic examples of a metaphor's reproducing a familiar and
thus reassuring schema of understanding in a new context (new in the
sense that the political arena is accompanied by uncertainties). Thinking
of the "book" of organic life as written in a chemical code based on four
"letters" called nucleotides is an example of how researchers working
on the frontiers of science are dependent upon the familiar patterns of
understanding (mind, in Bateson's sense) encoded in metaphor.

The "source domain" from which we derive our interpretative
schema that is then mapped onto new experiences, along with important personal variations in interpretation and insight, includes both bodily
experiences and the metaphorical frameworks already embedded in the
language of our community. In The Body in the Mind, Mark Johnson (1987)
makes the point that bodily experiences are a source of schemata used
for understanding the most basic relationships (up/down, near/far, left/
right, front/back, toward/away from, etc.) as well as other dimensions
of experience. Direct bodily experiences, for example, were used centuries ago as the basis of measurement encoded in the vocabulary of inch,
foot, yard, and mile. Thus the understanding of distance was based
on metaphorical thinking: The word mile comes from the Latin "milia
passuum," which encodes the practice of equating that unit of distance
with a thousand paces. The metric system of measurement simply

encodes according to a different metaphorical framework. But experientially derived schemata for understanding are also influenced by the more purely symbolic coding processes of a culture. It is culture, for example, that provides the schema for encoding the assumptions and prejudices (in Gadamer's sense of the term) that leads to viewing "up" as better than "down," "right" as better or worse (depending upon ideological orientation) than "left," and so forth. A more specific example of how metaphor encodes past ways of understanding can be seen in how the word *intelligence*, when used in educational settings, led to thinking about intelligence as an individual attribute that could be scientifically measured. The cultural assumptions encoded in the word during the early twentieth century were then reproduced in the thought process of subsequent generations of educators who viewed themselves as autonomous individuals making rational (scientifically based) decisions about the student's future prospects. Other words, such as *rationality, individualism, freedom, information*, and *literacy*, are examples of metaphors that enable us to understand the new in terms of schemata worked out at some earlier point in our cultural history and passed on as part of the tacit knowledge we acquire as members of a language community.

The bonds of language, or the "mental characteristics immanent" in the symbolic system, to paraphrase Bateson, can be seen in how three distinct views of educational empowerment have been influenced by a particular metaphorical image of the individual. That the individual has been viewed as the primary social unit is itself an example of how language provides the basis for making distinctions and seeing relationships. Over the last decade we have seen educational programs based on a metaphorical representation of the individual as free, authentic, and self-creating. The thinking of Carl Rogers is a particularly good example of this position. Educational empowerment, as dictated by the generative metaphor of the free and authentic individual, meant a classroom that allowed a wide range of choices and self-expression; the teacher's role in the empowerment process was to be a "facilitator" (Rogers, 1983, p. 135). B. F. Skinner started with an entirely different metaphorical image. The positivistic tradition led him to view the individual in terms of what could be observed (namely, behavior) and to view the individual's behavior like that of the laboratory pigeon—both were controlled and shaped by contingencies of reinforcement. Empowerment, given the encoding process of Skinner's metaphorical framework, meant organizing the environment so that the behavior deemed desirable by the behavior modifier would be reinforced. As the environment shapes individual behavior ("it not only prods or lashes, it selects," to quote Skinner [1972, p. 16]), the term *empowerment* disappears from the behaviorist's vocabulary only to be replaced by more metaphorically coherent phrases, such as *behavior management techniques.*

A more recent example of a theory of education's being framed by the metaphorical starting point, or what Donald Schön refers to as a "generative metaphor," can be seen in recent writings of Mortimer Adler and Allan Bloom. In describing how generative metaphors serve as a lexical and conceptual guidance system, Schön (1979) notes that problem solving usually begins in the stories that people tell about some troublesome situation. These stories, in turn, are centered around powerful metaphorical images that frame the structure of the story—the nature of good and evil (and its secular equivalents), how people should act to overcome the problem, the sources of empowerment, and so forth. In the educational theories of Rogers and Skinner, their stories centered around the metaphorical image of the free individual and the behavioral selecting characteristics of the environment. For Adler and Bloom, the metaphorical image that underlies their problem-setting stories about the educational roots of nihilism is that of the individual who, as a rational being, is capable of fulfilling the responsibilities of democratic citizenship. This image of the potentially rational individual is not compatible with Rogers's starting point, which is the natural freedom and authentic goodness of the individual. Nor can it be easily reconciled with Skinner's view of the individual, as his generative metaphor locates the source of authority for behavior in the environment. In effect, the generative metaphor that underlies the educational ideas of Adler and Bloom sets the conceptual boundaries and dictates the direction their arguments will take.

The curriculum recommended by Adler and Bloom makes no concession to the freedom, original sin, or natural goodness of the individual—all expressions of other metaphorical frameworks. Instead, the conceptual/metaphorical coherence is grounded in a list of great thinkers of the past whom the student "must have read, or rather lived with, to be called educated" (Bloom, 1987, p. 53). Although Adler and Bloom give their own distinctive stamp to the arguments for revitalizing the rational foundations of social and political life, it is, ironically, metaphor rather than pure reason that sets the initial direction for their analysis and recommendations. In effect, the generative metaphor represents the analog or pattern that is prior to rational thought. In the case of Adler and Bloom, their own deep and personally transforming experiences of reading Plato, Aristotle, Locke, Rousseau, and other Western philosophers becomes the analog (generative metaphor) for formal education.

One characteristic of the coding process that needs reiteration, when thinking about the nature of educational empowerment, has to do with how the metaphorical nature of our language causes us to view the current ecological crisis through the conceptual lenses of the past. The use of metaphors that encode ways of understanding formed during past struggles to rework traditions of thought and social practice means, in some instances, that we continue to use ways of thinking appropriate to Western Europe in the seventeen and eighteenth centuries as a basis of interpreting our present circumstances. In other instances, currently used metaphors serve as information cells that reproduce the patterns of thinking that go back to the origins of Western monotheistic religions. An example of the latter is our current way of viewing the environment as a resource to be exploited. The much older way of thinking, which involved the "animal/man/god interpenetration" essential to ancient peoples, who viewed all forms of life as interdependent, was displaced by a binary logic that separated the sacred from the natural environment. According to Herbert Schneidau, by investing the abstract Yahweh with absolute power, the cosmic continuum was disrupted; as a result, the earlier metaphorical coding process of ancient religions, which Schneidau views as a form of geography that "organized space into sacred configurations" (1976, p. 71), is now viewed as paganism. The binary logic that made the sacred a transaction between the person and God, rather than representing all forms of giving and taking of life as bound up together, alienated humans from a religious sense of the interdependence of all life forms.

With the strengthening and progressive modernizing of the metaphorical framework that privileged humans as superior to other life forms (the works of Plato, Descartes, and Locke being part of a tradition that culminates in the modern technocrat), we have now arrived at a point where it is difficult to comprehend that the metaphorical frameworks of ancient peoples may represent the information coding process essential for ecological survival. In The Primal Mind, Jamake Highwater (1981) gives two examples of lexical coding that suggest the nature of the double bind that characterizes the dominant culture. As a member of a traditional and what was formerly a bioregionally integrated culture, Highwater recalls his surprise at learning that in English the word wilderness is used to refer to the natural environment. Viewing the forest and plains as wild and in need of being tamed, controlled, and harnessed reflects the perspective of European immigrants, but from the point of view of traditional peoples, like the Blackfeet Indians, "the forest is the natural state" and it is "the cities that are wild and seem to need taming" (p. 5). He also observes the different conceptual mapping process associated with the word earth. For "primal" people, "the earth is so marvelous that their connotation of it requires it to be spelled in English with a capital 'E.'

How perplexing it is," he continues, "to discover two English synonyms for Earth—'soil' and 'dirt'—used to describe uncleanliness, soiled and dirty. And how upsetting it is to discover that the word 'dirty' in English is also used to depict obscenities" (p. 5). The double bind, as Highwater's example suggests, lies in basing our current and highly rational approach to the ecological crisis on a metaphorical language that encodes the perspectives, experiences, and cultural assumptions of earlier generations who faced an entirely different set of circumstances. We shall look at two other examples of how metaphor influences our approach to problem solving before taking up the question of educational empowerment. Both examples will also serve as a reference point for thinking about how the educational process can be used to free ourselves from the outmoded schemata encoded in our language. The two examples have to do with relationships: our relationship to technology and our relationships with one another. The latter, as the authors of *Habits of the Heart* point out, can be understood as the problem of whether commitment will connect people as part of a moral ecology or separate them (Bellah et al., 1985). Both areas of relationship, individual/technology and individual/community, are based on patterns of understanding rooted in metaphorical memory. The real problem is whether the domains of human experience from which the metaphorical information codes are derived are adequate for understanding the current situation.

The metaphor that guides our understanding of our relationship with technology is the image of a neutral tool or procedure that is ready-at-hand to be used for purposes we give it. But it is also understood on another level, particularly when the technology is perceived as created by a mode of thought concerned with rational control and efficiency, as an artifact of the culture of progress. We will address only the individual/technology relationship here and will use the educational use of computers as an example. Although early pioneers in the development of artificial intelligence anticipated that the computer would quickly surpass humans in the evolution of intelligence capabilities, the classroom use of the computer has retained for it a more lowly metaphorical standing as a neutral tool that facilitates drill and practice, simulations, and word processing, and serves as a powerful database. The generative metaphor of a neutral tool led to defining "computer literacy," itself a metaphor that served primarily a political purpose, in terms of learning the mechanical functions of the machine. It also led Seymour Papert (1980), the creator of the computer language LOGO, to claim that "working with computers can make it more apparent that children construct *their own* personal microworlds" (p. 162; emphasis added). And from Robert McClintock (1988), chairperson of the Department of Communication,

Computing, and Technology at a leading eastern university, we learn that "as we translate the stuff of culture into binary code and create more and more powerful *tools* for working with such binary code, we are increasingly able not only to store information in external objects, but to endow certain objects with the power to process information intelligently" (p. 351; emphasis added).

Both Papert and McClintock, who are highly representative of thinking within the field, frame the individual/technology relationship as one in which the individual remains the controlling agent. What is left out of their technology-as-neutral-tool metaphor is an awareness that technology mediates human experience. That is, the technology possesses characteristics that select out for amplification certain aspects of human experience—and reduce or cancel out other aspects (Ihde, 1979, p. 56). The use of a stick, for instance, amplifies the person's ability to reach the fruit in the upper branches, but reduces the ability to touch the fruit. Similarly, the telephone amplifies voice over distance, but selects out of the communication process the contextual cues (the metacommunication signals) that are often essential to understanding what is really being said. Although we continue to think of the computer as a neutral technology that is able to manipulate the data we input, it possesses, like the stick, its own selection, amplification, and reduction characteristics. The question of whether the selection/amplification characteristics reflect the metaphorical frameworks of the people who created the technology, or are technologically determined, is beyond the scope of our discussion. But it is intriguing to note that in educational settings the use of the computer selects for amplification procedural thinking, decontextualized data, and a conduit view of language. This tool, or what more accurately could be called a Cartesian machine, selects out of the information exchange the metaphorical nature of language, the tacit forms of knowledge, and the genealogy of the data—the latter being essential for understanding the power relations that surround how the data was selected and framed by a person who views the world through an interpretative framework influenced by the taken-for-granted assumptions of the cultural group.

All technology, regardless of whether it is mechanical in nature or takes the form of a social technique, mediates our relationships with one another and with the physical environment, and alters the inner sense of personal experience (what Foucault refers to as the "dividing practices"). Viewed within Bateson's framework, technology encodes the mental activity of the people who created it, as well as those who continue to refine it. It also mediates the information exchanges that Bateson views as the mental activity triggered by differences between the aggregate parts of a social/natural ecology. The metaphor of a neutral tool supports other culturally specific and historically rooted metaphors: that we are autonomous and rationally directed beings, that we are superior to and can act independently of other forms of life, and that we represent the most advanced stage in human evolution. But the metaphor, as schema, limits our participation in the information exchange that characterizes the social/natural ecology. Insofar as the metaphor of a neutral technology distorts our understanding of how we contribute to the deterioration of the ecosystem, the metaphor can be viewed as part of a pathological epistemology (Bateson, 1972).

We shall now turn briefly to the problem of how metaphorical thinking influences our individual/community relationships; more specifically, how the metaphor of individualism leads to commitments and ways of understanding that affect the social/moral ecology—to use another metaphor that helps connect a Batesonian perspective with the main themes of *Habits of the Heart* (Bellah et al., 1985). This book, which explores the moral and political implications of the language of individualism, can be viewed as a study in the genealogy of a metaphor. The process of understanding the new in terms of the familiar—particularly when the familiar represented the early stages of a postfeudal social order where people's identities, and thus potential, were largely fixed—provided a challenge to the metaphorical imagination of the early American settlers. But this was not exactly a period of social openness in which new guiding images could be freely chosen. The distinctive character of religious belief that led people to the new territory where a new moral order could be based on Biblical analogs also provided the generative metaphor for understanding the individual as morally interdependent. The heightened sense of political awareness surrounding the Revolutionary War and the founding of a republic provided a more secular, though no less collective, foundation for thinking about what it meant to be an individual. The Biblical and republican forms of individualism were both constituted by and served to reinforce the integration of the self as part of a social ecology. In more recent years, with the emergence of new metaphors for thinking about the self as an expressive, autonomous being, and as self-directing and competitive, the awareness of the self as part of a larger informational network, an ecology, was no longer metaphorically coherent. The new metaphors of expressive and utilitarian individualism, whose origins may have been more heavily influenced by the ideological fathers of modern science—Descartes, Newton, and Bacon—than by Emerson and Franklin (or Nietzsche, Weber, and Heidegger, for that matter) provided a way of thinking that magnifies the discrete nature of entities, wants, events, achievements, and failures. But the interpretative schema provided by these metaphors, as documented by the interviews recorded in *Habits of the Heart*, was unsuited to understanding that the supposedly discrete events of experience are always part of a context characterized by relationships.

Carol Gilligan provides a different perspective on how metaphor encodes a particular view of reality while preventing other aspects from being seen. In her study of gender differences, she found that the metaphorical self-representation of the men in her study involved references to personal attributes and achievements. Unlike the women, who identified themselves in terms of relationships, "individual achievement rivets the male imagination, and great ideas or distinctive activity defines the standard of self-assessment and success" (1982, p. 163). The gender issue raises important questions about the origins of our guiding generative metaphors; for example, are the analogs for the image of both the utilitarian and expressive forms of individualism derived essentially from masculine domains of experience and metaphorical frameworks? Gilligan's study, as well as the analysis of other feminists concerned with the gender/epistemology issue, highlights another critically important point; namely, that there are metaphorical images of the self as an individual that promote power through separation, and that other metaphors of the self, derived from a more contextual way of understanding, foster an awareness of the more subtle and complex information exchanges that characterize relationships.

When we start with the traditional view that rationality is an attribute of the individual, the problem of educational empowerment is a relatively easy issue to deal with. For those in the tradition of Adler and Bloom, the guiding analogs can be found in the great thinkers of the past. For those who think that the computer is an analog of how the mind works, empowerment becomes a matter of bypassing classrooms in order to "input" directly into the mind of the individual. According to Larry Snarr (1982), Director of the National Center for SuperComputer Applications at the University of Illinois, "The ultimate in new technology will be a computer system so fast and so powerful that it will be able to compute the output of the supercomputer directly into the eye-brain system. The human at this point will become the limiting factor in the computer cycle." As he told his audience at the 1987 annual meeting of the American Association for the Advancement of Science, "The distinction between artificial and real reality will begin to be hard to perceive simply by looking at it" (quoted in "Numbers Crunch' In," 1987, p. E-1). Both positions, from a Batesonian perspective, are incorrect because they fail to take into account the mental activity immanent in the system within which the person is embedded. The semiotic systems of a culture, which encode the mental activity of past generations and provide the basis of thought and communication, should be the unit we look at when assessing the nature of intelligence. As pointed out earlier, language encodes the schemata that largely set the boundaries and determine the pattern of thinking. Thus, the schemata made available by the culture for thinking about self-identity, work, technology, time, progress, and so forth, rather than the empowerment of an even more rational and autonomous individual, should be the primary focus in any discussion of education.

At this point it might seem that the bonds of language make the discussion of empowerment largely irrelevant, or make it seem like the atavistic expression of a pattern of thought that represents, with its anthropocentric view of the universe, a cultural experiment with the ecosystem. Although the language/thought connection is deeper than our Cartesian way of thinking allows us fully to recognize, it would be a mistake to reduce everything to the conceptual codes embedded in language. This would be like a linguistic version of Skinner's determinism. A more useful way of thinking about the language/thought connection would be to use Gadamer's (1976) notion of preunderstanding, which enables us to view understanding as based on the epistemic traditions of a language community. Within this horizon of possibility, people are capable of reorganizing the conceptual building blocks made available by the language, obtaining conceptual distance from their otherwise taken-for-granted nature, and of reworking them on a metaphorical level. The nature of metaphorical thinking itself points to the symbolic openness of our language: the same imaginative capacities involved in thinking of the new in relation to the familiar (the "computer is like the human brain") can lead to seeing new relationships ("the computer is like the brain center of the panoptican society"). Imagination, relational thinking, and critical reflection represent the human contribution to the mind immanent in the information exchanges that make up the ecosystem. The challenge is to figure out an approach to formal education that does not empower people as autonomous beings who are then, in turn, cut off conceptually and morally from the information exchanges that signal when the larger system is being threatened.

A starting point is to think of education in terms of the original meaning given to the phrase *cultural literacy*, before E. D. Hirsch, Jr., reframed the idea of cultural literacy to fit the Reagan administration's educational agenda. As worked out in *Cultural Literacy for Freedom* (Bowers, 1974), a book heavily indebted to a sociology-of-knowledge interpretation of how people's conceptual frameworks are constituted, sustained, and renegotiated through an ongoing process of communication, the central idea was that cultural literacy involves the ability to decode the taken-for-granted cultural patterns that otherwise control thought and behavior. For Hirsch, cultural literacy is based on the same Cartesian tradition of psychological research that he sees converging with the view of intelligence underlying current work in artificial intelligence. As he put it, "both approaches show that expert performance depends upon the quick deployment of schemata" (1987, p. 62). In equating information with building schemata (a term he uses in a way that is profoundly different from our previous discussion of how a metaphor encodes an earlier schema of understanding), the issue of cultural literacy becomes associated with the amount of information-type knowledge the person possesses. "A basic vocabulary of 50,000 schemata," he writes, "serves merely as a quickly accessible index to a much larger volume of knowledge. Any of the 50,000 schemata [he means here factual knowledge about places, events, people, things, etc.] can be related to others, and the further relationship can be *stored in long-term memory*" (p. 64; emphasis added). The italicized words suggest the way in which the computer metaphor directs Hirsch to think of cultural literacy as the factual knowledge needed to think quickly and effectively—thus, the famous list every literate person in America needs to know. Although I cannot disagree with his concern about how a lack of properly informed citizens imperils our collective interests as a society, or with the widespread nature of the problem, I disagree profoundly with the idea that information-type knowledge contributes to the form of empowerment needed in an ecologically interdependent world. Wendell Berry (1986) articulated what is missing in Hirsch's view of cultural literacy:

> The definitive relationships in the universe are thus not competitive but interdependent. And from a human point of view they are analogical. We can build one system only within another. We can have agriculture only within nature, and culture only within agriculture. At certain critical points these systems have to conform with one another or destroy one another. (p. 47)

Rather than the "great chain of being," which, in its modern form of expression, puts either the more traditional view of rational "man" (Bloom) or the new computer analog (Hirsch) at the top of the evolutionary process, Berry's view of interrelationship corresponds more to Bateson's warning about viewing mind as separate from the environment.

I would like to situate the original meaning of cultural literacy within a more Batesonian notion of empowerment, and then identify how a form of education that contributes to cultural literacy can be carried out in the classroom—at both the public school and university level. In discussing how we cannot indefinitely use technology to compensate for our epistemological errors (he refers to them as "pathologies"), Bateson (1972) notes that one of the most basic misconceptions "reinforced by thousands of cultural details" (p. 485) is that we are autonomous individuals who observe and make rational decisions about the external world. This view of the individual leads to a unilateral notion of power, where the individual acts on the external world in terms of a supposedly rational mode of understanding. By way of contrast, a Batesonian notion of empowerment would involve growth in the ability to participate fully in the information exchanges that contribute to the "fitting together" that characterizes a healthy ecology. The person's internal world of coherence, as well as the symbol systems of the culture, must, as Bateson (1980) put it, "fit the external requirements of the environment" (p. 159).

Viewed from this perspective, cultural literacy takes on an entirely different meaning, one that challenges the idea of the individual as having objective knowledge of the world, and a view of language as a conduit through which this objective information is passed between individuals. This view of the individual and language are part of the epistemological orthodoxy still dominant in both the public school and the university. Cultural literacy, when considered as a process of decoding the cultural patterns that give form to thought and social behavior, involves the dereification of those epistemological errors. The theoretical framework that corresponds closely to Bateson's way of understanding is the sociology of knowledge of Alfred Schutz, Peter Berger, and Thomas Luckmann. As the sociology of knowledge is particularly useful for understanding how the person acquires the interpretative framework necessary for participating in a shared social world, it will be used here as the primary basis for explaining both the difficulty of becoming aware of one's own cultural patterns and deep assumptions, and the dynamics of making them explicit in a classroom setting.

For the sake of brevity, only three concepts derived from the sociology of knowledge will be treated as critical for understanding the sources of resistance to cultural literacy. These include the person's *intersubjective* world of experience; the *natural attitude* that characterizes how the person experiences the cultural/epistemic patterns that are the basis of understanding, meaning, and imagination; and the central role that *communication* plays in sharing, sustaining, and reconstituting the shared view of social reality. We shall explain the process of primary socialization within the context of the classroom, with the understanding that communication outside the classroom also constitutes an ongoing process of primary socialization as well as reinforcement of already shared interpretative frameworks. While socialization occurs in the message exchanges that characterize all semiotic systems, the classroom involves several critical differences from the rest of the social world. These differences include greater reliance on the abstract representation of how to think about the social/cultural world, and the possibility of examining taken-for-granted beliefs and social practices without experiencing the penalties that often accompany the exercise of a critical attitude in other sectors of society.

In *Cultural Literacy for Freedom* (Bowers, 1974) the educational process of making explicit the cultural patterns and assumptions was framed in terms of an existential interpretation of the tension between freedom and self-alienation. The sociology-of-knowledge account of how the socially shared definitions of everyday life become part of the person's taken-for-granted beliefs, and thus contribute to a state of inauthentic being and a loss of existential freedom, seemed to provide a framework for an empowering form of education. But this existential interpretation of individual freedom, as I now view it, was compromised by an uncritical acceptance of important elements of Cartesian thinking: that reflection is individualistic, that tacit forms of knowledge contribute to inauthenticity, and that freedom is undermined by the acceptance of such supposedly external sources of authority as tradition. In actuality, the sociology-of-knowledge framework for understanding the dynamics of how social reality is constituted and sustained through the multiple channels of communication that make up the social/cultural world is more consistent with a Batesonian interpretation of the person as part of the ecology of mind that includes both cultural and natural systems. When viewed from this perspective, educational empowerment becomes more understandable in terms of enhancing the total system—and not just the autonomy and rational power of the individual. It is important to note that the ecological view of empowerment does not lose sight of the distinctiveness of the person, nor does it disregard the importance of personal meaning and the political role of critical reflection. As Alfred Schutz (1967) observed, each person's life has biographically distinct characteristics and, at the same time, is lived as an intersubjective self.

Cultural literacy, when understood within Bateson's metaphorical framework, still involves the ability to "read" or decode cultural patterns, particularly those embodying ways of thinking that are socially and environmentally destructive. The pedagogical task is to know what aspects of the culture need to be made explicit, how to enable the student to decode cultural patterns that are part of the natural attitude and thus taken for granted, and how to put the decoding process in a broader framework of understanding that will guide the reconceptualization process. Regardless of grade level, teachers mediate the normal process of socialization through their control of the language that will be made available to students for thinking about the aspect of culture to which they are being introduced. This mediation process is further complicated by the fact that teachers, in terms of their own prior socialization, have internalized as part of their intersubjective self the thought patterns embedded in their cultural milieu. In some instances teachers have made explicit certain cultural assumptions and patterns, added their own interpretation and sense of integration to others, while continuing in the grip of still other shared cultural patterns. Teachers who are aware of gender bias and view empowerment in terms of emancipating the individual from the authority of tradition are an example of the unevenness and atavistic nature of this process of cultural mediation.

The critical difference between a form of education that binds the student to the "ecology of mind" that characterizes the culture and the process of cultural literacy has to do with the teacher's ability to recognize the many channels of information exchange that operate in the classroom. In contrast to viewing the classroom as an arena in which individuals communicate ideas and information through the conduit of language, the classroom can be more accurately understood as an interacting set of semiotic systems—where the channels of communication include the verbal, kinesic, proxemic, paralinguistic, and even the use of time as a part of the message-exchange system. For reasons having to do with the teacher's own natural attitude, much of the information exchanged through these channels will be shared and, depending upon the cultural background of the student, processed by the student without the teacher being consciously involved. Thus the degree to which education contributes to cultural literacy will vary in accordance with the teacher's ability to recognize the cultural messages shared through these interactive channels of communication. As few teachers are educated to decode the metacommunication processes that frame, and in some instances provide resistance to, the more Cartesian exchange of information, we shall limit our discussion here to critical moments in the classroom process of primary socialization that teachers, as a first step, can focus attention on.

Primary socialization involves learning from a "significant other" how to think and act, with regard to a new area of cultural experience, in a manner congruent with other people's taken-for-granted patterns. Although students, depending upon where they are in the educational process, will bring to the moment of primary socialization an interpretative framework built up through their own previous socialization, they will be highly dependent upon the mental characteristics embedded in the message-exchange systems that characterize the ecology of the classroom: the teacher, verbal and nonverbal language systems (including books, films, etc.), organization of space, and so forth. We can see this dependency in the first-grade classroom, where the teacher introduces students to their first formal explanation of language (the spoken and written word being metaphorically represented as a conduit through which ideas and information are transmitted). We also see it in graduate classes, where students still have, though at a more sophisticated level, first encounters with how to think about new areas of the culture: learning about statistics, artificial intelligence, the sources of nihilism, and so forth.

Primary socialization can be viewed metaphorically as a language game, and the teacher as in control of how the "moves" in this game will be played out. The initial move that the teacher controls is in making available the language framework that will be used as the initial basis of understanding. If students share common elements of the teacher's symbolic world and are learning something for the first time (how to think about work, technology, community, social class, etc.), the language made available will both empower and bind at the same time. The patterns of understanding encoded in metaphors of the language, as well as the complexity of the language code made available, provide the schema for understanding while binding students to the embedded analogs worked out by earlier generations in response to a different set of social/environmental issues. As in the case of the other "moves" in the language game of primary socialization, the teacher's own pattern of socialization will be a critical factor in determining whether the educational process reinforces the "epistemological errors" of the past or provides an opportunity to assess the adequacy of the thought patterns that are being shared. If the teacher has a limited language code and has not critically examined its current explanatory power—a process of cultural clarification that is made difficult by the double bind we discussed earlier—it is likely that the student, at this critical moment, will have no other option than to use the limited language and encoded schemata as an initial basis of understanding. To paraphrase Bateson, "the mental characteristics of the system," which are under the legitimating authority of the teacher, will be shared with the new members being introduced into the system. Thus "the mental characteristics of the system are immanent, not in some part, but in the system as a whole," to reiterate Bateson's basic point (1972, p. 316).

This process of reproducing in the minds of students the state of intelligence that characterizes the larger system, which always involves disjunctures between the thought processes of the past and novel elements of the present, can be seen in the other moves in the language game of primary socialization. As the new language framework is being given special legitimation by the teacher, the teacher is also controlling (often unconsciously) whether aspects of the cultural ecology will be learned at an implicit level of understanding or will be made explicit to the student. And in instances where students see relationships still hidden from the teacher's level of awareness, the teacher can exercise a variety of pedagogical maneuvers intended to maintain the traditional relationship between explicit knowledge and the hidden cultural assumptions upon which it rests. While performing as the gatekeeper over how much of the implicit thought processes will be allowed into the arena of the explicit, the teacher also controls whether explanations will be represented as factual and thus reified, or as having a history that should be understood as part of what the students are being asked to learn. While students are not passive participants in primary socialization, the fact that they are learning something for the first time makes them highly dependent upon the teacher to make the implicit explicit, and to guide them to the genealogy often hidden by the practice of representing ideas and information as objective. They are also dependent on the teacher's ability to provide a comparative basis for recognizing the root metaphors—or paradigms for representing the deepest levels of the culture's epistemological framework—that frame and give conceptual coherence to the patterns of social life. If the teacher is unaware of the deep levels of the symbolic ecology, such as the assumptions that underlie our views about the nature of work, technology, and individualism, the socialization process may leave students with the ability to manipulate facts and data but not to understand that they are doing it in accordance with archetypal patterns dictated by the culture encoded in the language they have acquired. But if students do not share the teacher's symbolic world, or can only enter into parts of it, the process of primary socialization may become more ambiguous—with the students' primary cultural schemata becoming more critical to how the content of the curriculum is understood and interpreted.

When primary socialization uses language as a conduit and involves the limiting "moves" we have just described, it is likely that the students' way of understanding the message exchanges between self and the cultural/natural ecology will reproduce the epistemological errors of the larger system. I think this is what Joseph Tussman (1960) meant when he wrote that "our habits are our powers; they are bonds only when we try to break them" (p. 7). In effect, the taken-for-granted nature of the patterns will lead to repeating them, until we either choose to examine them or are forced to confront them because of ecological damage that can no longer be ignored. Cultural literacy, which involves the ability to "read" the cultural patterns that influence thought and behavior, requires that teachers understand culture, language, and thought as a symbolic ecology, and that the message exchange process can bind the thought patterns of the present to the metaphorical frameworks of the past. When translated into classroom practice, this understanding can lead to changing the dynamics of primary socialization. The gatekeeper role, in terms of fostering cultural literacy, involves not only providing a language code sufficiently complex for understanding the multiple dimensions of whatever aspect of the culture students are being asked to learn about, but also to attending to whether the metaphorical nature of the language that is part of the primary socialization process provides the appropriate schemata for understanding new relationships. Empowerment is also contingent upon helping students to recognize how the use of metaphor illuminates and hides at the same time.

A second change in the process of primary socialization involves attending to taken-for-granted beliefs—in books and other curricular materials, in the thought patterns of students, and in the teacher's own life world. Knowing when taken-for-granted beliefs impede the ability to recognize the message exchanges that are part of the life-sustaining process of an ecology is a major aspect of the teacher's responsibility.

A third change involves knowing when it is essential to illuminate how past thought patterns are embedded in what would otherwise appear to most students as an objective fact or datum. A student who is learning something for the first time, and who is initially dependent upon the language (metaphorical) framework provided by the teacher, will not automatically recognize the epistemological error of treating ideas and data as not having a social history. The teacher's responsibility involves bringing the historical perspective into the process of primary socialization. In Bateson's terms, this enhances the student's ability to recognize that the ecology of ideas has a temporal dimension, and that the failure to renew the forms of understanding encoded in the language derived from the past can lead to further ecological imbalance.

Lastly, the teacher must be sensitive to when it is important to make explicit the underlying cultural templates. This may lead to cross-cultural comparisons and, in terms of the problem of addressing the current anthropocentrism, to the use of the natural environment or ancient cultures as a source of appropriate analogs for understanding relationships and patterns.

Gary Snyder's discussion of Ezra Pound's view of the poet as the antennae of humanity provides a useful way of understanding the difference between a form of cultural literacy that contributes to the revitalization of the information pathways between the culture and the natural environment, and Hirsch's interpretation of cultural literacy that equates empowerment with the acquisition of information or, as Bloom advocates, furthering the cultural agenda legitimated by the mainstream of Western philosophy. Poets, as Snyder (1980) views them, "are like an early warning system that hears the trees and the air and the clouds and the watersheds beginning to groan and complain a little bit. And so they try to send a little bit of warning back. . . . They also can hear the stresses and the fault block's slippage creaking in the social batholith and also begin to give out warnings" (p. 71). This sensitivity to relationships—between language and thought, and between cultural patterns and natural environment—also seems essential to the teacher's role. But unlike the poet, who "effects change by fiddling with the archetypes and getting at people's dreams about a century before it actually effects historical change" (Snyder, 1980, p. 71), the teacher must systematically help students sort through and make sense of the current symbolic resources of the culture. The role of being a guide in the ongoing process of cultural transformation, rather than being the antennae of an early warning system, requires that teachers be able to "read" and put into perspective the conceptual foundations of their own culture. This decoding process, when viewed in terms of the mounting evidence of ecological disruption caused by modern technology and cultural values, requires the teacher to consider whether the patterns of thought being shared with students contribute to a greater sense of social and ecological interdependence. This now seems to be the primary educational issue that should frame our notion of cultural literacy.

Chapter 9

Implications of Gregory Bateson's Ideas for a Semiotic of Art Education

The conceptual categories that underlie the epistemology of the dominant culture influence the most taken-for-granted and seemingly straightforward patterns of thought and expression. Witness, for example, the explanations in the teacher's manual for *Art Works* (1989), which is part of a discipline-based art education instructional materials series:

> As students create their crayon etchings, comments such as the following may be helpful: *You* (the student) are pressing down hard on *your* crayons, which will help *you* as *you* etc. *Your* sense of humor is being reflected in *your* art. (p. 47, emphasis added)

This representation of the person as an autonomous source of agency and of art as an entity with an independent existence, which, if "good" enough, may be displayed for the purpose of viewing by others, carries over to the explanations that are to guide how the student thinks about the art of traditional cultures. For example, students are to be told that

> Kenojuak Ashevak is a contemporary Canadian Eskimo artist whose artwork reflects the traditions of her cultural heritage, the hunting and gathering Inuit, or "real people," of Northern Canada. Her stonecut print, Enchanted Owl, was included in a collection of Eskimo art in 1960, and in 1970, it was selected for use on a postage stamp. (p. 31)

The cultural epistemology that frames the student's artistic expression as autonomous and art as an entity also reframes the wide range of aesthetic expressions that characterizes traditional cultures into a reductionist and modern point of view in which art is an object—this time to be displayed on a postage stamp.

THE CARTESIAN FOUNDATION OF MODERN CONSCIOUSNESS

Although the epistemology of the dominant culture influences how we think and interact generally, I want to explore its implications for considering one aspect of the socialization of students in an art education class. In order to avoid the impression that I have chosen obscure textbooks to make my point about how socialization in an art class reproduces the conceptual assumptions that give a culture its distinctive mindset, I have purposely chosen examples from texts that many regard as the most outstanding in the field. But first I need to identify more precisely the epistemological origins of viewing the autonomous individual as the source of the creative process.

In her study of how Cartesian thinking became the foundation of modern consciousness, Susan Bordo (1987) notes that, in contrast,

> the medieval *aesthetic* imagination . . . shares with the perceptual world of the developing child the correlative structure of a not yet fully "desubjectified" world and a not yet fully "objectified" self—a self which does not primarily experience itself as "located," along with other objects of the world, within time and space. Subject and object are united through shared meanings, rather than rendered ontologically separate. (p. 69)

The introduction of linear perspective as a way of seeing appears some two hundred years before Descartes. Nevertheless, it was his work that helped crystalize the epistemological foundations of modern thought (Dupre, 1988) that underlie the current practice of viewing the self as an autonomous agent—an individual who views and acts on an external world that is made up of distinct entities. Locating the thought process in the mind of the individual created a division between inner and outer world, a distinction essential for the idea of the autonomous individual. Descartes' epistemology also provided the basis for what Heidegger (1977) saw as a new form of relationship—viewing the world as a picture, something that is objectively observed. "World picture," he writes, "does not mean a picture of the world, but the world conceived and grasped as a picture" (p. 129).

This Cartesian epistemology, in terms of one stream of its evolutionary development, leads to explanations, such as the following, which are to be shared with students:

> You can create art. You can create artwork about things you see and remember. . . . Artists learn to see *lines* in nature. . . . You are learning to create many kinds of art. What do you remember? . . . A *tradition* is something people have remembered for a long time. (Chapman, 1985, pp. 6, 10, 56, 66)

In terms of Heidegger's observation, such textbook explanations assume that there is an inner/outer relationship between the student and the world, and that the inner world of thought, remembrance, and imagination is stimulated by observing the external world. The "products" of this relationship, in the field of art, also take on a peculiar static quality that follows from this form of consciousness.

There are numerous examples of forms of consciousness among traditional cultures that point to the limitations of the Cartesian epistemology that underlies modern consciousness—including the mind-set encoded in the textbook art lessons just cited. Instead of going back in time or introducing cross-cultural examples, which could open me to accusations of being either unrealistic or romantic, I want to use the ideas of Gregory Bateson as well as basic concepts from the field of semiotics as a basis for arguing that the Cartesian epistemological foundation for thinking about the role of the student, and the nature of the artistic experience, is basically limiting and wrong-headed. I shall later return to how the view of art in traditional cultures represents a form of consciousness that is similar to Bateson's position.

BATESON'S ECOLOGY OF RELATIONSHIPS

Unlike the Cartesian view of the individual, where imagination, aesthetic judgment, and creative activity are viewed as expressions of the individual's inner mental state, Bateson presents a radically different way of understanding these phenomena. His starting point is the system or ecology of relationships. As he puts it: "The mental world—the mind—the world of information processing—is not limited by the skin" (1972, p. 454). The basic unit of information, what he also refers to as an idea or mental activity, is a "difference which makes a difference" (p. 318), as the aggregate parts of an ecological system interact. The information exchange is the expression of a cybernetic system, of circularity as opposed to the linear causality that characterizes the Cartesian view of the individual who unilaterally reflects and then acts on the world. In order to explain how relationships (the patterns that connect) are the sources of information exchanges that, together, characterize the mental state of the system as a whole, Bateson (1972) uses the example of a man felling a tree with an axe:

> Consider a man felling a tree with an axe. Each stroke of the axe is modified or corrected, according to the shape of the cut face of the tree left by the previous stroke. This self-corrective (i.e., mental) process is brought about by a total system, tree-eyes-brain-muscles-axe-stroke-tree; and it is this total system that has the characteristics of

immanent mind. More correctly, we should spell the matter out as: (differences in tree)-(differences in retina)-(differences in brain)-(differences in muscles)-(differences in movement of axe)-(differences in tree), etc. What is transmitted around the circuit is transforms of differences. And as noted above, a difference which makes a difference is an idea or unit of information. (pp. 317–318)

As Bateson demonstrates in this example, the information exchanges are in the relationships and it is their interactive nature that give rise to the "difference which makes a difference."

While Cartesianism leads to viewing the mental as an inner state of the individual (now often viewed as the activity of the right and left hemispheres of the brain), Bateson situates the person within the context of a larger mental ecology. As he puts it: " The individual mind is immanent but not only in the body. It is immanent also in the pathways and messages outside the body" (1972, p. 461). And in another passage, which challenges both the anthropocentrism and detached observer status of the Cartesian individual, Bateson warns that "in no system which shows mental characteristics can any part have unilateral control over the whole. In other words, the mental characteristics of the system are immanent not in some part, but in the system as a whole" (1972, p. 316). If the mental is in the pathways that connect, as Bateson argues, then individuals will experience the same pattern (including "pathologies") of thinking that characterizes the mental ecology of the larger system of which they are participating members. I will come back to this point later when I discuss the implications of basing a view of art education on a Cartesian view of the individual.

THE ROLE OF METAPHOR

Bateson's view of how individuals participate in the information pathways that make up an ecology is, of course, more complicated than what the casual reader might interpret "information processing" to be. Although genes, neurons, and membranes represent one level of participation in the pathways through which coded information is transmitted, Bateson recognized that among mammals, communication about relationships is encoded metaphorically. This is to say that kinesic and paralinguistic communication are analogic: The attitude about the behavior of another participant in a relationship is signaled through a body gesture or paralinguistic cue that is dependent upon a past association.

For example, the leader of a wolfpack was observed using the same pattern of pressing its open mouth on the neck of a usurping male that was used in the weaning process. If the message could have been spoken, it would not have been, as Bateson (1972) puts it, "don't do that"; rather it would have been a reminder of the analogic message: "I am your senior adult male, you puppy!" (p. 366). The use of metaphors among humans extends beyond the use of analogs to communicate about the "rules and contingencies of relationship"; metaphor is also the basis of understanding the information that is communicated through the multiple pathways that constitute an ecology.

Bateson's distinction between "creatura" and "pleroma," which roughly translates into the difference between conceptual map and territory, is essential for a deep understanding of the restrictive role that metaphor plays in constituting understanding. For my purposes here, however, we can establish an adequate basis for making the connection between semiotics and his way of understanding the individual as part of a field of relationships that is mediated by the epistemology shared by members of the culture. We can do so by focusing on two aspects of metaphor that are generally ignored when metaphor is dealt with outside of a Batesonian framework. Because metaphorical thinking, in its most basic sense, involves the imaginative act of recognizing a relationship (of correspondence or likeness between the new and the already familiar), we shall also be establishing additional connections with issues in art education that will be taken up at the end of this chapter.

Within the Cartesian framework it is natural to say "I think," "I see," "I imagine," and so forth. If we take seriously what Johnson (1987) and Lakoff (1987) are telling us about how metaphor provides the schema essential for thinking, it then becomes clear that what the person thinks or imagines is largely dependent upon the thought processes of others, which are encoded in the metaphor that becomes the conceptual scaffolding of the individual's understanding and imagining. Again, in Bateson's terms, language is part of the mental ecology; indeed, it is essential for communicating about relationships. As metaphors (e.g., "intelligence," "individual," "man," "data") encode other people's way of thinking, such activities as thinking and imagining become expressions of the larger mental ecology of which the individual is a part. Earlier processes of analogic thinking (e.g., where our understanding of "intelligence" was associated with explicit forms of knowledge, communicated in printed English and objectively measurable) encode the hidden cultural assumptions and associations that are established as the model, or schema, of understanding in an iconic (image) metaphor that subsequent

generations use at a taken-for-granted level. For example, such an encoded schema can be seen in the metaphor "New World" that has been
commonly used to refer to a territory whose inhabitants possessed forms
of culture much older than that of the European "discoverers"—which
itself is a misleading metaphor. It can also be seen in a colleague's com-
ment, referring to her style of dress, that "I am in my comfortable *mode*
today." In effect, metaphor as map illuminates only certain aspects of
the territory.

METAPHOR AND "DETERMINATIVE MEMORY"

The linguistic encoding of the metaphorical thought processes of others
is important in yet another way to Bateson's way of viewing the individual as part of the larger mental ecology. Although individuals participate in multiple pathways of information exchange, not all the information (as Bateson's distinction between creatura and pleroma suggests)
is understood or even recognized as important. Furthermore, some information is interpreted according to a schema of understanding that
reflects the metaphorical thinking of earlier generations who confronted
an entirely different set of circumstance. Bateson (1972) refers to this
process of current information being processed (understood) in terms of
past characteristics of the mental ecology as the "determinative *memory*"
within the system (p. 316). The encoding characteristics of metaphor,
where the prevailing analogs of the past continue to provide the schema
for understanding, mediate the information pathways. They do this by
causing some information to be unrecognized (what cannot be interpreted
according to the schema of understanding) and by contributing to anachronistic interpretations of other information For example, the early
efforts to understand the educational use of computers in terms of the
metaphorical image that represented technology as neutral led many
educators to ignore the message exchanges that did not fit with certain
assumptions. Ignored were assumptions about the neutrality of technology, the progressive nature of change, and the efficacy of data that were
part of their received schema of understanding. To cite one more example
of how metaphor mediates the information pathways of an ecology,
the image of self as an autonomous individual has contributed to the
nonrecognition of the larger informational network that constitutes
the person's relations with other people and the natural environment.
Bateson's image of the self as part of a larger mental ecology, on the other
hand, enables the person to recognize the multiple levels of connectedness.

SEMIOTICS AND CULTURE

Bateson's emphasis on the patterns that connect (i.e., what is communicated through relationships) relates directly to one of the more important insights that has emerged from the field of semiotics; namely, that culture, as Ju Lotman (1988) notes, consists of the "totality of nonhereditary information acquired, preserved, and transmitted by the various groups of human society" (p. 213). Using the language of semiotics, culture can be viewed as a system of signs, where the signifier and signified are encoded according to the symbolic (mythic) system of the cultural group. This encoding process, which corresponds to what Bateson means by "determinative *memory*," provides the basis for how the sign is to be interpreted; that is, the meaning that it is to have for the members of a cultural group. In traditional cultures, where the "living myth must include and speak of the interlocking cycles of animate and vegetable life, of water, sun, and even the stones, which have their own stories" (Turner, 1986, p. 19), members are enveloped in a fullness of meaning, where sounds, movement, space, and event are connected through the rhythms of ritual to a transcendent sense of time. By way of contrast, the anthropocentricism of our Cartesian culture leads to a different system of encoding, where signs connected with commercial activity and self-gratification tend to stand out as an instrumental network of meaning. Just as the food display of a Japanese vendor represents encoded messages of semiotic and cultural richness in a society that does not separate the everyday world from the aesthetic world (Barthes, 1982), the BMW, designer clothes, hair style, credit card, and bodily movements represent encoded messages about how success and class affiliation are to be recognized in our culture.

The field of semiotics has not adequately addressed the connection between myth ("epistemology," to the modern thinker), metaphor, and the encoding process that makes the person's cultural environment an ecology of signs. It has, however, brought to the foreground the importance of recognizing that culture has to do with relationships, that these relationships are communicated through a network of signs, and that these signs are, when recognized, the source of information necessary for the individual's sense of meaning and orientation in the world. Although the individual both acts in response to the signs and is acted upon by them, it is the deep and generally unrecognized assumptions of the culture—assumptions which underlie the encoding of the message— that the signs are intended to communicate. This brings the discussion back to Bateson and the problems associated with a Cartesian approach to art education, where thought, imagination, and creative expression are viewed as subjective processes that occur within the individual (i.e., art as self-expression).

ART AS "MAKING SPECIAL"

To summarize a major difference between Bateson and a Cartesian way of thinking: The former emphasizes relationships and circular causality (the patterns that connect), while the latter holds discrete entities that are subject to linear causality to be the central feature of reality. We can see this difference in two different ways of thinking about art. In the article "Art as Semiotic Fact," Jan Mukarovsky (1976) states that:

> the work of art, then, has a two-fold semiotic function, autonomous and informational. . . . [That is, art is] always some "thing," some "artifact." . . . Its semiotic function is in its power, as a sign, to characterize and represent the "age." (pp. 3–7)

This is the Cartesian (and modern) view of art as a discrete entity that may communicate to the observer. In Ellen Dissanayake's recent book, *What Is Art For?*, we find a view of art that is closer to Bateson's ecological perspective. Rather than asking "What is art?," she suggests that asking a different question, "What does art do for people?," leads to an entirely different approach to art. I do not have the space here to explore fully the nature and significance of her critique of how the modern view of art has diminished the role of art in comparison to its place in traditional (so-called primitive) cultures. Nevertheless I will identify several key ideas related to how an approach to art education as the individual creation of art objects differs from both a Batesonian and a semiotic perspective.

For Dissanayake (1988), art is not to be understood as an object (like a painting, dance, or poem) or a quality (such as beauty or harmony) that characterizes objects, but rather as a *behavior* that involves "making special." She writes:

> Making special implies intent or deliberateness. When *shaping* or giving artistic expression to an idea, or *embellishing* an object, or recognizing that an idea or object is artistic, one gives (or acknowledges) a specialness that without one's activity or regard would not exist. Moreover, one intends by making special *to place the activity or artifact in a "realm" different from the everyday.* [Part of the answer to the question, "What is art?" is that, in "making special,"] reality is converted from its usual unremarkable state—in which we take it or its components

for granted—to a significant or specially experienced reality in which the components, by their emphasis or combination or juxtaposition, acquire a meta-reality. (pp. 92–94)

In Dissanayake's view, art in the sense of "making special" can also transform ordinary things (clothing, household implements, and body language, to cite just a few examples) in such a way that relationships take on a fuller and a more enriching sense of meaning. In effect, "making special" represents the aesthetic dimension of the system of "signs" that we otherwise know as cultural patterns and artifacts. In terms of Bateson's observation about artists being "concerned with the relation *between* levels of mental process" (1972, p. 464), "making special" has to do with communicating, often in a highly metaphorical way, about relationships.

IMPLICATIONS FOR ART EDUCATION

If I can use discipline-based art education as an example of the way in which many students are being taught to think about art (as well as to do art), it seems that the questions Karen Hamblen (1988) asks about hidden cultural assumptions students learn along with their direct art experiences can be extended. One of her observations is that students, in learning to adopt the "expert's" view of art, may not be able to make the connection with the aesthetic dimensions of their own life worlds. My review of art teaching manuals suggests that her criticism is essentially correct. In learning the language of the modern art expert, and in achieving the integration of a more informed way of seeing with the physical skills of creation, students still end up with a highly abstracted, skewed, and limited way of thinking about art. Thus, Dissanayake's observations about the differences between the modern Western view of art and the more semiotically rich function of art in traditional societies seem particularly relevant here. The modern view of art, to summarize her observations, focuses on the aesthetic qualities within the art object; the ability, intent, and historical place of the artist; the art object as an entity that is free of context and has autonomous value. As Dissanayake (1988) observes, "an art object need serve no purpose other than its own existence as something for aesthetic contemplation" (p. 40). In terms of this view, the underlying cultural epistemology moves between the poles of an "individual-centered" and "thing-centered" view of art and clearly reflects the subject/object separation that characterizes Cartesian thought. In traditional societies, on the other hand, the "making special" associated with artistic behavior so permeates relationships and activities that "it is inseparable from daily life" (p. 44).

In one sense there is no difference between traditional and modern Western cultures—both involve complex ecologies of behavioral patterns, creation and use of technologies, and belief systems that influence how members view their physical environment and the purpose of existence. But in another sense, the differences are profound, for reasons that have to do with whether the person and social group live a meaningful and environmentally balanced life. In a traditional society, the child learns in context the semiotic systems that are illuminated and elevated through what has been "made special." Social message, performance, and aesthetic sensitivities are integral to an ecology that does not separate the human from the so-called natural world. The cognitive and subjective orientation toward making art that is learned in a discipline-based art education classroom reinforces the highly restrictive view of art as an autonomous act of creation that should lead to an equally autonomous art object. The relationships of everyday life (i.e., the patterns that connect the student to the larger mental ecology) may or may not possess the added aesthetic touch of having been "made special." In being educated to a more restrictive view of art, the student is less likely to recognize and thus to participate in the sense of specialness, even when it is present. Conversely, I think it would be fair to say that these students will be more tolerant of instrumental relationships where the aesthetic is deliberately used by communication experts as part of the semiotic system of the consumer society.

Let me end by citing two examples—one that reflects the Cartesian epistemology that underlies the school experience of art as informed individual expression and one that represents a view of art ("making special") that is as multidimensional as human relationships. In the section of *Discover Art* (Chapman, 1985) where a lesson on "Living with Art" is outlined for teachers, we find the following vocabulary: "art show, art gallery, mount." The objectives for student learning include:

> a) understand that artists exhibit their best work for many people to *see*. b) discuss their reasons for selecting a particular piece of artwork for a class or school-wide art show. c) mount and label one piece of artwork for a class art show. (p. 118)

The lesson is obviously simplified for the third-grade level; but its simplicity also serves to disclose more starkly the ideology that represents art largely as the products of individual creative expression— products that are to be given a special place where they can be seen, appreciated, and reflected upon.

The contrasting example is provided by Barthes's description of bow- ing as an expression of politeness in Japan—a social act that, he warns, might not be understood or appreciated by Westerners, who often regard politeness with suspicion. I am using it here as an example of the aesthetic ("making special") dimension of relationships that our Carte- sian epistemological orientation can grasp only in the most superficial and thus distorted way. As Barthes (1982) describes the semiotic and aes- thetic plentitude of the relationship:

> Two bodies bow very low before one another (arms, knees, head al- ways remaining in a decreed place), according to subtly coded degrees of depth. Or again (on an old image): in order to give a present, I bow down, virtually to the level of the floor, and to answer me, my partner does the same: one and the same low line, that of the ground, joins the giver, the recipient, and the stake of the protocol, a box which may well contain nothing—or virtually nothing; a graphic form (inscribed in the space of the room) is thereby given to the act of exchange, in which, by this form, is erased any greediness (the gift remains sus- pended between two disappearances). The salutation here can be with- drawn from any humiliation or any vanity, because it literally salutes *no one*; it is not the sign of a communication—closely watched, conde- scending and precautionary—between two autarchies, two personal empires (each ruling over its Ego, the little realm or which it holds the "key"); it is only the feature of a network of forms in which nothing is halted, knotted, profound. *Who is saluting whom?* (p. 68)

Bowing may be too archaic and undemocratic for us to take seriously, but if we recognize it as an example of how relationships can both com- municate a social message and be characterized by beauty and dignity that is experienced by the participants, perhaps then we can begin to shift the focus of attention from the plentitude of individual self-expression to the plentitude of relationships that we share with each other and other life forms. It is a plentitude of aesthetic experience that is nonindividu- alistic, but rather shared and participatory. In a word, it is what trans- forms our sense of community from the ordinary to the extraordinary and special.

Chapter 10

The Anthropocentric Foundations of Educational Liberalism

Some Critical Concerns

A discussion of the merits of an educational theory should start by establishing the set of conditions that are to serve as the basis for critical judgment. The conditions to be used here as the primary reference point include the decline of the life-sustaining capacity of natural systems: soil, water, vegetation, and atmosphere. The impact of human activity on the habitat has also contributed to an accelerating decline in other species of life, and in sources of energy essential to sustaining modern culture. Toxic spills, destruction of forests, problems of disposing of human wastes, and the decline of oil production receive near daily exposure in the media. Our task here is not to recapitulate the evidence of habitat abuse; rather, it is to examine, in light of the ecological crisis, the adequacy of liberal theories of education that are being represented as the highest and most progressive form of thinking. The question of where progressive spokespersons are leading us is particularly important at this time, especially since the discourse of the two most viable and often contending streams of educational liberalism are completely silent about the existence of the ecological crisis. This silence represents one of the ironies of the modern, progressive way of thinking.

It is possible to identify three distinct educational discourses that amplify different aspects of liberal thought. These include the technocratic, emancipatory, and the now less visible neoromantic educational reformers. The actual classroom practices, historical roots, and forms of rational justification that characterize these often contentious traditions of educational liberalism already have been dealt with in *Elements of a Post-Liberal Theory of Education* (Bowers, 1987). Our purpose here is to identify a cultural myth shared by all three traditions of educational liberalism, and to consider how this myth helps to constitute ways of thinking that ignore the culture/habitat crisis. The central aspect of this myth, which is reinforced through a variety of Western narrative traditions, is that the world must be viewed from the perspective of humans; that is, it is to be valued, understood, and utilized in terms of human needs. This can be called the myth of the anthropocentric universe.

As the thinking of technocratic educators can be traced directly back to the ideas of Descartes, Bacon, Newton, and others who helped lay the conceptual foundations for the modern quest of gaining control over nature, it is no great surprise that they would also retain the extreme form of anthropocentrism of these earlier thinkers. Prediction and more efficient control of those areas of experience not already routinized by technique required careful observation of a world where the primary goal was to reduce it to its most basic component parts. Taylorism, with its concern with using the procedures of scientific management as a template for human activity, has further served to desensitize technocratic educators to the dangers of their way of thinking.

Unlike the normative vocabulary of the technocratic tradition of educational liberalism, which makes no claim about the importance of questioning their guiding assumptions, the emancipating tradition of educational liberalism has made consciousness raising and the overcoming of all forms of domination its primary educational goal. The most recent mutations in this stream of educational liberalism have been articulated by theorists like Paulo Freire, Henry Giroux, and Maxine Greene. Their normative vocabulary gives the Cartesian dictum a new twist, with "I think, therefore I am" becoming "I think critically, therefore I am." This reference to Descartes is no slip on my part, but rather is critical to a partial understanding of why a group of educational theorists deeply committed to the emancipatory potential of the educational process are also furthering the very anthropocentric-based traditions of a culture that now threatens the viability of the world ecosystems. While these emancipatory educational theorists reject the Cartesian translation of the rational process into a procedural/problem-solving pattern of thinking, they have nevertheless retained other aspects of Cartesianism that have, in turn, exerted a powerful influence on how they have framed the nature of the emancipatory process. These aspects of Cartesian thinking are also basic to the anthropocentric nature of their educational goals.

Cartesianism is based upon the acceptance of important dualisms that have influenced the development of modern culture, two of the most important being the mind/body and "man"/nature distinctions. The identification of knowledge with mental processes occurring in the head of the individual discounted the importance of the body as a source of knowledge. This distinction is still part of the thinking of Freire, Giroux, and Greene. They also retain the Cartesian dualism that leads to view-

ing the individual as thinking about an external and essentially irratio-
nal world, but one that can be made rational by the critical reflection of
the individual. This aspect of Cartesianism can be stated in another way
that brings into focus basic differences separating their approach to emancipation from the forms of consciousness that seem to be part of traditional, preliterate cultures that have evolved along more ecologically sustainable paths. By emphasizing conscious reason, which is presumed to
have its locus in the individual organism, other forms and sources of
knowledge, which are encoded in the material and symbolic patterns that
collectively constitute a culture, are discounted as viable and legitimate
guides to human practices. Descartes (along with Locke and the other
founding fathers of modern consciousness) posited a view of the rational process that represented the individual as autonomous from the
influence of tradition and culture. As we shall see in the more prominent writings of Freire, Giroux, and Greene (to stay with the leading
emancipatory theorists), this Cartesian view of the rational process as
free of tradition and culture is represented as a potential to be attained
through a particular approach to education. Escaping the influence of
culture and tradition involved, as Descartes viewed it, the simple act
of setting aside "anything which admits of the slightest doubt." The
emancipatory educators, by way of contrast, view it as an ongoing
process that requires an external agent (the teacher) who may have to
problematize the taken-for-granted beliefs of students who are embedded in the distorting grip of culture/tradition to a degree that Descartes
failed to understand.

That the emancipatory process, as understood by Freire, Giroux, and
Greene, leads to an extreme form of anthropocentrism can be seen in how
they write about the process of empowerment. For example, in *The Dialectic of Freedom* (1988), Greene makes the attainment of human freedom
the basic issue facing our era. Freedom, as she defines it, is "a surpass-
ing of a constraining or deficient 'reality'"; it involves a critical understanding and the courage to respond to "the ambiguities of various kinds,
layers of determinateness"; and "it is the free act . . . undertaken from
the standpoint of a particular, situated person to bring into existence
something contingent on his/her hopes, expectations, and capacities"
(1988, pp. 5, 9, 70).

> It is because of people's embeddedness in memory and history,
> because of their incipient sense of community that freedom in educa-
> tion cannot be conceived as an autonomous achievement. . . . It is
> because of the apparent normality, the givenness of young people's
> everyday lives, that intentional actions ought to be taken to bring things
> within the scope of the student's attention, to make situations more

palpable and visible. And only when individuals are empowered to interpret the situations they live together do they become able to mediate between the object-world and their own consciousness, to locate themselves so that freedom can appear. (pp. 121–122)

Strengthening the individual's sense of autonomy in making choices, interpretations, and challenging the "deficient reality" in the layers of determinateness through critical reflection fits the moral/educational vision constituted by the normative vocabulary of liberalism, but it also perpetuates the cultural myths that have given this vocabulary its moral force.

These cultural myths, including the blindness to the culture/habitat relationship, are also retained in the thinking of Paulo Freire, the educational theorist who has gained a worldwide audience for his human-centered, Enlightenment-based pedagogy of liberation. Both his philosophic anthropology (his interpretation of "man's" essential human nature, which transcends all cultures) and his pedagogy are complex and deserve more extended analysis than can be given here—particularly Freire's failure to acknowledge the existence of the ecological crisis. However, one aspect of his philosophical anthropology that is especially germane to the problem of anthropocentrism is the way in which he frames the connection between language and the realization of human nature through the exercise of critical reflection and actions based on free choice.

The following quotation appears in *Pedagogy of the Oppressed*, and its centrality both to Freire's understanding of what it means to be a free human being—intended to apply equally to the Hopi, Chinese, Balinese, English, and so forth—and to the pedagogical practices he recommends, is reaffirmed in his later writings. In clarifying the distinction between a "true word" (associated with freedom) and an "inauthentic" or "false word" (associated with domination), Freire writes: "Human existence cannot be silent, nor can it be nourished by false words, but only by true words, with which men transform the world. To exist, humanly, is to *name* the world, to change it. Once named, the world in its turn reappears to the namers as a problem and requires of them a new *naming*. Men are not built in silence, but in word, in work, in action-reflection" (1974, p. 76). And by extension, each generation would reconstitute, according to their own powers of critical reflection, the knowledge encoded in the naming of the previous generation. In commenting on the authority and empowerment of tradition in people's lives (what Freire refers to as history), he states: "Again, my suggestion is that we attempt to emerge from this alienating daily routine that repeats itself. Let's try to understand life, not necessarily as the daily repetition of things, but as an effort to create and recreate, and so an effort to rebel" (1985, p. 199).

Perhaps more than the other emancipatory educational theorists, Freire fuses his anthropocentric view of the world with the Enlightenment myth that change based on critical reflection is inherently progressive. As a person who thinks "history is becoming," Freire argues for a position that he himself, in terms of the traditionalism of his own personal life, cannot achieve. For example, he writes in *The Politics of Education*, "I cannot permit myself to be a mere spectator. On the contrary, I must demand my place in the process of change. So the dramatic tension between past and future, death and life, being and non-being, is no longer a kind of dead end for me. And my response can be none other than my historical praxis—in other words, revolutionary praxis" (1985, p. 129).

As a longtime advocate of Freire's critical pedagogy, Henry Giroux helped expand and popularize a vocabulary intended to awaken classroom teachers to their role as "transformative intellectuals." Whether Giroux is writing about fostering "resistance," "struggle," or "sites of contestation," the purpose of education, as he views it, is to liberate "human beings not only from those traditions that legitimate institutional arrangements, *but also from their own individual history, i.e., that which society has made of them*" (1981, p. 118; emphasis added). In his more recent book, *Teachers as Intellectuals: Toward a Critical Pedagogy of Learning*, he suggests that this process of individual emancipation from the influence of culture requires that schools be viewed "as economic, cultural, and social sites that are inextricably tied to issues of power and control" (p. 126). In effect, the educational road to emancipation involves politicizing (that is, making problematic and thus negotiable in terms of the student's critical judgment) all aspects of cultural life—or as stated in the previous quotation, "that which society has made of them." As he put it, central to the role of the teacher as "transformative intellectual is the necessity of making the pedagogical more political and the political more pedagogical" (1988, p. 127).

While all three emancipatory educational theorists argue that the consciousness-raising process of critical reflection will strengthen the possibility of genuine dialogue and thus contribute to the emergence of a nonexploitive form of community, they have not considered how the cultural orientation embedded in their view of community reflects the assumptions of the Western subculture Alvin Gouldner (1979) referred to as the "culture of critical discourse," and how this culture of critical discourse has framed their view of the power and authority of the critical process. By defining the rules governing critical discourse for the rest of society, intellectuals elevate their status and authority because they possess, more than other social groups, the elaborated language code essential to a theoretical form of discourse.

One of the problems of the emancipatory educators' view of community is related to their one-sided and excessively narrow way of understanding the process of individual empowerment. The limitation of their anthropocentric position can be seen by considering the basic elements of Aldo Leopold's (1970) argument that the bottom line, in terms of both moral and intellectual judgments, is that "a thing is right when it tends to preserve the integrity, stability, and beauty of the biotic community. It is wrong when it tends otherwise" (p. 262). In effect, Leopold is suggesting a new basis for thinking about individualism, the root metaphors that underlie the symbolic systems of a culture, the practices that follow from these mental templates (which are not really separate from individual thought processes and behavior), and how we understand the challenges of emancipation. The basic characteristic of all life—which holds for all cultures—is what he calls the "biotic pyramid." The survival of human culture depends, over the long term, on preserving the natural systems that make up the larger biotic community. "Land," which he considers to be the basis of the biotic community,

> is not merely soil; it is a fountain of energy flowing through a circuit of soils, plants, and animals. Food chains are the living channels which conduct energy upward; death and decay return it to the soil. The circuit is not closed; some energy is dissipated in decay, some added by absorption from the air, some stored in soils, peats, and long-lived forests; but it is a sustained circuit, like a slowly augmented revolving fund of life. (p. 253)

As humans occupy only one of the layers in this biotic community, it is both absurd and suicidal to base a culture on an anthropocentric view of the world. This fact of interdependence is what led Leopold to propose a further development in human ethics. The earlier ethical systems in the West governed individual/societal and individual/God relationships; but, as Leopold notes, the ethics that regulated the social and spiritual community did not extend to the "land and to the animals and plants which grow upon it." The "land ethic," which Leopold proposes as a way of governing relationships with the environment, involves moving away from the anthropocentrism that underpinned earlier ethical systems. For Leopold, "the land ethic simply enlarges the boundaries of the community to include soils, waters, plants, and animals, or collectively: the land" (p. 239). When humans are understood as interdependent members of this enlarged sense of community, an ecologically based ethic, according to Leopold, can then be understood as involving a "limitation of freedom of action in the struggles of existence" (p. 238). Or, as Alexander Solzhenitsyn put it, "Freedom is self-restriction! Restriction of the self for the sake of others" (1975, p. 136). The "other" is understood here as the entire biota that constitutes the life of Leopold's enlarged view of community; that is, self-restriction for the sake of the long-term survival of soil, water, plants, animals, and so forth.

Leopold's "land ethic," which leads to a radical reformulation of the traditional view of individual freedom, does not cancel out the need to address the social justice issues of discrimination, cultural domination, poverty, and so forth. A form of education that contributes to the citizen's communicative competence and, thus, ability to participate in the democratic process, remains a legitimate concern. But the development of communicative competence, along with the ability to identify and think critically about outmoded cultural assumptions and practices, does not have to be grounded in the anthropocentric myth that underlies the emancipatory theories of Freire, Giroux, and Greene.

The full implications of shifting from the root metaphor of a human-centered universe to that of interdependent community (where community is understood to include the entire biota) have yet to be worked out for our society. But it is possible to see in traditional cultures that have evolved along more ecologically sustainable pathways patterns of thought and relationships radically different from the assumptions that underlie the normative vocabulary of the emancipatory educational theorists. The process of identifying cultural patterns of more ecologically sensitive cultures, however, *should not be viewed as dictating the pathway we must follow.* The traditions of other cultures are not like products on a supermarket shelf that we can appropriate for our own use. But understanding that ecologically sustainable cultures appear to share certain common characteristics may help us to recognize that some of our most taken-for-granted cultural assumptions may be an anomaly rather than the main pathway of human history. Gary Snyder (1980) makes this point by noting that the rates of population growth, resource extraction, and destruction of species that characterize the emergence of industrialized societies have no parallels in previous human history. What Snyder calls living "in a totally anomalous time," we call modern, progress, and, now, Information Age. Snyder's more long-range perspective on human development and the current evidence of habitat destruction both suggest that our guiding metaphors (what Theodore Roszak calls our "God words") need to be seriously questioned.

The earlier cited statements of Freire, Giroux, and Greene contain the godwords of the anthropocentric discourse that now needs to be juxtaposed against the characteristics of cultural groups that have evolved more ecologically responsive forms of consciousness. These godwords include *critical reflection, freedom, emancipation,* and, by extension, *individualism.* Given their cultural habit of thinking in dichotomous categories, where freedom and emancipation are understood only in terms of their opposite—namely domination (Freire and Giroux) and "determinateness" (Greene)—and critical reflection as the bulwark against the social forces of oppression and dehumanization, basic aspects of the human/cultural experience are simplified and thus distorted in a way that makes it difficult to move away from the anthropocentric worldview. In looking at traditional cultures, or aspects of our own pluralistic belief systems that are the basis of daily existence, it should be kept in mind that only the outlines of cultural patterns are being identified here, and that each cultural group has a depth and distinctiveness that requires a sense of caution in how far we extend our generalizations. However, the following generalizations about the differences between an anthropocentric-based culture and traditional cultures appear sufficiently valid, given the ethnographic record now available, to warrant further consideration.

Perhaps the most important point of contrast can be found in the writings of Freire, Giroux, and Greene that reflect the myth of modernity that equates rationally directed change with progress. As John Berger observes, after living within a peasant culture in France, modern cultures envisage an expansion of human possibilities. "They are forward-looking because the future offers ever larger hopes" (1979, p. 204). Cultures based on an awareness of scarcity, what Berger calls a "culture of survival," "envisage the future as a sequence of repeated acts for survival. Each act pushes a thread through the eye of a needle, and the thread is tradition. No overall increase is envisaged" (1979, p. 204). A basic difference that seems to be a demarcation line separating the modern anthropocentric culture advocated by the emancipatory educators and primal (including peasant) cultures thus has to do with the different attitudes toward experimentation with ideas, values, and social practices. Cultures that involve an awareness of how close they are to the margins of survival appear to possess a different attitude toward experimentation from that of modern cultures, which are able to develop technologies that have helped to maintain the illusion of a surplus of food and energy resources. Cultures of survival cannot afford the risk. Now that the ecological crisis is exposing the illusion of surplus for modern cultures such as ours, we have to ask whether equating every form of experimentation with progress is not in fact part of the cultural crisis we face.

The connection between the forms of knowledge regarded as having authority in people's lives and how human life is framed in relation to the nature of time is essential to understanding the ecological consequences of the form of modernity advocated by the emancipatory educators. The writings of Freire, Giroux, and Greene make occasional references to other-than-rationally-based forms of knowledge, but these are only momentary lapses from their basic belief that the dialectic of human existence is advanced through a critical, problematizing form of rational thought. In *Pedagogy in Process* (1978), Freire writes about the importance of "re-Africanization" of the colonized peoples of Guinea-Bissau, and then he promotes the use of Portuguese as a basis of an emancipatory literacy program. A more recent book, *Learning to Question*, which was published as a conversation between Freire and Antonio Faundez, contains a statement by Freire that suggests a more complex view of knowledge: "To a critical understanding of reality must be added sensitivity to reality, and to attain this sensitivity or develop it they [intellectuals] need communion with the masses. Intellectuals need to discover that their critical capacity is of neither greater nor less worth than the sensitivity of the people. Both are required for an understanding of reality" (Freire & Faundez, 1989, p. 29). Later in his conversation with Faundez, sensitivity becomes associated with naivety, and the primacy of critical reflection as the only true source of knowledge is reestablished, as it always has been in Freire's dialectic of practice being guided by critical reflection. Witness the following: "Rigorous thought must not deny naivety in *its attempt to go beyond it*. And so I feel I must mention . . . the ability to accept the naivety of other people so as with them to *progress beyond it*" (Freire & Faundez, 1989, emphasis added). He goes on to share his observation that even naive people have the capacity for critical thought—which he urges intellectuals to take seriously.

Maxine Greene's view of the human situation also singles out critical reflection as the only legitimate source of knowledge—one that underlies the expansion of human freedom. Critical reflection is what gives empowerment to the human capacity to interpret, or as Greene (1988) puts it: "To recognize the role of perspective and vantage point, to recognize at the same time that there are always multiple perspectives and multiple vantage points, is to recognize that no accounting, disciplinary or otherwise, can ever be finished or complete. There is always more. There is always possibility. And this is where the space opens for the pursuit of freedom" (p. 128). Unlike the "cultures of survival" Berger refers to, Greene's vision is one of ever-expanding possibilities for individuals. The irony of her position, as well as that of Freire and his chief follower, Henry Giroux, is that they argue for totalizing the form of knowledge that is the most experimental and, in terms of its accompanying cultural baggage, the least suitable for encoding and transmitting to future generations ecologically sound cultural practices. In effect, their anti-tradition stance prevents them from recognizing that critical reflection is important because it is a powerful means of *renewing* the threads of cultural life, which Berger calls "tradition."

The other forms of knowledge, which must also be viewed as sources of community empowerment in the broadest sense of the term, can be seen by looking at *certain* areas of our taken-for-granted experience —particularly those areas that Wendell Berry, Wes Jackson, and Gary Snyder write about. But as too many aspects of our bodily, tacit, and analog forms of knowledge are filtered through the metaphorical framework that separates humans from nature, and privileges a Cartesian view of the rational process in a way that obscures our place in the information exchanges flowing through the pathways that make up the cultural/natural ecology, we will turn to examples taken from traditional cultures. Again, it must be stressed that we are looking at forms of knowledge, and not arguing that the forms are shared in identical ways in all traditional cultures or that they all represent, in their particularity, profound forms of understanding. Just as critical reflection has the potential of being used in both constructive and destructive ways, the other forms of knowledge should not be romanticized. But if we are to recover from the consequences of the hubris of Western consciousness, we must work our way back to an understanding of, and an appreciation for, those forms of knowledge that connect us with our habitat in long-term sustaining relationships.

The investigations of Joseph Campbell, Marshall Sahlins, J. Donald Hughes, as well as the representation of the native point of view by Jamake Highwater, Vine Deloria, Jr., and Black Elk (to cite just a few sources of a very complex and rich literature), point both to an extraordinarily wide range of knowledge (perhaps better expressed as knowledge pathways) connecting people to the characteristics of their habitat and to proven (that is, ecologically sustainable) practices. Learning how to live in a habitat, whether we are talking about the Koyukon hunters and gatherers of the subarctic regions of the North or the Hopi of the arid Southwest, involves learning from elders (survivors), generations no longer present, plants, animals, soil, weather patterns, and all other elements of the habitat. Knowledge, context, continuity, and practice seem to be intertwined and holistic. Ecologically sustainable forms of knowledge include tacit and analog ways of knowing; these forms of knowledge also involve a more complex view of the environment as a system of signs—that is, a language that allows for interspecies communication and for understanding what ecosystems are communicating about their own condition. Relationships that characterize, in Gregory

Bateson's sense, the ecology of which the person is an interactive member, are the source of semiosis that enabled the traditional mind to experience the habitat as alive and full of meaning. In this sense, traditional peoples who were sensitive to the importance of reading and decoding the signs of their environments were the first semioticians. Unlike the emancipatory orientation of critical reflection, which incorporates Western assumptions about knowing being based on an individual perspective and a distancing/objectifying relationship, traditional forms of knowing seem to have the characteristics of contextualizing and unifying in the sense that the person is not viewed as the primary repository and legitimator of knowledge. The whole environment appears to be understood in a manner that corresponds to Bateson's observation about the individual mind being part of a larger mental process.

The following observation by Bateson, which frames these characteristics of traditional people's epistemological orientation in more contemporary terms, points to another dimension of their knowledge that is fundamentally different from the position of Freire, Giroux, and Greene. Writes Bateson: "Thus, in no system which shows mental characteristics can any part have unilateral control over the whole. In other words, *the mental characteristics of the system are immanent, not in some part, but in the system as a whole*" (1972, p. 316). Further on he suggests we begin to think of the individual mind as not limited to being in a self-contained body, but as "immanent also in the pathways and messages outside the body." Furthermore, this ecological perspective leads to the recognition that "there is a larger mind of which the individual mind is only a subsystem," and was perhaps what people were attempting to represent by such terms as *God, the Great Spirit,* and so forth (p. 461).

For traditional peoples this awareness of the interconnected planetary ecology represents a form of spiritual knowledge that provides the basis for living a moral life; that is, one that is in harmony with the patterns of sustainable ecological order. Notions of emancipation from group knowledge, empowering the authority of critical reflection (i.e., individualism), and expanding the horizons of freedom would be viewed as fragmenting and subverting this spiritual order. Incidentally, what Leopold is arguing for on a rational basis is an integral part of what traditional peoples learn as they undergo vision quests and other rituals that encode and transmit spiritual knowledge.

Other forms of knowledge that differ from the singular focus on critical reflection as the source of empowerment include a wide range of narrative traditions, dance, song, initiation rituals, ceremonies, and mentoring relationships. If we examine closely these encoding and storage processes we can recognize that each often involves the aesthetic element of "making special" relationships and activities that otherwise would be experienced as mundane. This capacity for artistic expression, according to Ellen Dissanayake (1988), converts everyday reality "from its unusual unremarkable state . . . to a significant or specially experienced reality in which the components, by their emphasis or combination or juxtaposition, acquire a meta-reality" (p. 95). What is shared through these pathways for maintaining the continuity that binds the present and past together involves great complexity and, over a time span exceeding what we are accustomed to thinking within—and certainly the relevant time span of the emancipatory educators—has to meet the test of maintaining a viable eco-system. And not all traditional cultures met this test, as we can observe today.

Some elements of what would be involved in a shift to a more nonanthropocentric approach to education can be identified here in outline form. Keeping in mind that we *cannot* borrow (like we do another country's technology) the patterns of other, more ecologically responsive cultures, and that we have special political problems connected to the cultural diversity and economic orientation of the dominant cultural groups, it seems there are still a number of areas that can be addressed by classroom teachers. No single educational reform will be adequate in itself in bringing our cultural practices into balance with the life-sustaining capacities of natural systems. For the sake of brevity, I shall identify classroom reforms in terms of two general categories. The first has to do with fostering what (in 1974) I called "cultural literacy." Before that phrase was associated with a more recent educational agenda, it was used to mean using the educational process to become aware of cultural assumptions and social practices that are ecologically disruptive. Cultural literacy thus meant to decode our own taken-for-granted cultural patterns. This would involve examining such aspects of culture as our approaches to technology, work, competition, individualism, and so forth; taken-for-granted assumptions embedded in textbooks, everyday experiences of students and members of the community, and the way in which the metaphorical nature of language encodes culturally based patterns of thinking would be essential curricular resources for this aspect of the educational reform process.

But making the taken-for-granted explicit, and putting it both into historical and cross-cultural perspective, does not take us much beyond the critical form of consciousness advocated by Freire, Giroux, and Greene —though it would radically decenter the anthropocentric position they advocate. The other category encompasses a wide range of educational/ cultural activities that seem closer to what Snyder views as reconnecting people to the "spiritual disciplines" that had been the main preoccupation of humanity until the emergence of the myth of modernization, with its preoccupation with technological proficiency and maximizing individual choice. Some of these educational/cultural activities, such as the rediscovery of the importance of narrative forms of communication and how they differ from literacy, are beginning to be more widely accepted in classrooms. Other curricular activities that have the potential to expand the sense of connectedness, meaning, and thus an awareness of self as a part of a larger community, are dance, music, and art. Of course these ways of knowing can be framed by, and in turn help to promote, the ideology of individual self-expression. But they can also provide experiences grounded in ecological metaphors that make the sense of both community and continuity vital in a way fundamentally different from recent expression of our more politicized artforms. When we look at the typical art class, however, we can see how far away we are from uniting metaphorical expression with "making special" the everyday relations of community life. What art students now "produce" are largely art objects that are supposed to have autonomous aesthetic merit—which reflects an anthropocentric form of aesthetic appreciation that depends on the perspective of the individual.

What is now needed in teacher education is a shift from the Cartesian position of an autonomous, culture-free individual to a Batesonian framework that starts from the premise that we must expand our understanding of mind outward to the point where we can recognize self as part of the information-exchange processes that constitute the ecology of which we are a part. Our ability to participate fully in the information exchanges that characterize this ecology of pattern and relationship is dependent, as Bateson points out, on the metaphorical framework we use (and that uses us) in the interpretative process we call "thinking." Shifting from the root metaphor of a human-centered universe to that of an "ecology" seems fundamental to getting right the complex relationships between the culture/language/thought connection and the habitat, and to helping teachers recognize that we must begin to make a shift from the modern and transitory to values and beliefs that contribute to cultural patterns based on long-term sustainability and interdependence within a larger sense of community.

Chapter 11

Contingency, Irony, and the Ecological Crisis

The Reactionary Nature of Richard Rorty's Liberalism

Richard Rorty's *Contingency, Irony, and Solidarity* (1989) serves as an important example of the double bind the ecological crisis now places us in. That a highly esteemed philosopher who has taken on the task of aligning our epistemological assumptions with a vision of liberalism that seems half John Stuart Mill and half John Dewey completely ignores the ecological crisis suggests the real depth of the difficulties that lie ahead—at least for those of us who expect philosophers to address the paramount issues of the day. Rorty's silence is not so much the problem as is his influence on that part of the discourse where philosophy and ideology merge in a more self-conscious manner. This brings us to the real source of the double bind; namely, the form of liberalism Rorty proposes we adopt in the name of progress is reactionary in terms of bringing our cultural patterns into sustainable balance with the life-sustaining eco-systems. Before considering why Rorty's arguments lead to one of the most reactionary and nihilistic formulations of modern liberalism, it is essential to summarize what has now become part of the daily news coverage on the damage being done to different systems that constitute the biosphere upon which human life depends.

According to a report of the National Academy of Sciences, *One Earth, One Future* (Silver & DeFries, 1990), the demands of a rapidly expanding human population (which increased from 2.5 billion in 1950 to over 5 billion in 1987) on natural systems are contributing to a greenhouse effect that threatens major disruptions in other areas of the biosphere, including the fertility of soils already depleted by our overuse of petrochemicals and availability of usable fresh water. The report also notes the increasing devastation of tropical forests (about 27 million acres a year) and species diversity among plants and animals. To this alarming list must be added the vast amounts of toxic wastes being poured into the atmosphere, onto the land, and into the water systems. That human cultures may be close to crossing critical thresholds in the capacity of natural systems to sustain life is a possibility that is being given serious consideration by both national and international agencies who are monitoring a growing body of scientific evidence.

Aside from the numbers of people in Africa and Asia who are starving (or perilously close) in numbers that overwhelm our capacity to comprehend fully what is happening and how to respond, we must recognize that the wealthy countries of the world (which constitute only one-fourth of the population) consume 80% of the world's commercial energy and that 40% of all the carbon dioxide building up in the atmosphere is emitted by the seven wealthiest countries of North America and Europe. The figures and trends cited here should now be familiar to anybody who has even the most casual contact with the media. But what the daily news reports on the worsening condition of the environment fail to address is the way in which cultural beliefs and practices contribute to the deepening crisis.

It is against this background of rapid environmental degradation that Rorty's ideas must be judged. Rorty's arguments on the nature of language and thought, as well as his attempt to extrapolate a coherent set of ideological guidelines for living a personally and socially meaningful life, are framed in a vocabulary that has wide appeal to people who still believe in the emancipatory and progressive vision of liberalism. Unfortunately, readers who identify with his messianic political vocabulary may lose sight of the fact that the ecological crisis is the most important challenge we face. In assessing the adequacy of Rorty's ideas for meeting this challenge, we must keep in mind that the stream of liberalism he proposes to revitalize served as the ideological engine of the Industrial Revolution, which treated the earth as an exploitable resource. As one of the central arguments being advanced here is that this stream of liberalism (as well as its more technocratic mutations) reinforces the cultural forces that continue to degrade the earth's ecosystems, we cannot treat the vocabulary of liberalism as sacrosanct. We must also be open to considering the possibility that primal cultures that have evolved ecologically sustainable ways of knowing may have more relevance for addressing the current imbalance between cultural demands and life-sustaining capabilities of ecosystems than the ideas of leading philosophers such as Richard Rorty.

Rorty's vision of a liberal society that optimizes the individual's need for self-creation, and at the same time reduces suffering, is based on a radical view of language, which he attributes to Donald Davidson. Although Rorty does not acknowledge it, this view of language also has roots in several other academic disciplines, including the sociology of knowledge, which treat all beliefs and values as contingent (that is, as relative). The following statements by Rorty sum up the two main threads of his argument about the language/thought connection and the form of liberal society his contingency view of language leads us to. Following the lead of Nietzsche, Freud, and now Derrida, Rorty suggests that we should "treat *everything*—our language, our conscience, our community— as a product of time and chance" (p. 22). He also reiterates the competitive model of classical liberalism when he writes: "A liberal society is one which is content to call 'true' (or 'right' or 'just') whatever the outcome of undistorted communication happens to be, whatever view wins in a free and open encounter" (p. 67). Rorty's view of what will hold together the ideal liberal society, what he terms the "glue," is also quite interesting, given the expressions that anomic individualism have taken in the last few decades. The necessary "glue" is a shared "consensus that the point of social organization is to let everybody have a chance at self-creation to the best of his or her abilities, and that that goal requires, beside peace and wealth, the standard 'bourgeois freedoms'" (p. 84). But perhaps the most critically important statement by Rorty, given the relativism of these previous quotations, is that the charge of relativism "should not be answered, but rather evaded" (p. 54). That is, the argument that his position is built upon the shifting sands of relativism (*nihilism* would be a more accurate term) must be viewed as an expression of a "deep metaphysical need." The antidote he prescribes for this archaic intellectual and moral condition is to invent new vocabularies that will reframe how the problem is understood.

As his liberal ideology is based on what he sees as the successful overturning of the epistemological/metaphysical problems that have bedeviled philosophers from Plato to the present, we shall focus on the adequacy of how he represents the language/thought connection. This is the connection, from his point of view, that has been incorrectly understood, thus leading to a long and varied history of false claims about the correspondence between thought and the external world. In claiming that the world is indifferent to how humans describe and think about it, Rorty is taking a position that would be supported by thinkers who identify with different streams within the sociology of knowledge (from Marx to Peter Berger) and even by cultural anthropologists such as Clifford Geertz. But they avoid the problem of relativism by recognizing the intersubjective nature of human understanding and the fact that most of the shared cultural knowledge is experienced as part of the person's natural attitude toward everyday life. Rorty omits these considerations by adopting Donald Davidson's instrumentalist view of metaphor as the primary basis for understanding the language/thought connection. This strategy enables him to build an argument for thinking of the individual in the atomistic and voluntaristic terms required by his desire to give new life to a now largely defunct interpretation of liberalism. But his position is made especially vulnerable by the fact that Davidson, with the characteristic penchant of British philosophers for treating language as a culture-free phenomenon, adopts one of the most narrow interpretations of metaphorical thinking in the literature.

Rorty's more general views of language would be accepted today by many scholars as conventional wisdom: that humans create language, that language helps to constitute how the world is understood and experienced, and that language is used to express the inherently metaphorical nature of human thought. Or, as Rorty puts it, the history of thought "is the history of metaphor" (p. 16). But few would accept his way of understanding the role that metaphor plays. Citing Nietzsche's definition of "truth" as a "mobile army of metaphors" (p. 17), Rorty sees himself establishing the basis of another Nietzschean-like pronouncement; namely, that philosophy is dead. Epistemological and metaphysical concerns, in effect, cannot be taken seriously when we recognize that thought is metaphorical, and that metaphorical constructions are a result of historical contingencies (that is, chance occurrences that reflect the absence of an inherent purpose and order in the world). As there is no basis for a final vocabulary, Rorty turns away from philosophy and toward ideology. Had he adopted a more culturally grounded view of metaphorical thinking, he might have avoided a problem that has contributed to the sterility of Western philosophy; that is, the failure to recognize that such words as *truth, rationality, justice, language, individualism, equality,* and all the other godwords of professional philosophers cannot be properly understood apart from the cultural groups who use them. This is, in part, the message of Alasdair MacIntyre's (1988) *Whose Justice? Which Rationality?* Rorty refers to *culture,* but in treating the word as another expression of his abstract theory of contingency, he fails to recognize that the patterns of a culture, whether we are talking about linguistic forms, social interaction, or forms of aesthetic expression, are experienced by its members as part of their natural attitude—like the taken-for-granted patterns of the cultural group Rorty reproduces in both his form of communication and patterns of thinking (e.g., his unquestioning acceptance of the myth of progress).

In his more general statements about the history of thought being based on metaphorical thinking, Rorty inadvertently gives support to a view of metaphor he wants to deny in his more direct explanations of how we use metaphors. But as his more focused explanation of the rela-tivistic foundations of language serves as the fulcrum upon which he bal-ances both his image of the "ironist," who is the new hero figure, and his views on the nature of liberal society, we shall turn to this more pivotal part of his argument.

According to Rorty, we will face up to the contingent nature of human existence when we develop "a willingness to face up to the 'con-tingency' of the language we use" (p. 9). And we can understand the con-tingent nature of language by taking seriously Donald Davidson's way of thinking about language and, more specifically, his view of metaphor. The strength of Davidson's position, as Rorty puts it, is that "he does not view language as a medium for either expression or representation" (p. 11). This leads to the claim, which Rorty accepts, that metaphors do not have "a special meaning, a specific cognitive content" (p. 262). But if metaphors do not possess cognitive content (that is, do not provide a schema for understanding), then what function do they perform? Davidson's (1984) answer is: "What distinguishes metaphor is not mean-ing, but use—in this it is like assertion, hinting, lying, promising, or criti-cizing" (p. 259). That is, metaphors (which Rorty equates with language) are like tools, and thus must be assessed in purely instrumental terms. According to Rorty: "We should restrict ourselves to questions like 'Does our use of these words get in the way of our use of other words?' This is a question about whether our use of tools is inefficient, not a question about whether our beliefs are contradictory" (p. 12).

This view of language, as a vocabulary that elicits responses in the same way as grunts, groans, and pauses, provides the basis for Rorty's view of the ironists who have "radical and continuing doubts" about the vocabulary they use, who realize that their "present vocabulary can nei-ther underwrite nor dissolve their doubts," and who do not consider that their current "vocabulary is closer to reality than others" (p. 73). This instrumentalist view of metaphor serves to provide the conceptual foun-dation for Rorty's arguments that language should be understood as part of the process of natural evolution, "as new forms of life (metaphors) constantly kill off old forms—not to accomplish a higher purpose, but blindly" (p. 10). But it differs radically from the views of metaphor advanced by Mark Johnson, George Lakoff, Donald Schön, and Michael Reddy—to cite just a few of the scholars who make a convincing case that metaphors provide a schema of understanding and thus have cog-nitive content within a language community. I should like to summarize this more mainstream view of the connection between metaphor and thought by situating the discussion within a cultural context. This is essential both for understanding a major area of silence in Rorty's theory, as well as for bringing into focus how Rorty's view of a liberal society would further exacerbate the ecological crisis.

What the Rorty/Davidson view of metaphor cannot account for is how the root metaphors of a cultural group (which can also be understood as metanarratives, worldviews, paradigms, etc.) influence the process of analogic thinking, and the subsequent encoding of the schema of understanding worked out in the process of analogic thinking in the iconic metaphors that do their work at the taken-for-granted level of understanding characteristic of everyday discourse. If we consider the symbolic world of cultural groups not overwhelmed by the syncretism of modernity, we find a shared way of thinking, communicating, developing and using technologies, and expressing aesthetic preferences that are made coherent by their root metaphors. An example is the Kwakiutl of the Pacific Northwest, whose culture is organized in terms of a master schema of understanding (root metaphor) that represented all life as part of a process of eating and being eaten by others. Stanley Walens (1981) describes their root metaphor in the following manner:

> Thus, the Kwakiutl moral universe becomes united, not by any vague religious sense but by the fact that the entire universe contains all beings within its bounds, and that all beings are subject to the principle of being both hungry and the food of other beings who are themselves hungry. The Kwakiutl universe is a universe of related beings, all of whom have the moral responsibility to control their eating. Eating is a universal property of the world, and thus it is the basis of morality. (p. 6)

Masks, dwellings, implements, dances, and narratives are given a form that expresses metaphorically this way of understanding the universe. The root metaphor also serves to frame their way of understanding what constitutes a moral life—which is synonymous with being Kwakiutl. Because the world is viewed as discordant and self-destructive, as life is sustained only by making a meal of other life, it is "only when its inhabitants agree to cooperate to maintain order at the expense of their own personal desires, agree to suppress their hunger, and to modify it into its proper proportion can the world operate" (Walens, 1981, p. 12). This basic organizing schema influences how relationships are understood as well as bodily actions and forms of knowing—as witnessed in how the rights to various forms of food are organized, how the life of an animal may be taken, and how the preparation of food is divided along gender lines. Each cultural pattern has metaphorical significance.

We can see in our own history how a root metaphor provides a master schema for the process of analogic thinking. When Johannes Kepler wrote in 1605 that "my aim is to show that the celestial machine is to be likened not to a divine organism but to a clockwork" (quoted in Merchant, 1980, pp. 128–129), he was helping to establish the foundations of a new root metaphor that would, like the Kwakiutl cosmology, provide the master schema for organizing the culture—including the early development of science, the technological revolution, and our way of thinking about nature. For example, William Harvey broke with the final vocabulary used by medieval thinkers, to use Rorty's phrase, when he referred to the human heart as a "pump." Though separated by nearly 400 years, the Cal Tech professor who said, "In a sense the hardware for making a man is 23 chromosomes" (quoted in Kidder, 1989, p. 14), was engaging in a process of analogic thinking framed by the same (slightly updated) root metaphor. It would be highly unlikely that the Cal Tech professor working on the frontiers of molecular biology would be aware of how a deeply rooted cultural template had influenced him to represent a human being in mechanistic terms. Root metaphors partially expressed in such images as fallen man (or original sin), a human-centered universe, a mechanistic universe (and now as a giant computer), and Gaia, as well as iconic metaphors that encode earlier processes of analogic thinking (e.g., artificial intelligence, individualism, freedom, data, and so forth), provide schemata that connect individual thought/experience to the deeper symbolic levels of a cultural group. And this "determinative memory," to use Gregory Bateson's phrase, operates largely at the level of the individual's natural attitude; that is, the individual is largely unaware of how the cultural episteme influences the process of thinking.

Mark Johnson (1987) sums up in the following way the complexity of conceptual patterns, continuities, and the layered nature of metaphorical thinking:

> Understanding does not consist merely of after-the-fact reflections on prior experiences; it is, more fundamentally, the way (or means by which) we have those experiences in the first place. It is the way our world presents itself to us. And this is a result of the massive complex of our culture, language, history, and bodily mechanisms that blend to make our world what it is. *Image schemata and their metaphorical projections are primary patterns of this "blending."* Our subsequent propositional reflections on our experience are made possible by this more basic mode of understanding. (1987, p. 104)

It should be added that our "propositional reflections" are also framed by these taken-for-granted schemata of understanding. The Rorty/Davidson view of metaphor lacks this depth of cultural contextualization, and thus represents a serious misunderstanding of the metaphor/thought connection.

Rorty's view of ironists as strong poets (that is, individuals who endlessly metaphorize without needing assurances that language has any cognitive relationship to the larger ecology of which they are a part) leads him to embrace a view of liberalism that contains an inner tension between the rights of the individual and the responsibilities of community membership. Although Rorty has an aversion for all final vocabularies, he nevertheless acknowledges "that Western social and political thought may have had the last *conceptual* revolution it needs. J. S. Mill's suggestion that governments devote themselves to optimizing the balance between leaving people's private lives alone and preventing suffering seems to me pretty much the last word" (p. 63). As a number of recent theorists have addressed the problem of how to reconcile the areas of conflict that arise from this formulation, most notably William Sullivan, Benjamin Barber, and Robert Bellah, I shall frame my criticisms of Rorty's liberalism in terms of the ecological crisis—which now seems to be the paramount political as well as existential issue.

Rorty's view of the ideal political system that will maximize the freedom of ironist individuals (i.e., autonomous individuals) is based on a number of cultural assumptions that can be traced back to early Hebrew and Christian theology and to the Enlightenment tradition of thinking that now underlies modern society: the linear organization of time that trivializes the cycles of the natural world, the progressive nature of change, the efficacy of abstract ideas, the individual as an autonomous rational and moral agent, and the anthropocentric universe. The identification of these cultural assumptions is critical to understanding why Rorty's liberalism represents the ultimate irony; that is, how the anthropocentric cultural assumptions underlying what many Western thinkers regard as the most progressive and enlightened way of thinking have been turned into a reactionary position by the ecological crisis.

For all Rorty's protestations about metaphysical thinkers who want to discover truth and then impose their final vocabulary upon others, his own thinking is deeply rooted in the Western myth of progress. For example, in the struggle between metaphysicians and ironists, he sees the latter prevailing. This same sense of progress is expressed in his argument that we should "see language as we now see evolution, as new forms of life constantly kill off old forms" (p. 19). While he rejects the idea of cosmic design or a purpose being worked out in the evolutionary process, he nevertheless retains the assumption that a life based on continual doubt, and the acceptance of contingency, represents a progressive process—just as his reference to Mill's formulation of a liberal society is framed by a view of political evolution that is progressive in nature.

Rorty's embeddedness in the Western view of progress can also be seen in his way of understanding tradition. Part of the legacy of the Enlightenment was to frame tradition in binary terms. Tradition represented the dead weight of the past on the living present; it was also regarded as circumscribing the individual's potential for rational self-direction. Progress was (and still is) understood as moving away from tradition. This binary way of thinking precludes the possibility of considering tradition and progress as complementary, just as it is impossible within this binary framework to view social change as the renewal of tradition. Rorty's Enlightenment attitude toward tradition can also be seen in the intellectual and emotional traits he associates with ironist thinkers whose task of self-creation is dependent upon continually questioning the authority of tradition. According to Rorty, "ironists are afraid that they will get stuck in the vocabulary in which they were brought up if they only know the people in their own neighborhood" (p. 80). For the ironist individual, tradition poses a particularly difficult existential challenge because there are no criteria for judging whether the basis of their continual questioning is justified. Rorty writes:

The ironist spends her time worrying about the possibility that she has been initiated into the wrong tribe, taught to play the wrong language game. She worries that the process of socialization which turned her into a human being by giving her a language may have given her the wrong language, and so turned her into the wrong kind of human being. But she cannot give a criterion for wrongness. (p. 75)

In another passage, Rorty states that "the opposite of irony is common sense. For [common sense] is the watchword for those who unconsciously describe everything in terms of the final vocabulary to which they and those around them are habituated" (p. 74). The common sense (what others might call the taken-for-granted patterns) and the habituated are, to Rorty's way of thinking, synonymous with tradition, and thus a source of authority external to the individual. In good Enlightenment fashion, Rorty wants to locate authority in the reflective doubts of the individual, even if that "reminds herself of her rootlessness."

Irony is also an appropriate word for understanding Rorty's view of tradition, as the authority for his actions and thoughts is embedded in traditions that are part of his own natural attitude—or what he terms "common sense." These include, in terms of what is visible to the reader, the patterns of writing from left to right; organizing and expressing thoughts in terms of a subject-verb-object pattern shared by the rest of his language community; using the conventions of capital letters, spaces between words, and paragraphs; and holding the belief that explicit and propositional representations of knowledge have more authority and legitimacy than tacit or orally communicated forms of knowledge. The reader would probably be correct in surmising that Rorty also takes for granted such other forms of tradition as money (and royalty payments), technologies, libraries, clothes, and nonverbal patterns of communication—to cite just a few of the areas of daily life that involve the reenactment and, over time, transformation of traditional patterns. The problem with Rorty, as philosopher and liberal ideologue, is that he is embedded in what Edward Shils (1981) refers to as an "anti-tradition tradition"; that is, a tradition of thinking that has as its mission the denigration of all forms of knowledge considered as limiting the possibility of human emancipation. The problem is that this tradition, which has split into intense rivalries, has given legitimacy to a limited number of ways of knowing—and most of these are highly experimental, in that they make a virtue of newness and originality. Knowledge learned through bodily experience, tacit forms of understanding and performance, spiritual knowledge, and knowledge encoded in technologies and cultural patterns simply have been ignored by philosophers such as Rorty who are in the anti-tradition tradition of Enlightenment thinking.

Rorty's view of the ironist individual reflects another assumption that has been a mainstay of many liberal thinkers; namely, that the intentions and acts of critically reflective individuals (ironists) will be essentially good. Whereas James Madison argued for institutionalizing checks and balances in order to protect society from selfishly motivated misuses of power, Rorty represents the ironist individual as possessing a natural proclivity toward treating others in a way that enhances solidarity and the alleviation of pain and suffering. This natural proclivity, however, should not be "thought of as a recognition of a core self, the human essence, in all human beings." Nevertheless, he states that "the view I am offering says that there is such a thing as moral progress, and that this progress is indeed in the direction of greater human solidarity" (p. 192). Perhaps the best example of Rorty's optimism can be seen in how he frames the problem of reconciling responsibility toward others and the ironist's pursuit of self-interest—which he refers to as "self-creation." Writes Rorty: "Our responsibilities to others constitute *only* the public side of our lives, a side which competes with our private affections and our private attempts at self-creation, which has no *automatic* priority over such private motives" (p. 194). What a moral obligation means is also to be worked out by ironists, who do not consider that their "vocabulary is closer to reality than others . . ." (p. 73). In the final analysis, the moral relativism of Rorty's position is defensible only because of his optimism about the proclivity of ironist individuals—an optimism that is not historically grounded.

The above quotations provide a good picture of Rorty's view of community as an ongoing set of relationships wherein all members attempt to reconcile self-creation with their equally individualistic inter-pretation of the meaning of solidarity. But there is another aspect of his view of community that is particular relevant to the ecological crisis. Rorty's way of understanding community, like both the classical liberal and Deweyian traditions he resonates with, involves humans only. In effect, Rorty's efforts to envision human life lived without the false se-curity of final vocabularies remains embedded in the root metaphor of an anthropocentric universe. It is his unconscious acceptance of this root metaphor that frames his understanding of community in a way that ignores the interdependence of humans with other life forms that make up the biosphere. When we recognize this interdependence, which in-volves the viability of food chains that are far more basic to life than fi-nal or any other form of vocabulary, both Rorty's liberalism and his naive epistemological formulations begin to unravel. There are indeed abso-lutes that govern relationships, and one of the most critical ones is that humans (including "strong poets") cannot survive the destruction of their habitat. The well-being of humans and habitat, over the long run, go to-gether—although the habitat would not be adversely affected if humans were to disappear.

There have been a number of thinkers who have used the natural ecology as a root metaphor for challenging key elements of liberal thought. Aldo Leopold, for example, argues that humans must be understood in terms of their place in the food chain. Whereas Rorty's anthropocentrism leads him to limit moral obligations to the domain of human relationships, Leopold extends the boundaries of moral obliga-tion to include all the other elements, contributing to what he describes as "energy flowing through a circuit of soils, plants, and animals" (1970, p. 253). He even argues for a moral absolute: "A thing is right when it tends to preserve the integrity, stability, and beauty of the biotic com-munity. It is wrong when it tends otherwise" (p. 262). That is, freedom is to be understood as self-limitation for the sake of others. But this is not meant to be understood in altruistic terms; "others" include the entire biotic community that is the source of energy for sustaining life. Viewed in ecological terms, self-limitation is essential over the long term to the sustenance of the individual's own life—and that of his or her progeny.

Gregory Bateson is another thinker who has challenged the anthropocentric foundations upon which Rorty's intellectual edifice rests. Unlike Rorty, who views thought as a mental activity occurring in the head of each individual, Bateson argues that mental activity ("information," in its most simple form of expression) is synonymous with an ecological system. As he puts it, "the mental characteristics of the system are immanent, not in some part, but in the system as a whole" (1972, p. 316). A system, for Bateson, should be understood in cybernetic terms, where a "difference which makes a difference" represents the most primitive and basic unit of information. Bateson also recognizes that the information exchanges that occur in the relationships that characterize a natural "ecology" (where humans are not necessarily the principal actors) are understood by humans on a metaphorical and thus conceptual level.

The metaphorical constructions are, in Bateson's terminology, the conceptual maps, or schemata, that make interpretation possible; the ecology of differences which make a difference represent the territory. Conceptual maps are not always adequate for recognizing the characteristics of the territory. Or, in more Batesonian terms, many of the information exchanges occurring in the system are not thought about or adequately understood because of the individual's conceptual (cultural) way of knowing. One expression of this possible incongruity between map and territory is the metaphorical representation of the individual as an autonomous thinker—which is the position Rorty adopts. Another example of a conceptual map being inappropriate to understanding the information exchanges that are part of a cybernetic system was the long-term failure to recognize the relationship between the use of pesticides and the decline of animal populations. Before Rachel Carson challenged the conceptual maps that characterized 1950s thinking, pesticides were thought of in terms of controlling "pests"—which is itself an interesting metaphor that illuminates and hides in accordance with a cultural group's root metaphors. A third example is the long-held belief in a form of progress that involves the depletion of nonrenewable resources. The purpose of Bateson's metaphorical distinction between map and territory is to highlight how our lives are inextricably embedded in natural systems, and how all human activities involve relationships with other elements that make up an ecosystem. Two statements by Bateson sum up the basic difference that separates him from the anthropocentrism of Rorty. The first: "The total self-corrective unit which processes information, or as I say, 'thinks' and 'acts' and 'decides,' is a *system* whose boundaries do not at all coincide with the boundaries either of the body or of what is popularly called the 'self' or 'consciousness'" (p. 319). And in addressing the question of whether individuals can survive while the natural systems that make up their habitat fail, he states that "*the unit of evolutionary survival turns out to be identical with the unit of mind*" (p. 483). It must be remembered here that, for Bateson, the unit of mind is the ecological system, of which the individual is an interactive member.

Western philosophy has been a part of a nearly 2,500-year effort to establish a new regime of truth that led to viewing primal peoples as intellectually and culturally inferior. These mostly agrarian preliterate cultures have been studied scientifically and used as a source of artifacts for museum curators. They have also been used as a reference point for determining how far the rationally based cultures of the West have evolved. One of the possibilities denied by this regime of truth is that there is anything really important to learn from these cultures. But with the growing awareness that the values and ways of thinking underlying Western technological practices are degrading the habitat at an alarming rate, there is a growing recognition that primal cultures may be important for reasons that go beyond our fascination with their forms of aesthetic expression. Of particular interest now is their ability to live in sustainable balance with their habitat. That they have been able to do this over a span of time we are not likely to match, even with our "superior" forms of culture, makes their achievement even more remarkable.

Although primal cultures vary widely in their belief systems, technologies, and patterns for guiding daily life, there are a number of shared traits that relate directly to their ability to live within the margins of their habitats. A brief identification of these characteristics may help put in focus why Rorty's more progressive and rationally based ideas would likely contribute to further accelerating the destruction of the environment. These characteristics are not meant to be taken as ready-made patterns we can adopt for our own culture. But they can suggest new pathways we might evolve along in our own distinctive way.

In the concluding chapter of *Pig Earth*, John Berger (1979) identifies a basic difference that separates modern cultures from tradition-oriented primal cultures. He notes that peoples who live within the limits of their bioregion tend not to be experimental in terms of new ideas, values, and technologies; nor do they view the future as an ever-expanding horizon of new possibilities. As a people who have survived where others have perished, their chief concern is to hand on to the next generation the means of survival, which means ideas, values, and technologies that have been proven within the context of their own lives. The exemplary models or analogs for how to live are thus located in the past, but the obligations are to insure that the possibilities for survival of future generations have not been diminished by current practices. Berger points out that the Western approaches to modernization are based on the opposite way of thinking. We view the future in terms of expanding knowledge, power, and consumer conveniences; that we might already be close to the margins of survival in terms of availability of topsoil, uncontaminated water and air, and other nonrenewable resources is not a concern of most modern thinkers. For example, Rorty makes experimentation with ideas and values the highest achievement of the ironist individual; in fact, he represents moral and intellectual relativism as synonymous with progress.

Another contrasting characteristic of primal cultures is the manner in which their root metaphors (epic narratives, mythic accounts of origins, etc.) situate humans *within* the natural world, rather than separate from it or in a hierarchical relationship in which humans are given a privileged position that allows the rest of the biotic community to be treated as a "natural resource." The root metaphors are constitutive of the cultural group's way of knowing, sense of moral obligation, and use of technology—just as our root metaphors have been the foundations upon which our cultural beliefs and technological practices rest. One of the implications of primal root metaphors that represent humans as interdependent with other life forms, while avoiding the separate conceptual categories that keep certain forms of knowledge and technological practices isolated from moral considerations, is that their technological practices are guided by their understanding of moral and spiritual relationships. In effect, the technological, moral, and spiritual are not separate domains of experience; it should also be pointed out that their knowledge of local habitats often represents a depth of knowledge and technical skill that exceeds what is now possessed by all but the most specialized modern person (and the modern expert generally has a very narrow range of competency).

The last characteristic that will be used as a basis for asking about the relevance of Rorty's thinking for living in sustainable balance with the ecosystem has to do with how primal cultures have chosen the pathways of developing the spiritual languages of dance, song, narrative, and art rather than the more political pathways that characterize Western cultures. These spiritual languages, as Gary Snyder (1980) points out, are a cultural storage of collected and tested wisdom about how to live in a balanced relationship with the rest of the biotic community. That is, the spiritual languages provide the moral/political/spiritual templates for regulating group life. In effect, primal cultures appear to have evolved in a way that expanded the symbolic world for its members, while reducing the political domain. They also provide members of the culture a means of active participation in the celebration, sanctification, and renewal of these highly metaphorized templates. Lastly, it should be pointed out that participation in these spiritual languages does not require the degradation of the physical environment, which has not been the case in our efforts to provide for the forms of happiness and success demanded by the self-creative form of individualism that seems to be at the center of popular culture.

The difference that separates the form of liberal culture needed to maximize the freedom of Rorty's ironist individual from primal cultures who use their marginal bioregions to construct complex symbolic worlds brings into question another assumption Rorty takes for granted. The characteristics of thought Rorty associates with the ironist individual contribute to politicizing more areas of cultural life—which appears to be the exact opposite of the situation in ecologically sustainable cultures. That is, questioning the final vocabularies and common sense that provide the sense of authority (taken-for-grantedness) for the patterns that guide daily practices has the effect of relativizing them. Questioning the cosmology and ceremonies that maintain the temple system for regulating the irrigation water essential to the ecosystems of Bali, to cite a concrete example, might create more ironist individuals (Rorty's goal), but it would threaten the food-production patterns that are dependent upon the complex integration of social and natural cycles worked out over the past several centuries by the Balinese. Furthermore, if every individual emulated Rorty's ironist as a cultural model, the relativizing process would be extended by the need of individuals to rely upon their own interpretations and need for self-creation. The political process of reconstituting the patterns upon which relationships are to be based and resources allocated would thus become even more fractious. But Rorty does not acknowledge this problem. The difficulty of achieving new grounds of consensus opens the door to a form of politics based on the illusion that technicist solutions are politically neutral. Either way, the epistemological foundations of Rorty's liberalism would contribute to furthering an experimental approach to the political process, rather than using the political process within a moral framework committed to sustaining and improving ecologically viable cultural patterns

The basic issue posed by primal cultures' ability, and our inability to live in sustainable balance not just within our bioregion but within the earth's ecosystems, is whether primal cultures are more relevant guides to the future than the ideas of a philosopher who is totally unaware that the fate of humans is dependent upon the fate of other forms of life that make up the biotic community. The forms of knowledge recognized by primal cultures are very close to what Bateson is getting at when he says the mental characteristics are immanent in the system as a whole, and to what Dogen, the Zen master, meant when he answered his own question, "Whoever told people that 'Mind' means thoughts, opinions, ideas, and concepts?" by saying "Mind means trees, fence posts, tiles, and grasses" (quoted in Snyder, 1990, p. 20). This view of knowledge does not lead to final vocabularies, in Rorty's use of the phrase, but it does put in focus what should be understood as the principal relationships.

Chapter 12

Cultural Diversity and the Ecological Crisis

Addressing the Double Binds in Teacher Education

The two major changes that will dominate the educational/political scene over the decades ahead—the growing awareness (and pride) in distinct cultural identities and the ecological crisis—should not be viewed by teacher-educators as pulling them in opposite directions. While on one level the two phenomena may appear to be separate and distinct, and thus requiring different responses, they are, in fact, related. Both, for quite different reasons, signal that the assumptions underlying modern culture are no longer sustainable. The viability of the earth's ecosystems is being seriously threatened by the technological practices and ever-expanding demands on nonrenewable "resources" deemed necessary by the modern individual. And the myth of personal success that prompted generations of people to turn their backs on the web of relationships and patterns that constituted their ethnic heritage by entering the competitive and highly individualistic mainstream culture is now becoming increasingly illusory. Unemployment, drug use, alienation, structural poverty, stress, and toxin-induced illnesses represent the reality that now overshadows this myth. The flaws in this modern form of consciousness are now being challenged by both environmentalists and groups attempting to recover their ethnic identities—African Americans, Hispanics, and Native Americans (Sioux, Nez Percé, Cheyenne, etc.). To put it another way, the ecological crisis and the emergence of ethnic consciousness have their roots in the same dominant cultural values and practices that are now seen as increasingly problematic.

The ecological crisis and the challenge of achieving a genuinely multicultural society (as opposed to using the rhetoric of "multiculturalism" to mask the continuing dominance of the Eurocentric mind-set) are connected in two other ways that must be understood by teacher-educators.

To focus only on culturally responsive approaches to teacher education, in the belief that the problem of cultural diversity should now be the primary focus, overlooks the multiple ways that the degradation of ecosystems impacts those cultural groups who are already the most politically and economically disadvantaged. Technologies that spew out toxic wastes are often located in areas inhabited by these politically and economically disadvantaged ethnic groups. The fouled atmosphere of urban areas impacts these ethnic groups more than the white middle class, who tend to live in the suburbs. And the groups who are most likely to experience the greatest economic impact resulting from a declining resource base and from changes in environmentally disruptive technologies are ethnic minorities. In effect, they are more exposed to the consequences of environmental destruction. Thus, it would not be too simplistic to assert that addressing the cultural practices contributing to a degraded habitat is an indirect way of dealing with the problem of social injustice in a multicultural society.

The other connection between the ecological crisis and the meeting of diverse cultural traditions is even less understood, even though it may represent one of the most powerful justifications for a multicultural society. The Eurocentric mind-set, with its human/nature dichotomy, its emphasis on competitive individualism and technological/economic practices, and its experimental approach to ideas and values (guaranteed by a belief that change is inherently progressive), is clearly not ecologically sustainable over the long term. With mainstream cultural beliefs and practices now being recognized as part of the ecological crisis, there is a need for a wider understanding of cultural patterns (ways of knowing, technological practices, communal relationships) that are sustainable. Many of the cultural groups who have not abandoned their traditions in order to attain the autonomous individuality celebrated by mainstream culture (and preyed upon by commercial interests) continue to sustain practices, values, and forms of knowledge that are more ecologically viable. The valuing of extended family relationships (including the sense of interdependence), ceremonies that provide members an expanded sense of meaning and identity, and the oral traditions that serve to strengthen the community of memory and frame commitments to unborn generations—all these seem essential to living more interdependent lives and stand as ecologically sound alternatives to the substitute forms of gratification that characterize a consumption-addicted society.

Some ethnic groups (particularly American Indian cultures) have developed complex symbolic representations of how humans are intertwined with animals, plants, and all the other elements of a multilayered cosmos. Their diverse ways of understanding citizenship within the larger biotic community represent powerful and particularly relevant analogs that help illuminate cultural pathways previously not recognized by Eurocentric cultural groups. The multiple forms of cultural storage they have developed for insuring that the moral/spiritual analogs of how to live in sustainable relationships also represent a legacy that other cultural groups can learn from. Just as the European immigrants learned valuable lessons about a democratic and representative form of government from the chiefs of the Iroquois nations, we might learn what Franklin and the others failed to grasp in their meetings with the chiefs—namely, that the political/moral community must encompass all forms of life. We might also learn something about the nature of moral education (which avoids the pitfalls and wrong-headedness of both values clarification and Kohlberg's stages of moral development) and how metaphorical thinking can serve to strengthen the sense of interdependence rather than to represent the environment as a "natural resource." This legacy, as well as the sustaining cultural patterns of other groups, is still fragile, and might be further subverted by teachers who are both in denial about the ecological crisis and committed to socializing ethnic students to the seemingly progressive and liberal beliefs that underpin the mainstream culture.

In the area of education, the cognitive foundations of modernism (the individual who is perceived as free of cultural baggage, the reductionist way of viewing the component parts of cause-and-effect relationships, the association of knowledge with "mental" processes that can be made explicit, the view that education is a matter of acquiring objective information and factual knowledge) are also creating a unique set of double binds. The more objective scientific and technicist educational practices become, the less students become educated in a reflective sense that would enable them to become aware of their own taken-for-granted cultural patterns. This double bind becomes particularly visible (i.e., expressed in early dropping out and alienation) among students with a strong ethnic identity. This educational double bind also contributes to the effect that mainstream cultural patterns have on diminishing the prospects of future generations.

In my own attempts to address the phenomenon of the double bind in teacher education, I discovered a unique set of problems that make culturally and linguistically sensitive reforms difficult to achieve. As a member of a teacher-education department that had an established record of adapting its program to take account of every major innovation that swept the country—career education, competency-based teaching, mastery learning, the Holmes Report, and so forth—I assumed there might be a similar receptivity to rethinking those aspects of the program that seemed at odds with the growing awareness that society is becoming increasingly multicultural in a way that defied the old solution of a melting pot that transformed differences into the respectable patterns of the white middle class. But discussions of how a teacher-education program could address both multiculturalism and the ecological crisis by exposing future teachers to an in-depth understanding of cultural and linguistic patterns in the learning and communication processes that characterize the classroom, as well as an understanding of the non-neutrality of technology (print, computers, such social techniques as mastery learning and behaviorism), quickly brought home the realization that the faculty was receptive only to innovations that fit the technicist mode of thought. They had great difficulty in taking a genuine cultural and linguistic turn in their thinking about the foundations of teacher education. The discussion of culture was reduced to the old clichés about recognizing "individual differences." The discussion of language could not transcend the conventional view that it is a symbol system for communicating objective information and the individual's own thoughts. And the possibility that teachers might be introduced to understanding the culturally specific mediating characteristics of technology was transformed into proposals for greater exposure in how to use overhead projectors and different computer applications in the classroom. But the problem goes beyond the inability of a teacher education faculty to reconstitute the epistemological foundations that led to an industrial model of teacher education.

One of the achievements of modern culture has been to hide from consciousness an awareness of culture—its taken-for-granted patterns, contextual nature, and multiple layers. The problem of taking seriously the cultural/linguistic foundations of human experience is further complicated by the view that many teacher-educators have of themselves as being progressive, cutting-edge, humanitarian thinkers. In effect, the ecological crisis, and the recognition that cultural differences mean profoundly different ways of knowing and valuing, turn the ideology of modernism on its head. That modernism is now a reactionary position seems too difficult to grasp—and too much against the grain of daily experience. Yet it is these aspects of the problem, which challenge in the most fundamental ways the modern idea that rational thought is simply a matter of making sense of the evidence, that must be understood if we are going to address the challenge of evolving ecologically sustainable forms of culture.

The specific nature of the double binds that contribute to ecologically destructive cultural practices was clearly visible in the taken-for-granted ways of thinking I encountered among students going into our fifth-year education program. These same patterns of thinking are equally visible in textbooks, educational software, journal articles on teaching methods (even innovative and supposedly progressive classroom practices), and the many approaches that characterize the amorphous field of staff development. It should also be recognized that many of the patterns of thinking I will be identifying as the source of the cultural/ecological crisis are reinforced in other university departments. The problem is much broader than teacher education, but there it stands out more clearly as a critical issue because teachers are engaged (supposedly) in a more self-conscious and reflective approach to the cultural, linguistic, and cognitive processes we call education. To put it more simply, the medium shared by students and teachers is a cultural one. And this has special implications in terms of their professional decision making.

The following six areas of misunderstanding seem especially critical to professional decision making in the classroom, and to the specific problems of multiculturalism and the alarming rate of environmental degradation:

1. *Teachers are continually serving as mediators in the cultural transmission process, but most teacher-education programs do not provide an in-depth understanding of culture as a symbolic ecology.* If students are going to understand their relationship with the environment and with one another, they will need to understand the multiple dimensions of culture. But most teachers I have encountered reinforce in the classroom a culturally specific way of knowing that represents the rational process as individualistic and a correspondence view of language in which ideas stand for the external world of objects and events. These epistemological biases serve to reinforce the more widely held commonsense view of the individual as a spectator of an external world. The response to this external world may be rational or emotive, but according to prevailing mythic thinking it is individually chosen, which may contribute to the despair of those teachers who want students to make informed judgments. This reinforcement of a cultural orientation to how the individual self is understood as an autonomous agent is part of the double bind of a cultural pattern that makes itself invisible.

Teacher-education programs need to become more culturally centered; that is, to help teachers understand that forms of intelligence, communication, behavior, self-identity, and technical practice are expressions of shared cultural patterns. This claim of the deep presence of culture in human experience does not preclude the possibility of highly individualized expressions of shared cultural patterns. In terms of professional decision making in a multicultural classroom, and in helping students recognize cultural patterns that misrepresent the sustaining capacities of natural systems, there seem to be several aspects of culture that are more critically important than others.

The first has to do with understanding how cultural patterns are generally experienced as part of the person's natural attitude (or taken-for-granted sense of everyday reality). This sounds simple, but it is actually one of the most difficult aspects of culture to translate into classroom practice. There are also the pedagogical decisions relating to knowing which taken-for-granted values, beliefs, and technical practices to make explicit. A second aspect of culture that needs to be part of the teacher's professional knowledge has to do with the complex processes associated with cultural storage; that is, how forms of symbolic representation are encoded (stored) in objects, technologies, and patterns of communication (dress, body language, architecture, spoken and written discourse, etc.). Cultural storage can also be understood as the living (and outmoded) traditions of a cultural group; or to put it another way, as part of the temporal dimension of the shared mental ecology.

Recognizing that the scientific method, a technology such as the computer or the automobile, and one's self-concept have grown out of a specific cultural way of knowing (and that that way of knowing may have been based on deeply held taken-for-granted assumptions about the separation of humanity and nature or an evolutionary view of human/ cultural development) seems critical to being able to understand the problems of intercultural education and to addressing the even more vexing problem of environmentally destructive cultural practices. To put it another way, teachers need to have a deeper and more complex understanding of how tradition serves as a medium of cultural storage. The ability to make explicit for students the symbolic way of understanding of previous generations seems essential to understanding the nature of current cultural patterns and to addressing the question of whether the patterns will leave future generations with a diminished habitat. Unfortunately, more courses on natural systems and teaching about recycling will not begin to compensate for the destructive consequences of an educational process that retains a professional silence on the constitutive role that culture plays in human experience.

2. Teachers tend to misrepresent the culture/language/thought connection by treating language as a conduit through which ideas and "factual" information are passed. Consequently, they fail to recognize professional decisions relating to the metaphorical nature of language and thought. The conduit image of language is also an expression of a complex set of cultural traditions, but it deserves separate treatment in our discussion of teacher-education programs. As I have already written a great deal on the implications of the metaphorical nature of the language/thought connection for decision making in the classroom (1984; 1988; with D. Flinders, 1990), I will summarize the issues that relate most directly to those aspects of language that create a double bind in addressing multiculturalism and the ecological crisis.

The double bind for teachers (and subsequently for students) results from treating language as a conduit into which they put their representations and meanings. In recent years language has become more fully understood as metaphorical in nature; that is, it encodes the schema of understanding that serves as an initial way of understanding novel situations and of reinforcing previously held ways of understanding. To summarize the essential relationships, the process of analogic thinking is framed by the master or root metaphors of a cultural group (which may also be referred to as worldview, paradigm, etc.). A mechanistic root metaphor, for example, is part of the encoding process that emerges from the process of analogic thinking (such as thinking of computers as like "artificial intelligence" and the heart as a "pump"). The process of analogic thinking that prevails over others becomes, over time, the taken-for-granted schema, or image (iconic metaphor), that "thinks us" as we think and express "ourselves." The following textbook explanation (Visual Education Corporation, 1985, p. 37) serves as an example of how metaphors encode the mentality or form of intelligence expressed in earlier processes of analogic thinking that were framed by even more deeply embedded root metaphors: "The first step in choosing *your work* is to set some goals" (emphasis added). Among all the metaphorical images strung together in this sentence (thought), we can recognize at least two distinct schemata of understanding that were worked out in earlier dialectic processes of root metaphor/analogic thinking: "your" as expressing an autonomous agent that makes choices, "work" as an activity involving the exercise of a skill and the output of "energy" that will be remunerated.

If we want to consider how the intelligence/cultural patterns of earlier cultural groups influence current thought patterns, we have only to consider such expressions as "man and nature," "student as product," "natural resources," "intelligence testing," and "ecosystem." Although different cultural groups may share similar schemata of understanding, at some point in their conceptual/linguistic mapping processes there will be significant differences in their experiences that lead to such taken-for-granted iconic metaphors as "earth," "individualism," "community," "death," "tradition," and so forth being associated with fundamentally different ways of understanding.

Teaching in a multicultural classroom must take account of the possibility that students may possess, as part of their natural attitude, schemata of understanding framed by very different root metaphors from those that underpin the dominant technicist, consumer, individualistic, middle-class culture. By continuing to treat language as a culturally neutral conduit, teachers put themselves in the double bind of professing a sensitivity to multicultural education while engaging in the most subtle yet powerful forms of cultural domination.

The connection between metaphorical thinking and the problem of cultural demands exhausting the life-sustaining capacities of natural systems is even more critical. The mental process (cultural schema) encoded in such iconic metaphors as "individual success," "science," "technology," "progress," "freedom," and "Information Age" (to cite just a few examples) points to the problem that teachers must be able to recognize at this juncture in the process of cultural mediation that we call education. These metaphors, like so much of the storage of metaphorical thinking that constitutes the curriculum, were constituted at an earlier time when frontiers, resources, and progress seemed endless. The discovery of the "New World," the Industrial Revolution that followed from the "exploitation" (a positive term then) of natural resources, and the unification of scientific methods of investigation with the development of new technologies were made coherent and compelling through metaphorical thinking.

Evolving cultural patterns that are ecologically sustainable will require a taken-for-granted attitude toward different root metaphors— metaphors that represent humans as interdependent with the rest of the biotic community. And this will lead to reframing how we understand "individualism," "technology," "success," and so forth. Good intentions and viewing oneself as a progressive and socially conscious teacher are no substitute for understanding the connection between language, taken-for-granted patterns of thinking, and the very real possibility that we have only a few decades to change ecologically destructive practices. The consequences of not waking up to this double bind are beyond the scope of anything humans have experienced in the past.

3. *The view of community reinforced in the classroom reinforces an anthropocentric approach to the ecological crisis.* Most teachers are socialized to a culturally specific view of community that undermines efforts to evolve a more ecological sense of community. The cultural orthodoxy reinforced indirectly in teacher-education programs is that community is to be understood as a collection of autonomous individuals. The more direct accounts of how to think about community are found in textbooks,

where students may learn to think of community in terms of historical development, geographical context, and functional relationships (employment, services, etc.). These diverse representations, however, share a common cultural way of thinking that has roots deep in Western thought; namely, community is understood as humans living together. It can also be understood as an expression of anthropocentric thinking that creates a double bind in attempting to address the cultural roots of the ecological crisis. This anthropocentric orientation also puts American Indian students (that is, those who have retained their cultural group's core beliefs) in an even more complex double bind.

The view of community is directly related to how the individual is understood. Thus a new (or recovery of a more ancient) way of understanding community will affect what it means to be an individual. A variety of theoretical frameworks can be used to argue that the Cartesian (and Lockean) view of the individual is wrong-headed and ecologically destructive. The sociology of knowledge, social linguistics, a Batesonian ecological model, or even the Buddhist doctrine that everything is linked in an intricate, interdependent web (making individual autonomy—and self-creation—an impossibility) can be used to challenge the view of the creative, autonomous individual that still seems to be the prevailing orthodoxy in many teacher-education programs. But perhaps the most compelling argument for a radically different view of community has been articulated by Aldo Leopold, who lays out the evidence that humans are part of a larger information and energy web. That is, humans are interdependent members within the larger biotic community, which also includes topsoil, aquifers, and so forth. This enlarged, nonanthropocentric view of community has profound implications for reframing the nature of moral responsibility to the other forms of life that share a bioregion. Leopold gives us a Golden Rule for ecological survival that might serve as a basis for constituting ways of thinking and behaving that are sustainable over the long term. Writes Leopold: "A thing is right when it tends to preserve the integrity, stability, and beauty of the biotic community. It is wrong when it tends otherwise" (1970, p. 262).

Teacher-education programs are not likely to become sites for deep discussions of the educational implications of Leopold's land ethic. But it is reasonable to expect faculty to address how their operational view of individualism relates to understanding the nature of community, and by extension, the form of education that contributes to a sense of responsible citizenship within this community. This discussion needs to be framed in a manner that takes account of other cultural groups' way of understanding community and, most importantly, the long-term consequences of excluding from the moral community other forms of life upon which humans depend. As there are few analogs in the larger society of nonexploitive and nonwasteful relationships with the rest of the biotic community, the classroom might serve as a setting where students and teachers could develop a fuller understanding of how (and why) the sense of community became so narrowly anthropocentric in Western thought, how ecologically sustainable cultures have understood community, and how these sustainable cultures stored and passed on the moral analogs for living in sustainable relationships within a larger sense of community. This might serve as a basis for the recovery and development of moral analogs within the dominant culture.

4. *Teachers tend to reinforce the cultural myths that represent technology both as culturally neutral and as an expression of modern progress. Both ways of understanding technology work against a multicultural approach to the classroom, and against being able to recognize forms of technology that are environmentally destructive.* Although technology is viewed in the dominant culture as either neutral (as a tool or technique whose user decides its purpose) or as an expression of progress, it actually contributes to yet another cultural double bind. It is particularly problematic when this double bind becomes part of classroom socialization. Again, the teacher's understanding of the cultural patterns to which students are being exposed becomes critical. Teachers deal with technology as part of the curriculum (at both the explicit and implicit levels) and use it as part of the teaching/learning process. The latter involves use of complex social techniques, print and other media-based discourse, and, increasingly, computers. It is both part of the background of every educational situation, and often mediates the processes of communication. Technology also influences the forms of knowledge students will encounter and, at the same time, eliminates other aspects of cultural experience from being considered. Given the evidence of the non-neutrality of technology, and that its progressive nature must be judged against the increasing evidence of environmental disruption, it is surprising (*shocking* might be a more appropriate term) that most teachers still uphold these mythic ways of thinking about technology.

Because a cultural way of thinking about technology is part of the curriculum, and so much of teaching involves the use of different forms of technology, a strong case can be made that teachers need to be exposed in a more explicit and critical way to understanding the cultural non-neutrality of technology. They also need the opportunity to consider the cultural assumptions built into the dominant culture's approach to technology, how these assumptions relate to the destruction of ecosystems, and, conversely, the forms of technology that amplify those aspects of human thought, behavior, and relationships that are minimally disruptive.

Briefly, a consideration of what we experience through the use of a technology helps to illuminate the distinctive mediating (that is, existentially and culturally non-neutral) characteristics. For example, communicating through electronic–mail may not be meaningful for cultural groups who are accustomed to more contextual and relational forms of communication. Computer technology amplifies rapid and accurate sender/receiver communication in which explicit messages are reduced to bits of discreet information. In terms of its amplification/reduction characteristics, it can be said to prevent tacit, contextual, and analog forms of knowledge from being communicated. We can also see how technologies such as the alphabet emphasized vision over the other senses, analytic and decontextualized thinking over communal participation, and so forth. The point is that technologies, by virtue of their characteristics, alter human experience. And their use is framed (and driven) by deep cultural assumptions. If we approach the scientific method as an example of a technique that cannot be separated from a specific set of cultural assumptions, we can see that the desire to understand what this interpretative framework illuminates is grounded in deep and often unconsciously held cultural patterns of thought. For example, some advocates of scientific investigation will argue that it involves a disinterested, non-technologically driven pursuit of knowledge for its own sake, others may argue that it is essential to human progress, and still others may connect the scientific method with the highest expression of a rationally based existence. Each of these justifications for the "will to knowledge" (some might say "power") reflects a cultural orientation that becomes more visible when we compare the secularizing and reductionist pattern of thinking required by this mode of inquiry with what other cultural groups regard as sacred and whole.

This example of a technique's possessing cultural amplification and reduction characteristics was deliberately chosen because many teacher-education programs are represented as scientific and technologically based, and thus as being politically and culturally neutral. This stance should now yield to that of a teacher-education faculty that is more reflective about what teachers should understand, as part of their professional knowledge, about the cultural nature and ecological consequences of technology.

5. *The liberal ideological orientations that guide the more socially conscious teachers, while appearing to be progressive, actually strengthen cultural practices that weaken cultural diversity and degrade the environment. As I have*

written extensively on the limitations of various streams of educational liberalism in the postmodern world we are now entering (1987) and the inadequacy of the conservatism of Allan Bloom, Mortimer Adler, and other advocates of reviving the Western canon (1992), I will summarize only those aspects of the argument that illuminate how the ecological crisis and the awakening of people to their cultural identities make liberalism a reactionary position. Although classroom teachers often embrace an ideological patchwork of guiding assumptions about the nature of reality, it is nevertheless possible to recognize a shared set of bedrock assumptions that have served as the foundations of modern liberalism. The technocratic, emancipatory, neoromantic, and just plain mainstream teacher who believes in the American dream of individual success all accept the following assumptions as common sense: The individual is the basic social unit, and the purpose of the educational process is to contribute to some form of rational empowerment and self-direction; the world must be understood in terms of human needs and sense of purpose; the human/social sense of time is experienced as a continuum where the future represents an ever-widening sphere of opportunities and progress and the past is considered as either an impediment or so entirely irrelevant that it can be ignored; and lastly, the progressive nature of change makes continual experimentation with new ideas, values, and technologies a matter of common sense that separates the modern person from the culturally backward. While teachers may overlay these foundational liberal assumptions with more specific personal and group agendas (emphasis on behavioral outcomes, developing critical thought, learning factual knowledge, etc.), most of them would also take for granted that these assumptions should be the basis for educating all students. That is, they subscribe to the tenet of modern liberalism that wants to extend its progressive interpretation of modernization to the entire world.

The irony today is that many of the cultures increasingly represented in the classroom have remained viable in the face of the society's homogenization pressures because they have refused to accept the foundational tenets of liberalism. The retention or recovery of their own language and the conscious practice of traditional patterns (including valuing a sense of responsibility to the extended family and cultural group) are expressions of cultural conservatism. For them, the commonsense attitude toward the past is to view it as the source of traditions that are lived in the present and that will provide the analogs or templates that will serve as guides into an uncertain future. Some of these forms of cultural conservatism (e.g. Asian American, Jewish American, and Hispanic cultural groups) share the anthropocentrism of modern liberalism (but for reasons that are quite different for Confucian-based cultural groups), while others, such as various American Indian cultures, do not. To put the double bind in its simplest form of expression: Teachers who proclaim the importance of multicultural education, and who consciously or unconsciously embrace the foundational assumptions of liberalism, cannot avoid turning the educational process into an exercise in political/cultural conversion.

I suspect that cultural identities (even in ideal circumstances) cannot be pure and unadulterated (I would prefer to think of this blurring process in terms similar to a person having a first and second language —and perhaps even a third language). But as important as it is, the prospects of a multicultural society must still be put in perspective. The most challenging problem posed by the various expressions of educational liberalism relates to the ecological crisis. Exceeding the life-sustaining capacities of the earth's ecosystems is the most fundamental issue we face, and when this is recognized, the nature of the double bind caused by liberal assumptions reminds us of the early Greek understanding of tragedy, where strengths, when carried to an extreme, become the sources of decline and death. When framed against the decline of species diversity, loss of topsoil, and poisoning of soil, water, and atmosphere, the promises of technological progress, human emancipation and freedom, and the expansion in emotional well-being and longevity sound increasingly problematic, since these successes can only be achieved through further exploitation of the environment. Instead of progress and continual experimentation, we will need to frame cultural practices in terms of political metaphors that foreground the importance of conserving values and practices. To put it another way, long-term sustainability will more likely be achieved through various forms of an ecoconservative ideology (culture) than through liberalism.

As control of teacher-education programs often represents the competing interests of technocratic and emancipating liberals (with a few anthropocentric-type conservatives thrown in), the ecological crisis poses a particularly difficult challenge. The shift from an emphasis on change, experimentation, and the authority of technical experts or individual judgment, to an emphasis on passing on sustainable values and practices, and an awareness of being dependent upon a larger energy and information ecology, will require the most fundamental changes in thinking. Indeed, teacher-education faculties cannot be expected to be the principal agents of this cultural transformation. But it would not be too unreasonable to expect them to begin recognizing the problematic nature of the liberal assumptions that now underlie most aspects of teacher education (as many of them have begun to rethink how gender bias permeated so many aspects of teacher education). Nor would it be unreasonable to expect them to be more open to the analogs that are part of the commonsense attitudes of more ecologically sustainable cultural groups, and to more public discussions of the cultural dimension of the ecological crisis.

   6. The continued privileging of high-status forms of knowledge in the classroom will further strengthen cultural practices that exceed the sustaining capacity of natural systems, and further discriminate against the forms of knowledge valued by other cultural groups. Depending upon their own ideological orientations, teachers reinforce the forms of knowledge appropriate to the status system of different sectors within the dominant culture: the forms of knowledge favored by the technological/economic sector, the humanistic traditions favored by the university community, and the knowledge related to life skills and life experience favored by teachers who are primarily focused on the self-development and self-expression of the individual. There is, of course, a mixing of these genres in many classrooms. But what is prominent in all of them is the "expanding the frontiers" mentality, where the promise is that learning a particular way of knowing will extend the frontiers of technology, human self-expression, freedom, and (teachers continue to hope) rationality. Knowledge of the characteristics and interdependencies of the bioregion, knowledge of how to live in relationships that minimize the impact on the larger biotic community, and knowledge of technological practices that take account of the nature of the ecological vulnerabilities in which they are used, will not be part of the curriculum in most classrooms. Nor will students encounter the forms of knowledge (including moral analogs) that ecologically responsive cultures encode in their narrative traditions, songs, dances, and dramatic rituals.

   The problem of high-status forms of knowledge being made problematic by the ecological crisis confronts us with a set of issues that go beyond the capacities of teacher-education faculties. But the long-term consequences of the dominant culture's increasing demands on increasingly degraded ecosystems should now be obvious enough to teacher-educators that they would begin addressing the connection between what is taught through the formal and informal curriculum and the declining condition of our environment. They might also begin to consider the possibilities of using new guidelines for the selection and organization of relevant knowledge. For example, instead of using an anthropocentric schema for organizing our understanding of historical development, perhaps we should consider an ecological model wherein the history of new ideas, technologies, and other "advances" are understood in terms of their impact on local and regional ecosystems. For example, what changes in the conditions of soils, water, ground cover, and species diversity resulted from the introduction of a particular set of master ideas, like Christianity, Cartesianism or Marxism? How did the European settlers change the ecosystems in the "New World"? What has been the impact of an industrial model of agriculture on topsoil and aquifers? Another guiding principle in the selection of ecologically relevant knowledge might be to give more attention to passing on folk practices and technologies that have enabled people to live a sustainable existence without the need for exploiting the reserves of other bioregions. A third guiding principle might be to consider how the biases incorporated into the Western humanistic tradition have served to denigrate cultures that have evolved along more ecologically sustainable pathways.

The privileging of certain forms of knowledge in the classroom is also critical to how education within the context of multiple cultural groups gets worked out. The "expanding frontiers" mentality of the dominant culture is not shared by all cultural groups; and, as pointed out earlier, many of the minority cultures have developed technologies and forms of knowledge more attuned to maintaining the dynamic balance within ecosystems. If metaphors such as "sustainability" and "ecology" can become more prominent in the thinking about teacher education, perhaps we can then begin to bring together multiculturalism and the ecological crisis in our thinking about the content of the curriculum. If this new discourse does not emerge as part of teachers' professional education, it is likely they will rely upon the taken-for-granted patterns of thinking acquired as part of their own educational experience. And these patterns, for the most part, encode the status distinctions that are part of the Western anthropocentric mythology.

The nature of the double bind, to reiterate the central point, must be understood in terms of the growing disparity between the ideals of the modern era and current changes in consciousness and habitat. The ideals of modernism were basically imperialistic in that their realization required assimilation into the technological/consumer mainstream culture, and imperialistic in the sense that the natural world was surveyed as a "resource" to be exploited for immediate economic ends. The ideal of further individual empowerment, generally measured in terms of material well-being, represented the form of intelligence attuned to the social and political projects that were the driving source of energy over the last two to three centuries. The reemergence of cultural identities that have their own pathways of development (as opposed to occupying a distinct stage in the linear development of a modern, progressive form

of consciousness—like an "underdeveloped" or "backward" culture wait-
ing to be lifted to the level of literacy) can be viewed as a challenge to
the mono-intelligence of modernism. The growing recognition of multiple forms of intelligence parallels the recent awareness that the modern mind-set, for all its emphasis on basing thought on information, over-
estimated the power of technology to sustain the dream of unending
progress and underestimated its disruptive impact on entire ecosystems.
Further attempts to utilize the basic premises underlying the modern
mind-set, whether in the areas of technological/economic development,
social policy, or teacher education, will involve adopting a reactionary
stance—that is, attempting to return to the imperialistic mind-set associated with the spread of modernism that accompanied the Industrial Revolution.

While the double bind may be transcended through the recognition
of multiple forms of intelligence (culture), and by framing current reform
efforts in terms of the criterion of long-term sustainability within a worldwide interdependent network of ecosystems, teacher-educators will not
have available to them the stock of ready-made conceptual guidelines
that enabled them in the past to focus primarily on problems associated
with technological implementation. The acknowledgment that cultural
differences can no longer be interpreted in terms of a theory of cultural
deprivation, and that the modern pathway to economic/technological
development has in fact been an experiment with natural systems that
was understood in terms of misleading metaphors, gives us a clearer
sense of what aspects of the past we should not repeat than answers to
questions that we can now only partially formulate. We are, indeed, in a
state of liminality where we are "betwixt and between" the received
answers of the past and answers that help to assure the future of the larger
biotic community of which we are a part.

Given this condition of liminality, the steps we can take in finding
an ecologically sustainable sense of direction in the reform of teacher
education include (1) sustaining an ongoing conversation that provides
an opportunity to reconsider the guiding premises of teacher education
and (2) encouraging communication between teacher-education faculty
and faculty in disciplines where issues of culture and environment are
central concerns. The nature of the double binds identified here might
serve as one starting point in this process of thinking and talking a new
guiding paradigm into existence. Although these suggestions seem modest
in comparison with the challenges we face, taking these first steps will
be the real test of just how complex and difficult the process of transforming consciousness really is, even when we recognize that our future
survival is at stake.

Chapter 13

Toward a Deep Cultural Approach to Environmental Education

What Urban Teachers Can Learn from Traditional Cultures

Urban planners are beginning to address the multiple crises caused by the burgeoning population through policies that reflect a growing ecological awareness. The initiation of recycling programs, efforts to empower local neighborhoods, retrofitting public buildings for renewable (or less polluting) forms of energy, and developing less ecologically damaging transportation systems are examples of current efforts to green our cities. But are similar efforts being made to green the urban classroom? The argument might be made that urban planners are simply engaged in crisis management, and that if they do not address the problems of pollution and inefficient use of energy the resulting increase in crime, loss of jobs, disease, and civic unrest will make urban life intolerable—and uncontrollable. Urban educators also must deal with the multiple crises of urban life—street violence, poverty, physical and psychological problems resulting from polluted air and inadequate housing, and so forth. The concern with drugs and firearms in the classroom, along with the less life-threatening challenges of students too unmotivated to take seriously the goals of the curriculum, it might be argued, may make the greening of the classroom seem irrelevant to the immediate challenges facing the urban teacher. The beliefs, values, and cultural practices that are communicated to students, and the question of whether they are part of the solution to the ecological crisis or part of the problem, are given lower priority by teachers—if they are considered at all.

As I have argued elsewhere in this collection, the ecological crisis (immediately manifested in toxic wastes and loss of employment opportunities) touches everyone's life, but the impact is greatest on the minority populations who live in urban areas where the greatest environmental abuses have been tolerated for decades. For example, 60% of

African American and Hispanic youth in the United States live near haz-
ardous waste sites; and in urban areas they are twice as likely to be
exposed to dangerous levels of lead poisoning than are white youth.
Although seemingly far removed from the immediate challenges of
urban life, the loss of fish stocks, topsoil, clean water, species diversity,
and so forth will have an impact on all urban dwellers—particularly as
population growth in other bioregions of the world leads to the collapse
of already fragile ecosystems. David Orr's observation that "all education is environmental education" (1992, p. 90) can be interpreted to mean
that everything taught in schools influences how students understand
the human culture/natural environment relationship. Unfortunately, the
curriculum reinforces the dominant cultural orientation that represents
the environment as a resource for humans.

If implemented, Orr's recommendation that classrooms foster "ecological literacy" would help contribute to overcoming the dominant myth,
perpetuated in mainstream culture, that social progress is primarily a
function of maintaining a permanent state of disequilibrium between
technological innovation and consumer demand. Ecological literacy, as
he defines it, involves three components: (1) fostering "a broad understanding of how people and societies relate to each other and to natural
systems, and how they might do so sustainably," (2) understanding the
"speed of the crisis that is upon us" (magnitude, rates and trends of
changes in ecosystems), and (3) a "broad familiarity with the development of ecological consciousness" (pp. 92–94). But like so much of environmental literature, ecological literacy might be viewed by many as an
opportunity to provide yet more "information" on the nature of the problem. This information, when framed in terms of how ecosystems work,
may provide a few students with momentary insights into what could
become the basis of a new (actually, an ancient) root metaphor for a radically different form of culture. But I suspect the insight will not be widely
shared, nor survive long in the streets and shopping malls where the
students continually encounter messages designed to sustain the current
cultural myths. The problem that Orr's recommendations help illuminate
is that we have a wealth of information about the destruction of species
and contamination of the environment, but we have few analogs of how
to live in a sustainable relationship with one another (including other supposedly less advanced cultural groups) and with the rest of the biotic
community.

Contrary to the current orthodoxy, which holds that information is
the basis of thought, people's lives are mostly based on cultural analogs—
and in terms of our society these taken-for-granted patterns encode the
Western cultural assumptions that represent the environment as an infi-

nitely exploitable resource. These analogs are sustained after the student leaves the classroom where there might have been an interesting (and perhaps alarming) discussion about the rate at which species are disappearing. Because the problem of the prevailing "natural attitude" toward everyday life will be a challenge to every approach we take to ecological literacy, I think it is especially critical that a deep cultural approach to environmental education be based on presenting students (and others) with analogs that can become the basis of an ecologically sustainable form of existence. But the recommendation that we supplement information about changes in ecosystems with cultural analogs for living in sustainable patterns creates a major problem for urban educators.

While many folk traditions of minority cultural groups kept alive patterns that contributed to a sense of community and fulfilled psychological/social needs without contributing to major disruptions in the habitat, these traditions have not been perceived as high-status forms of knowledge. Thus they have largely been marginalized in terms of the school curriculum. Even more critical is the fact that little attention has been given to how various folk traditions impacted the natural environment. Since the deep wisdom and practical guides stored in the vernaculars of folk knowledge have been ignored, discussions of ecologically sustainable cultures now are limited either to traditional cultural groups as they existed before being subverted by the fetishes of Western consumerism, or intentional communities that are attempting to adapt their lifestyles to the characteristics of their bioregion. Both types of cultural groups provide an important source of analog knowledge of how to live rich symbolic lives while reducing physical demands to a level that leaves the environment habitable for future generations. But the critical question is whether modern, urban people can learn anything from them that could become the basis for changing the patterns upon which their own lives are based. To put the question somewhat differently, can premodern ecologically oriented cultures be viewed as a source of analog knowledge for modern cultures? And would learning from them take the form of copying their patterns of technology, ceremonies, and eating habits? That is, can we learn, in a way other than by copying, how to use their knowledge of fundamental relationships to reconstitute our own patterns?

I would like to challenge the conventional wisdom of the dominant intellectual and economic class who have contributed to our current environmentally destructive path by arguing that premodern cultural groups may possess the forms of understanding essential to the radical reform of our own approach to education. But in suggesting this, it is important to clarify the distinction between the symbolic motifs or themes shared by different cultures and the specific way a cultural group works them out in practice. For example, premodern ecologically sustainable cultures appear to share in common cosmologies transmitted as mythopoetic narratives that connect the destiny of humans with the destiny of other forms of life. But in suggesting that common motifs of ancient peoples have relevance to modern urban dwellers, I am not suggesting that we indoctrinate students of an at-risk urban culture with the specific Kwakiutl account of how animals and spirits lead lives that are exactly equivalent to those of humans or the Balinese practice of propitiating the process of growth by pouring a bottle of holy water onto the ground while speaking a mantra that names half a dozen deities. If we can focus on the shared motifs and patterns rather than the specific form of elaboration that gives traditional cultures their specific identities, I think we can identify a number of cultural analogs that have immediate relevance to urban populations who have become largely insulated from the natural world by modern technology—but who now face the twin threats of depleted energy resources and being overwhelmed by the waste products of a consumer-oriented culture.

The traditional cultures I find interesting examples of having evolved a particularly good record of living in relative balance with their habitat (that is, before they were impacted by Western cultures) include the Hopi, Koyukon, Kwakiutl, Balinese, and, of course, the tribal groups we know collectively as the Australian Aborigines. Modernization now poses difficult challenges for these cultural groups, not the least of which is the rapid loss of ancient knowledge as narrativizing becomes a less central aspect of communal life. Their resistance to modernization, particularly in the face of the deepening ecological crisis, helps frame the importance of the motifs and patterns they are attempting to sustain. The irony today is that the knowledge they evolved over centuries of learning to live as interdependent citizens of their biotic communities is largely disparaged or entirely ignored by a culture that is betting the future of unborn generations on highly experimental knowledge that only makes sense because of a myth that equates progress with the exploitation of nonrenewable resources. This point is being brought out here in order to emphasize that the ultimate test of a culture's symbolic world is not dependent upon the judgments of Western intellectuals, but upon whether it provides its members a symbolically meaningful existence in a manner that does not diminish the prospects of future generations. Modern urban peoples are accustomed to using criteria associated with the wide range of choices made available by our consumer-oriented society, high literacy rates, and the vast body of scientific knowledge that has increased our technological efficacy as the basis of assessing what constitutes a meaningful existence. Consequently, many of the characteristics of ecologically sustainable cultures will seem, at first, both strange and backward looking. But the use of modern criteria suggests how confused we have become about the most fundamental priorities of human/cultural existence.

MYTHOPOETIC NARRATIVES IN ECOLOGICALLY CENTERED CULTURES

A common characteristic (that is, ontological motif essential to how each cultural group centers and elaborates itself over time) is a mythopoetic narrative that frames how time, space, origins, and relationships with the Other are to be understood. While fundamentally different in the account of events that happened at the beginning of time, the forces that govern what now happens, and the principle of order that governs the future, the mythopoetic narratives of these different ecologically oriented cultures appear to perform the same essential functions. The stories of origins—whether we are considering "The Dreaming" of the Australian Aboriginal peoples, the Hopi creation myth, the Balinese understanding of how the three worlds came into being and are kept in balance, the life cycles of the Kwakiutl world sustained by spirit forces, or the Distant Time when Raven made the world of the Koyukon peoples—provide a sense of coherence that encompasses all aspects of psychic and social existence. Ways of knowing, relationships with others, self-definition, uses of technology, aesthetic expression, ways of organizing time and space, and attitudes toward death—all are part of a coherent whole whose authority is rooted in the natural attitude that goes with membership in a language/epistemological community and all have been tested against the challenges nature has thrown up over past centuries. It is also interesting to note that these cultures do not have institutionalized sanctuaries for intellectuals whose primary function is to sustain the dialectic of progressive change by demystifying the many ways the mythopoetic narratives provide the symbolic patterns to which human behavior is to conform.

The power of mythopoetic narratives to keep ecologically sustainable groups morally centered in terms of fundamental relationships can be seen in W. E. H. Stanner's (1979) account of The Dreaming, which explains the sacred origins of humans and nature:

> The tales are a kind of commentary, or statement, on what is thought to be permanent and ordained at the very basis of the world and life. They are a way of stating the principle which animates things. I would

call them a poetic key to Reality. The Aboriginal does not ask himself the philosophical-type questions: What is 'real'? How many 'kinds' of 'reality' are there? What are the 'properties' of 'reality'? How are the properties 'interconnected'? This is the idiom of Western intellectual discourse and the fruit of a certain social history. His tales are, however, a kind of answer to such questions so far as they have been asked at all. They may not be a 'definition', but they are a 'key' to reality, a key to the singleness and the plurality of things set up once-for-all when, in The Dreaming, the universe became man's universe. The active philosophy of Aboriginal life transforms this 'key', which is expressed in the idiom of poetry, drama, and symbolism, into a principle that The Dreaming determines not only what life is but also what it can be. Life, so to speak, is a one-possibility thing, and what this is, is the 'meaning' of The Dreaming. (p. 29)

The Kwakiutl have an entirely different set of mythopoetic narratives, which lead to the elaboration of different technologies, ceremonies, taboos, understanding of self, and so on. Yet they share a similar motif of a morally unified world, and the human need to sustain the balance (the reciprocal relationships) of the life forces within the world by living according to the principles laid out in the narratives. According to Stanley Walens (1981):

The Kwakiutl moral universe becomes united, not by any vague religious sense but by the fact that the entire universe contains all beings within its bounds, and that all beings are subject to the principle of being both hungry and the food of other beings who are themselves hungry. The Kwakiutl universe is a universe of related beings, all of whom have the moral responsibility to control their eating. Eating is a universal property of the world, and thus it is the basis for morality. . . . Sacredness occurs in all situations in which the spirits and/or their spirit-power is present. It can occur suddenly when a man is out hunting and a spirit comes into his presence. Such a situation is considered to be fraught with intense danger, and many texts speak of the blinding pain and death that the visits of spirits bring to unprepared and unprotected humans. The prayers, speeches, and songs with which a person codifies and thereby mediates his relationship to spirits are thus, in part, a defense against the overwhelming potency that spirit-power presents. Prayers thus simultaneously elicit the power of the spirits and direct it toward human benefit rather than destruction. Various ceremonial and ritual activities combine these methods in differing proportions. Everyday acts, such as fishing and food preparation, may require merely a single ayer expressing the relationship of fisherman to fish; at the same time, however, the fish are willing to be caught because the chief, who holds the name giving him the right to permit his kinsmen to fish at that place, has performed all those rituals for which he is responsible. (pp. 6, 32)

Richard Nelson's observations about how narratives encode the moral/spiritual principles that guide the Koyukon's daily practices provide a third example of ecological centeredness. Distant Time stories, as Nelson (1983) observed them being told in Koyukon villages, "provide the Koyukon with a foundation for understanding the natural world and humanity's proper place in it. When people discuss the plants, animals, or physical environment, they often refer to the stories" (p. 16). Survival in a literal sense means paying close attention to the patterns and inhabitants of local ecosystems. But local knowledge and the meeting of immediate human needs are subordinated to the moral analogs encoded in the Distant Time stories. As Nelson noted, the stories "contain many episodes showing that certain kinds of actions toward nature can have bad consequences, and they are taken as guidelines to follow today" (p. 18).

The ecological wisdom contained in mythopoetic narratives of the Hopi and, to cite an example of a Hindu/Buddhist culture, the Balinese also deserve careful study by modern thinkers concerned with the irony of why the vast body of knowledge we have accumulated in our libraries and now being supplemented (and overturned) by the findings of scientists and deconstructionist thinkers has not mitigated the destructive pressures on natural systems. The narratives that guide the Hopi in terms of technological practices, ceremonies, and ways of understanding the natural world as part of a spiritually unified, if not always harmonious, world reinforce the point I want to make here; namely, that we further imperil ourselves by not giving serious consideration to the common characteristics that seem to be shared by ecologically successful cultures. J. Stephen Lansing's (1991) study of the complex relationship between the Balinese temple system and irrigation patterns (which have worked successfully for hundreds of years), and the breakdown in the rice-growing ecosystem when Western agricultural practices were temporarily introduced, is particularly relevant. Also relevant to any discussion of cultural analogs of how to live harmoniously within the natural world is the way in which the Balinese have made the arts (dance, theater, poetry) the center of community life. As we begin to realize that a technologically centered culture, even when made more efficient, will further degrade the environment, it becomes all the more useful to have models of cultural groups who have taken fundamentally different pathways.

To return to the basic questions raised by these traditional, ecologically sustainable cultures: Do they provide useful analogs for modern people who live in urban contexts? Do they provide a means of recognizing our own taken-for-granted patterns? How can their wisdom influence the nature of the environmental education that goes on in every classroom?

If these questions are interpreted to mean incorporating the cyclical calendar system of the Balinese into the curriculum, teaching urban youth the Songlines of Aboriginal peoples, or incorporating any other specific pattern of traditional cultures, the argument being presented here will have been grossly misunderstood. This would be a case of copying, and copying does not necessarily involve learning what these preurban peoples can teach us. But I think there is much that urban cultures can learn from common motifs and patterns shared by these culturally diverse, bioregionally centered peoples.

All cultures, including our own consumer, largely urban culture, are based on mythopoetic narratives. But what appears to separate the reality constituting narratives of ecologically sustainable cultures from the master analogs that give legitimacy and form to our modern culture is the way in which the former possess a sense of moral coherence. That is, the relationships involved in all aspects of the culture—ceremony, use of technology, social activities, eating, giving birth, and dying—are morally coherent, and still grounded in the stories of "what life is, and what it can be." This is fundamentally different from our modern form of culture, where art, religion, economic/technical practices, and so forth are segmented and controlled by a narrow form of expertise. For us, art may be judged by a set of criteria very different from our segmented understanding of religion, and technological practices and scientific discovery may be at odds with the folk traditions that sustain what is now our attenuated experience of community. For the modern person, the part is not seen as an expression of the whole, nor is a specific activity (design of a building, clothes, use of body, etc.) understood as a way of communicating about relationships. The part/whole pattern of understanding gives more emphasis to recognizing relationships as a form of communication. The languages used to communicate about relationships—dance, dress, style of greeting, technology used to provide food and shelter—are thus moral languages. Although our languages are also used to communicate about relationships, we tend to foreground discrete objects, events, information, and the judgments of the individual. For example, the glass box style of urban architecture reproduced until recently in cities around the world communicated the modern way of understanding relationships. But the moral order reinforced by these steel and glass signifiers was that context, tradition, and ecological systems were totally irrelevant to (indeed, impeded) the need to express individuality on a monumental scale. In the same way most classrooms, in the name of modernization, have transformed what members of ecologically sustainable cultures would regard as moral/spiritual relationships into economic, political, and technological relationships and, finally, expressions of individual need. In spite of this cultural atrophy, the modern languages of science, technology, art, consumerism, and so forth cannot avoid communicating about relationships. Unfortunately, the moral imperatives derived from modern culture's most fundamental analogs represent human achievement as separate from the fate of the environment.

But the lessons of traditional cultures are more fine-grained than this. If we consider the moral/conceptual coherence of a traditional culture such as Balinese or Koyukon (before the impact of television and other Western technology, including literacy), we see that their technology, languages, forms of aesthetic expression, patterns of social interaction, knowledge of food production, and so forth are based on stories and patterns of behavior (analogs) that distil down to what has proven essential to long-term survival. That is, every aspect of cultural life is based on a sensitivity and respect for life-sustaining traditions—and one of these traditions has held that humans must continually strive to restore the disruptions that threaten what Marshall Sahlins (1972) calls the "balanced reciprocity" of life. Although he gives the term primarily an economic and social interpretation, it also applies to the whole range of relationships involving other forms of life. Negative reciprocity, which Sahlins defines as the attitude wherein one of the participants in a relationship attempts "to get something for nothing with impunity," characterizes the ethos of modern culture. The challenge of restoring the balance in reciprocal relationships should not be romanticized, as it usually occurs in situations where human needs are met at the expense of other forms of life. Gary Snyder (1990) understood this when he wrote:

Everyone who ever lived took the lives of other animals, pulled plants, plucked fruit, and ate. Primary people have had their own ways of trying to understand the precept of nonharming. They knew that taking life required gratitude and care. There is no life that is not somebody's food, no life that is not somebody's death. . . . Subsistence people live without excuses. The blood is on your own hands as you divide the liver from the gallbladder. You have watched the color fade on the glimmer of the trout. A subsistence economy is a sacramental economy because it has faced up to one of the critical problems of life and death: the taking of life for food. Contemporary people do not need to hunt, many cannot even afford meat, and in the developed world the variety of foods available to us makes the avoidance of meat an easy choice. Forests in the tropics are cut to make pasture to raise beef for the American market. Our distance from the source of our food enables us to be superficially more comfortable, and distinctly more ignorant. (1990, pp. 183-184)

This distinction between balanced and negative reciprocity might lead urban educators to see the cultural messages in the curriculum in a new light. My own examination of curriculum materials, as well as observations of teacher/student discourse, strongly indicates that negative reciprocity has become an ideal that frames how we understand the nature of the individual (particularly individual success), economic practices, purpose of technology, and just about everything else learned in the classroom. But the use of different criteria, like balanced reciprocity and long-term sustainability, as the basis for changing the form of environmental education being carried on in urban classrooms can still be reduced to giving students information—albeit, different and arguably more important information. In order for the information to be transformative in terms of actually changing cultural patterns, students (like the rest of us) need exposure to analogs—that is, stories and exemplary models of how different individual/cultural needs can be expressed. This is where the motifs (general patterns and characteristics) of traditional cultures may serve as useful guides in recovering ecologically sustainable practices in our own cultural traditions and in reconstituting others that threaten our future.

ANALOGS THAT COMMUNICATE ECOLOGICAL CENTEREDNESS

The argument that environmental education in urban classrooms needs to be radically changed, and that the direction of curricular reform can be positively influenced by an awareness of the characteristics of ecologically sustainable cultures, requires that the nature of analog knowledge be more fully explained. The clarification of the difference between analogic and digital forms of knowledge, however, also needs to be placed within the context of a sociology of knowledge account of how the individual's intersubjective self is socially constituted and experienced as the natural attitude toward everyday life. As I have elsewhere addressed this process, the discussion here will focus primarily on the nature of analog knowledge, and on examples of analog knowledge developed by ecologically advanced cultures.

The phrase *analog knowledge* is used here to refer to patterns that become the basis of future behavioral and thought processes. Analogs (or patterns) include the cultural group's way of preparing and eating food, greeting friends and strangers, using paralinguistic cues, playing a game, using technology, and so forth. They represent the knowledge of "what is" and how to act and think in terms of these basic cultural definitions—but they are contextual, mostly experiential and tacit, and involve redundancy, with the old patterns being repeated as reliable guides to future behavior. Analog knowledge encodes the patterns worked out over time for how to understand and deal with relationships, and its contextual and tacit nature means that most of this form of cultural knowledge will be part of the person's natural attitude. That is, it represents a form of knowledge that the individual may not be explicitly aware of.

Digital knowledge, on the other hand, represents the discrete bits of information that may be communicated as facts or data. In being abstracted from the analog patterns of cultural life, it is represented as a context-free form of knowledge (like data on an airline schedule or street crime) that can be universally communicated. Another characteristic of digital knowledge is that its communication reinforces the ideological and accompanying analogs of modern consciousness, which holds that rational individuals use abstract, context-free information (data) to constitute their own ideas about relationships and how we should act in terms of them. Where analog knowledge involves adapting the new to the familiar (the elements of modeling and redundancy), digital knowledge reinforces the analogs of modern consciousness, which are predicated on the belief that context-independent data free individuals to escape from the influence of past traditions, and thus to become autonomous agents of progressive change.

These basic differences should not be interpreted to mean that all forms of analog knowledge are socially or ecologically desirable, and that all digital knowledge contributes to false consciousness and ecologically destructive practices. Nor is the case being made that because traditional cultures rely more on analog than digital forms of knowledge they are, contrary to popular thinking, somehow superior to cultures that have emphasized digital forms of knowledge—though a strong case can be made that part of the problem that modern cultures face can be traced back to the overemphasis on abstract, context-free (and thus experimental) forms of knowledge. The critical issue in assessing either analog or digital knowledge relates to how it contributes to an ecologically sustainable form of existence. The double bind is that the tacit nature of analog knowledge makes it difficult to recognize. Digital forms of knowledge are accompanied by a legitimating ideology that makes questioning of its authority tantamount to opposing progress—which involves another kind of double bind.

Given these qualifications, I would like to suggest that the challenge facing urban educators is to make explicit the analogs or patterns that are taken for granted in modern culture, and to begin laying the foundations for analogs that meet the test of long-term sustainability. Making explicit the cultural analogs that are contributing to the destruction of the habitat is relatively easy, but the recovery and reconstituting processes associated with fostering a natural attitude toward life- and community-sustaining patterns is far more difficult. The following examples of analogs that seem to be shared by many traditional, ecologically centered cultures may provide a useful starting point for both the demystification process that needs to go on in every classroom, and for reconstituting the student's natural attitude toward fundamental relationships. While our analytic pattern of thinking allows us to organize the analogs of traditional cultures into separate categories, it should be remembered that the mythopoetic narratives of the culture influence every aspect of daily life—and even provide for how ambivalence for constituted authority may be expressed (Diamond, 1987).

ANALOGS THAT REINFORCE AN INCLUSIVE SENSE OF COMMUNITY

Ecologically sustainable cultures have evolved a wide range of patterns for expressing how the individual is connected to the larger biotic community. While the diversity of patterns seemingly defies generalizations, it is nevertheless safe to claim that no traditional culture has taken the pathway of development that leads to our notion of the autonomous, self-directing individual who stands outside the natural world. For example, the inclusive sense of community for the Koyukon is expressed in the analogs that govern all human/nature relationships. Patterns of behavior ranging from food gathering, walking, and even talking about the multiple aspects of the natural world are framed in terms of living in a world of moral consequence. As Nelson (1983) puts it: "The proper forms of conduct are set forth in an elaborate code of rules, brought down from the Distant Time. Through this code, deference is shown for everything in the environment, partly through gestures of etiquette and partly through avoiding waste or excessive use" (p. 240). The inclusive community for the Balinese is framed by the invisible forces that work in the upper world (inhabited by the spirits of life and growth) and the lower world (inhabited by evil spirits that cause decay and death). Humans occupy the intermediate world, and their activities must be directed to keeping these two realms in balance. The energy unleashed by this awareness is directed to maintaining the essential balance that allows the cycles of life to continue. At the end of his essay on the Balinese cockfight, Clifford Geertz (1971) observes that "the mass festivals at the village temples, which mobilize the whole local population in elaborate hosting of visiting gods—songs, dances, compliments, gifts—assert the spiritual unity of village mates against their status inequality and project a mood of amity and trust" (p. 29).

Clan names, use of kinship terms to refer to animals and plants, and the awareness that human power is limited and thus must be used with great care and respect for the Other—all these reflect an awareness that humans are part of an interdependent world. The failure to incorporate this awareness into everyday behavior is fraught with danger that cannot be overcome simply through the development of a new and more powerful technology. But the sense of inclusive community has other implications that influence how distinctive personal qualities are expressed.

Contrary to the modern conception of preliterate cultures as being authoritarian to the point where individual expression is thwarted, careful observers of both modern and traditional forms of consciousness present a profoundly different view. While traditional cultural analogs provide the models to which much of human behavior is to conform, they do not eliminate the possibility of members giving individualized expression to the shared patterns. Indeed, Stanley Diamond (1987) argues that the so-called primitive expression of individualization is "the antithesis of ideological individualism" (p. 160). After many years of field work, Paul Radin (1953) summed up the latitude allowed for the individualized expression of cultural patterns:

> Free scope is allowed for every conceivable kind of personality outlet or expression in primitive society. No moral judgment is passed on any aspect of human personality as such. Human nature is what it is, and each act, emotion, belief, unexpressed or expressed, must be allowed to make or mar a man. . . . Limitations to this expression naturally exist—but these flow directly from an intense and clear-cut appreciation of the realities of life and from an acute sensitivity to group reaction. (p. 152)

Writing about how individualization is expressed within his own traditional culture, Jamake Highwater (1981) notes: "The relatedness of the individual and the tribe extends outward beyond the family, band, or clan to include all things of the world, thus nothing exists in isolation. Individualism does not presuppose autonomy, alienation, or isolation . . . but the far more fundamental right to be yourself" (p. 172). Individualized expression for the gifted person takes the form of restating a tradition within the culture, just as personal growth involves acquiring a knowledge of the deepest wisdom of the group and developing the inner discipline necessary for modeling this wisdom in daily life.

METAPHORICAL LANGUAGE THAT REPRESENTS HUMANS AS INTERDEPENDENT MEMBERS OF A BIOTIC COMMUNITY

Technology, particularly computers, is increasingly influencing both the understanding and use of language in modern culture. And the linguistic trajectory we are now following is taking us even further away from what can be regarded as one of the chief characteristics of language in ecologically sustainable cultures. The modern emphasis on using language to communicate "objective" information through electronic networks not only undermines the influence that cultural context has on communication and thought, but also strengthens the erroneous view of language as a container into which we put our ideas and information. As I have argued elsewhere in this volume, the practice of fitting language to the capacity of digital technology hides its metaphorical nature—even as the promoters of the new technicized language continue to use metaphors in all areas of their communication that has not yet been mathematized. But their metaphors for understanding both technical and human processes are derived from machine analogs.

One of the characteristics of the languages of traditional cultures we have been considering is that the natural world is used as a source of analogs that become encoded in their respective metaphorical languages. The use of the wolf, bear, eagle, salmon, and so forth as analogs for understanding both the human's relationship to the rhythms of ecosystems and what constitutes appropriate models of behavior, seems to represent the deeper awareness that language is a means of communicating about relationships. The metaphorical languages that utilize the patterns of the natural world as the basis of understanding appear to possess two other characteristics that separate ecologically oriented cultures from modern ones. The languages that represent humans as interdependent with the natural world serve as a primary form of storage for the moral wisdom of how to live in harmony—even when it is recognized that "there is no death that is not somebody's food, no life that is not somebody's death," to recall Snyder's reminder that harmony should not be romanticized. Stories of tricksters (often represented as coyote), of humans being transformed into animal form (e.g., "The Women Who Married a Bear," "He Who Hunted Birds in His Father's Village," and the Songlines [Aboriginal maps of spiritual geography]), are examples of how patterns in the natural world are used to illuminate human weaknesses (pride, selfishness, failure to respect tradition, etc.) and to provide the moral patterns that people must live by. Often the behavior of animals was seen as source of spiritual wisdom for humans, and in vision quests the deepest truths and forms of empowerment were communicated to humans through animals. Metaphorical language, in effect, provided for interspecies communication, thus connecting humans at the deepest symbolic level with all forms of life. "Self-limitation for the sake of others" was not the narrow form of self-enlightened thinking that modern thinkers associate with responsible "stewardship" of the earth's natural resources; rather it was an outgrowth of ways of knowing that were attuned to the voices and wisdom of other members of the biotic community.

The second characteristic is that in utilizing the environment as the source of metaphorical thinking, the language becomes contextualized. "Contextualized language," as Jim Cheney (1989) notes, "is tuned to quite specific situations and forgoes the kind of totalizing coherence with which we have been so preoccupied in the modern world" (p. 121).

ANALOGS OF TIME

An examination of the traditional cultures identified here as having evolved along more ecologically sustainable pathways reveals a variety of ways of making sense of time; but this diversity does not include the linear construction of time that has become the hallmark of modern consciousness. That they have not reduced time to mechanically measured units, or embedded it in a mythic view of progress that allows changes to automatically deauthorize living traditions, raises the question of whether the analogs that encode modern ways of understanding time are not fundamentally flawed. The patterns of the dominant culture, which vary the unit of meaningful time from the individual's sense of immediacy to what individuals hope to achieve in their own lifetime (or what corporations hope to achieve within the time frame set by stock holder reports), seem totally out of touch with the temporal patterns of the natural world. How long did it take to accumulate the fresh water in the aquifer that supplies the San Joaquin Valley (now being pumped out at the rate of a half a trillion gallons a year)? How long did it take to evolve the genetic storehouse of plants and animals, and the topsoil essential for their (and our own) continued existence? The Onondaga pattern of making decisions that takes account of the seventh unborn generation expands the temporal framework for morally responsible behavior well beyond what is imaginable to modern consciousness. Ecologically, it seems to be more profound (certainly more sustainable) than our sense of progressive time.

There are other characteristics of ecologically sustainable cultures that help to put in focus our own patterns. The Australian Aborigines, as noted earlier, view time in a manner where the patterns established at the beginning of time are still reliable guides to the present (indeed, they still have unchallengeable sacred authority to tribal members who have not been "educated" to a modern form of consciousness). That they have lived on the land for at least 40,000 years suggests their sense of time should simply not be dismissed as archaic and backward, particularly when compared with the degradation that has resulted from approximately 250 years of the Industrial Revolution. The Hopi, Koyukon, and Kwakiutl also have creation narratives in which the original wisdom of how to live in sustainable relationships provides the point of departure of the individual's spiritual growth. That is, the patterns of time, whether represented as cycles of change or as the present reenactment of eternal analogs, lead to a sense of responsibility that connects the individual to both past and future generations. Survival of life systems, as opposed to our concern with consumerism, is the test of the tribal member's sense of time and centeredness.

Another aspect of traditional cultures that may enable us to recognize the highly experimental nature of our own cultural pathways is the way in which rituals, particularly the use of music and dance, are used as individual/communal ways of transforming the ordinary into the experience of the ineffable forces of the primordial world. The communal dance, rich in rhythm and bodily movement, transcends chronological time by putting the dancer into touch with the eternal cycles. The sense of temporality used to frame all human activity, whether it be the dance or technological practices, is summed up in Joseph Epes Brown's (1985) observation that "the ultimate bearer of culture is a person who is religiously human within the context of a traditional heritage" (p. 123). To put this in another way, time in ecologically responsive cultures is experienced as sacred; and the persons who experience time in this way (and sustain the proven traditions of their cultural group) are living lives that are in balance. This is profoundly different from the cultural patterns of the modern person, who views time as an unending quest to get ahead.

RELEVANCE OF TRADITIONAL CULTURES
TO URBAN EDUCATORS

An examination of how ecologically centered cultures subordinate their technologies to the sense of moral order that defines their existence, and how they have developed much further than our urban-based culture the spiritual languages of dance, music, and narrative (and made them a central aspect of community life), would be useful to understanding why our own cultural practices are environmentally destructive. It would also help clarify what modern educators can learn from cultural groups that would be labeled by many modern thinkers as primitive and undeveloped. The attractiveness of New Age thinking, strengthened by liberalism's emphasis on self-creating individuals choosing their own values and visions, may lead some educators to introduce into the classroom the practices of more ecologically centered cultures—like the third-grade teacher who filled the classroom with Indian artifacts, the smell of burned sage, and, later, had the students instructed in the use of astrological charts. The practice of borrowing and mixing cultural practices, unfortunately, reflects the modern form of liberal consciousness that is totally insensitive to the context and authority of tradition. Incorporating into the classroom the specific practices of a traditional culture, whether it be its metaphorical language, mythopoetic narratives, view of time, or forms of technology, may under the best circumstances lead to some understanding of how sustainability has been worked out by a specific cultural group. But the pressures of modernism that impinge on most students will lead most of them to view any understanding they acquire from the encounter with ecologically sustainable cultures as largely irrelevant to their own lives.

The problem of using the analogs of other cultural groups as part of the curriculum is further compounded by the narrow form of education that most teachers have been subjected to, where they too often expect reform efforts to be immediately translated into classroom techniques. Even more daunting is the fact that cultural patterns that reflect a deep understanding of our place in the food and energy web, when introduced into the curriculum, further politicize the classroom. Scientific and religious fundamentalists (albeit different genres of fundamentalism), advocates of free market forces, not to mention ordinary parents and taxpayers who take for granted the myths of technologically guaranteed progress and the anthropocentric universe, would be highly critical of any serious consideration of cultures who have worked out self-limitation and reciprocal balance as ecological imperatives. To put it more directly, a deep approach to ecological literacy, where cultural patterns and beliefs are judged against the criteria of long-term sustainability, will be a highly political process—and the populist tradition in American education provides little security for teachers who engage students in this level of demystification. A third challenge to educators who are seriously concerned with the educational/cultural implications of the growing evidence that we are moving toward environmental catastrophe is that the development of critical awareness and the initial (and often experimental) classroom modeling of sustainable patterns will be overwhelmed by the cultural messages that sustain the current economic and technological orientation. Immersing students in the multiple dimensions of decision making that involves a time frame incorporating the rights and interests of unborn generations (like the Onondagen's concern with the quality of life of the seventh unborn generation) would be eclipsed for most students by the mesmeric qualities of the latest Nike television commercial.

Keeping in mind the complexities that surround attempts to affect deep cultural changes, we still are faced with the givenness of the teacher's situation: passing on a culture that deepens the double bind for the next generation who will inherit a form of progress that degrades the earth's natural systems. At some point in classroom discussions, data about the condition of the environment will lead to the question of how we can act differently. This is the question that leads to addressing the patterns (analogs) of thought, values, technical practices, and social/ environmental relationships that are being brought into question by the data on the destruction of the environment, and the nature of the cultural patterns that might be more appropriate in the years ahead. This is where knowledge of ecologically sustainable cultures becomes critically important to the teacher who takes the discussion to the next step beyond presenting information about the condition of the environment.

Given the mix of ideological orientations that have shaped the teacher's background knowledge and way of understanding the current situation, the intensity of political forces directed toward using the classroom to compensate for the breakdown in other areas of social life, and just plain apathy, it seems that a useful way to address the possibilities of a deep cultural approach to ecological literacy would be to identify four different levels of environmental education. The background knowledge teachers will need, which has implications both for teacher-education programs and colleges of liberal arts and sciences, can thus be more easily identified.

Level One: Providing Information on the Scope of Natural Systems That Are at Risk

Information about the human impact on the atmosphere, biodiversity, soils, and oceans is critically important to putting individual and social priorities in perspective. Many teachers are already engaged in this level of environmental education. Television, newspapers, magazines, and an increasing number of university-level courses provide a basic level of information that teachers can introduce into class discussions. This level of environmental education, however, does not involve exploring the connections between the information on changes in natural systems (and events such as major oil spills) and the cultural beliefs and practices that contributed to them. At this level of education few students are likely to recognize what makes this information more significant than all the other information to which they are exposed.

Level Two: Use of Environmental Information to Question Guiding Cultural Beliefs and Practices

Helping students recognize the nature of culture (particularly how it is experienced as the natural attitude toward everyday experience), how specific mainstream cultural practices have altered natural systems, and the beliefs and values that legitimate these practices represents the second level of environmental education. It can also be viewed as the first essential stage of a deep cultural approach to ecological literacy. Whereas the information approach to environmental education is likely to be limited to science and social studies classes, the examination of the culture/habitat relationship can be carried out in all areas of the curriculum—including literature, the arts, and vocationally oriented classes. The ways of understanding technology, individualism, success, work, community, creativity, progress, and so forth within the dominant culture have a history that needs to be understood. These basic building blocks of cultural practice and personal identity need to be made explicit within the context of finite and, now, declining natural systems.

While imaginative teachers now use literature to foreground the current assumptions about individualism or how nature is understood, most teachers are still limited in their ability to make explicit the earlier thought processes encoded in the culture's guiding metaphors, their historical development, and how the ecological crisis now makes them problematic. Understanding culture at this level requires a deep knowledge of the culture/language/thought connection that is currently not part of their professional education; and the failure of liberal arts faculty to agree on what constitutes an essential core body of knowledge (and the failure to escape the hold of the modern form of hubris that has contributed to deepening the crisis) further strengthens the current belief that all forms of knowledge, in the end, must be judged by what is felt to be relevant to the student. A level-two approach to ecological literacy would require a shift in teacher education away from the Cartesian framework that has dominated the field since its professionalization at the turn of the century, and toward the more cultural and linguistic bodies of knowledge that illuminate the culturally mediating role of the teacher. Liberal arts faculty would need to redirect their inquiry away from the traditional focus on the achievements of humanity, and toward understanding human/environment relationships. This shift away from the traditional anthropocentric liberal arts curriculum will be essential if teachers are to have the opportunity to learn about the characteristics of ecologically sustainable cultures. The irony is that the current (and past) understanding of a liberal education excludes the study of ecologically successful cultures while glorifying the great thinkers who failed to recognize that humans must learn to limit their demands on natural systems to levels that are sustainable, or become extinct.

Level Three: Recognizing Analog Forms of Knowledge in Mainstream and Minority Cultures That Are Ecologically Sustainable

Information will enable students to participate in the largely ritualistic forums that now pass for public discourse; and making explicit the cultural basis of practices and beliefs that contribute to pollution and other environmental problems may contribute to minor changes in personal behavior, and to changes in public policy. But the really constructive aspects of environmental education involve being educated to recognize the forms of knowledge (including technologies) both within the dominant culture and within minority cultures that enable a community to fulfill its economic, psychological, and spiritual needs without jeopardizing the prospects of future generations.

Teachers, like the rest of us, need help in recognizing sustainable forms of cultural practice. That is, consciousness raising must go beyond criticism of what was previously taken for granted; the process must also include a recognition of traditions that do not have an adverse impact on the environment. The present concern with more energy-efficient technology is an example of a viable tradition within mainstream culture that needs to be nurtured. But what other folk aspects of mainstream culture are ecologically sustainable? And how do teachers help to reinforce these patterns? Equally important is the teacher's ability to recognize the cultural patterns evolved by ethnic groups now represented in most classrooms that reflect either the expression of ecological wisdom or forms of human activity that represent non-consumer-oriented ways of fulfilling individual/communal needs. Most Native American cultures still retain elements of their mythopoetic narratives, moral coherence, inclusive sense of community, sense of temporality, and metaphorical language that allow for the contextually grounded form of communication discussed earlier. The educational challenge is to bring these traditions into the curriculum in a way that allows them to be understood as sources of wisdom that everybody can learn from.

But what about the storehouse of folk knowledge of African American, Latino, and Asian American ethnic groups? Most of their traditions have been judged against the criteria of the mainstream, technologically driven, consumer-oriented culture, with the result that they have been viewed as both inferior and backward. We now need to reconsider their traditions in terms of more ecologically based criteria. Their respective ways of expressing an emphasis on family, how success is to be judged and competition expressed, may turn out to represent a more profound form of wisdom than Western prejudices have allowed to be recognized. The folk knowledge of these survival-oriented cultures is just now beginning to be given serious attention, but the current focus is primarily on those areas of folk knowledge that may represent alternatives to the failures of modern technology.

As part of their education to the curricular and pedagogical implications of culturally diverse classrooms, teachers now need to consider whether folk practices of the ethnic groups are part of the problem or part of the solution to living more harmoniously in an increasingly crowded world. Understanding some of the characteristics of the ecologically sustainable cultures discussed earlier may help teachers to identify the more obvious aspects of folk knowledge, but we need a major reorientation in our approach to learning about nonmainstream Western cultural groups. An approach to ethnic studies that illuminates ecological issues would help, but another need is to address how the marginalization of minority cultures may have led to the development of more convivial and interdependent patterns of existence. Until this knowledge can be more effectively presented in classrooms, teachers will be largely dependent upon reinforcing the dominant cultural patterns that are part of the problem.

Level Four: Learning to Experience and Value
Ecologically Sustainable Patterns

Learning cultural analogs premised on respectful relationships and self-limitation for the sake of others, rather than exploitation of the earth's natural resources, occurs naturally and effortlessly for persons living in cultures where all the patterns of signification are morally coherent and directed toward these ends. But learning these analog patterns in a classroom that is a product of the Industrial Revolution involves several double binds. Limited knowledge and a contradictory outside world, however, do not make efforts at this level of ecological literacy entirely futile. The new (and ancient) patterns will have to be learned somewhere.

Although the classroom is an artificial environment, the initial basis for alternative ways of knowing and being can be established in the student's experience.

With the rapid dissolution of the foundations of modernism (particularly with regard to the previously unquestioned belief in individualism, purposive rational thought, and progress), the task of knowing what knowledge should have authority in people's lives is now more difficult to determine. For teachers, curricular decisions are like plotting a course without fixed reference points. Although teachers must be careful about simply borrowing the analog patterns of ecologically sustainable cultures, they can nevertheless use them as a general basis for determining whether the cultural patterns encountered by students will be viable in the years ahead.

Let me be more specific about the liminality that surrounds this level of ecological literacy. If teachers know from studying cultures like the Hopi, Koyukon, and Australian Aborigine that they have a strong oral orientation that carries through from their respective mythopoetic narratives to how they utilize the life patterns of other species as a basis for understanding moral relationships, they would have a basis for concluding that oral communication strengthens community and a more contextualized way of thinking. Learning how to listen and to speak as part of an ecology that includes all forms of the life that are part of the larger message-exchange process, rather than as a modern, ego-centered individual, is far more important and complex than learning to read and write. While I am not suggesting that ecological sustainability will require the abandonment of literacy-based discourse, I am suggesting that if teachers give more emphasis to involving students in the patterns associated with oral culture, they may be reinforcing micropatterns that will be consistent with the macropatterns of an ecologically sustainable culture. Patterns (or analogs) that have been tested over generations in terms of the peculiarities of a local ecosystem are more likely to be learned through the spoken word than the abstract (decontextualized) and thus highly experimental form of knowledge contained in books. Long-term sustainability means, in part, conserving what has been proven in the network of relationships within which the problem of group survival has been worked out. Learning to listen to the community's bearers of folk knowledge, and to speak in ways that clarify and improve upon this knowledge, should be an essential part of the curriculum. The knowledge of how to listen, and to speak in ways that actively engage the participation of others, involves learning as part of the natural attitude the shared patterns of the community, and it is learned most effectively from people who can model the patterns.

A study of primal, ecologically oriented cultures could also lead to other curriculum possibilities. What modern people designate as art will have different content and form of expression in cultures more oriented toward communicating about relationships. Learning how to use imagination, knowledge of traditions, and aesthetic sensitivity to transform the material objects of culture (clothes, tools, physical spaces) and ways of communicating, from the ordinary and banal into the extraordinary and special, should be part of level-four learning. Modern art, with its emphasis on creating an object to be displayed and (to meet the highest criteria of success) sold, is as wasteful in terms of the earth's energy systems as it is spiritually impoverished. Traditional cultures, as well as ethnic minorities who have been made poor by our economic system, can serve as guides in how to shift our approach to music and dance toward a more sustainable pathway. Traditional cultures use these forms of expression as spiritual languages that connect the individual to the larger whole. They also represent forms of cultural storage of moral wisdom, and thus have a pedagogical function. There are analogs in dance and musical expression, and there are analog patterns in how to learn from others these forms of expression. They are generally learned in context, and they may be strengthened by critical reflection on modern practices. But they are not always learned well when taught within a framework that strengthens the critical judgment and autonomous authority of the individual.

Other analog patterns that can be introduced into the curriculum have been suggested in Deborah Tannen's recommendation for more gender-sensitive communication, in Gregory Bateson's way of understanding information exchanges and relationships as the fundamental aspect of existence, and in Michael Oakeshott and Ivan Illich's understanding of how technologies are learned through mentoring relationships. To do more than identify general characteristics of this level of ecological literacy would be to contradict the basic insight that learning, context, and long-term sustainability are part of a single whole. Teachers need a rudimentary understanding of what is essential for a morally coherent relationship between culture and environment, as well as an openness to the forms of local analogs that can be clarified, legitimated, and made part of classroom experience. The other generalization that needs to be repeated is that teachers should be able to develop the appropriate curriculum at each level of environmental education before proceeding to the next level. That is, starting out at a level-four approach to ecological literacy would not be appropriate for most students. And given the cultural nature of the ecological crisis, level one would not be adequate in itself.

SELECTED BOOKS AND ARTICLES
BY THE AUTHOR

REFERENCES

INDEX

ABOUT THE AUTHOR

Selected Books and Articles by the Author

BOOKS

1969. *The progressive educator and the depression: The radical years.* New York: Random House.
1974. *Cultural literacy for freedom.* Eugene, OR: Elan.
1984. *The promise of theory: Education and the politics of cultural change.* New York: Longman. (Reprinted by Teachers College Press, 1987.)
1987. *Elements of a post-liberal theory of education.* New York: Teachers College Press.
1988. *The cultural dimensions of educational computing.* New York: Teachers College Press.
1989. *Responsive teaching: An ecological approach to classroom patterns of language, culture, and thought.* New York: Teachers College Press. (Co-authored with David Flinders.)
1990. *Culturally responsive supervision.* New York: Teachers College Press. (Co-authored with David Flinders.)
1993. *Education, cultural myths, and the ecological crisis: Toward deep changes.* Albany: State University of New York Press.

ARTICLES

1965. Existentialism and educational theory. *Educational Theory, 15*(3), 222-230.
1967. The messianic tradition in American education. *The Educational Forum, 31*(2), 203–209.
1972. Education and its discontents. *American Teacher, 56*(7), 5–8.
1972. The uses of power in education. *Main Currents in Modern Thought, 28*(4), 140–145.
1974. An alternative proposal for the schools. *Manas, 21*(9, 10, 11), 3.
1976. Curriculum and our technocracy culture: The problem of reform. *Teachers College Record, 78*(3), 53–69.
1978. Educational critics and technocratic consciousness: Looking into the future through a rearview mirror. *Teachers College Record, 80*(2), 272–287.
1979. Accountability: The ideological-historical context of an educational metaphor. *Theory into Practice,* Summer, 21–32.

1980. Ideological continuities in technicism, liberalism, and education. *Teachers College Record, 81*(1), 293–321.

1980. The technological conscience: An essay review of Manfred Stanley's *The technological conscience: Survival and dignity in the age of expertise. Teachers College Record, 82*(1), 139–145.

1981. Orthodoxy in neo-Marxist educational theory. *Discourse,* March–April, 54–64.

1982. Reproduction of technological consciousness: Locating the ideological foundations of a radical pedagogy. *Teachers College Record, 83*(4), 529–559.

1983. The problem of individualism and community in neo-Marxist educational thought. *Teachers College Record, 85*(3), 365–390.

1984. Metaphor, education, and the politics of language. *Kairos, 1*(3), 1–22.

1985. Culture against itself: Nihilism as an element in recent educational thought. *American Journal of Education,* August, 465–490.

1985. Education and the politics of modernization: Implications for a theory of education. *Discourse, 5*(2), 39–53.

1988. Master Ideas in a World of Data. *Kairos, 2*(2), 45–55.

1990. Educational computing and our ecological crisis: Some questions about our curriculum priorities. *Journal of Curriculum Studies, 2*(l), 72–76.

1991. Educational computing and the problem of cultural amplification. *Journal of Australian Computing,* September, 30–33.

1991. An open letter to Maxine Greene on the problem of freedom *in* an era of ecological interdependence. *Educational Theory,* Summer, 325–330.

1991. Questions about the anachronistic elements in the Giroux–McLaren theory of a critical pedagogy. *Curriculum Inquiry,* Summer, 239–252.

1992. The conservative misinterpretation of the educational/ecological crisis. *Environmental Ethics, 14*(2), 101–129.

References

Althusser, L. (1971). *Lenin and philosophy.* New York: Monthly Review Press.

Apple, M. W. (1978). Ideology, reproduction, and educational reform. *Comparative Education Review, 22,* 367–387.

Apple, M. W. (1979). *Ideology and curriculum.* London: Routledge & Kegan Paul.

Art works: Teacher's manual level 4. (1989). Austin, TX: Holt, Rinehart & Winston.

Barthes, R. (1982). *Empire of signs.* New York: Hill & Wang.

Bateson, G. (1972). *Steps to an ecology of mind.* New York: Ballantine.

Bateson, G. (1980). *Men are grass: Metaphor and the world of mental process.* West Stockbridge, MA: Lindisfarne Letter, No. 1.

Bell, D. (1977). The return of the sacred? The argument on the future of religion. *British Journal of Sociology, 28,* 419–449.

Bellah, R. N. (1970). *Beyond belief: Essays on religion in a post-traditional world.* New York: Harper & Row.

Bellah, R. N., Madsen, R., Sullivan, W. M., Swidler, A., & Tipton, S. M. (1985). *Habits of the heart: Individualism and commitment in American life.* Berkeley: University of California Press.

Berger, J. (1979). *Pig earth.* New York: Pantheon.

Berger, P. L. (1967). *The sacred canopy: Elements of a sociological theory of religion.* New York: Anchor.

Berger, P. L., Berger, B., & Kellner, H. (1974). *The homeless mind: Modernization and consciousness.* New York: Vintage.

Berger, P. L., & Luckmann, T. (1967). *The social construction of reality.* Garden City, NY: Anchor.

Berger, P. L., & Neuhaus, R. J. (1977). *To empower people: The role of mediating structures in public policy.* Washington, DC: American Enterprise Institute for Public Policy Research.

Berger, P. L., & Pullberg, S. (1964–65). Reification and the sociological critique of consciousness. *History and Theory, 4,* 196–211.

Bernstein, B. (1971). On the classification and framing of educational knowledge. In M. F. D. Young (Ed.), *Knowledge and control* (pp. 47–69). London: Collier-Macmillan.

Berry, W. (1986). *The unsettling of America: Culture and agriculture.* San Francisco: Sierra Club Books.

Black, M. B. (1973). Belief systems. In J. J. Honigmann (Ed.), *Handbook of social and cultural anthropology* (pp. 57–84). Chicago: Rand McNally.

Bloom, A. (1987). *The closing of the American mind.* New York: Simon & Schuster.

Bordo, S. (1987). *The flight to objectivity: Essays on Cartesianism and culture.* Albany: State University of New York Press.

Bowers, C. A. (1974). *Cultural literacy for freedom.* Eugene, OR: Elan.

Bowers, C. A. (1984). *The promise of theory: Education and the politics of cultural change.* New York: Longman.

Bowers, C. A. (1987). *Elements of a post-liberal theory of education.* New York: Teachers College Press.

Bowers, C. A. (1988). *The cultural dimensions of educational computing: Understanding the non-neutrality of technology.* New York: Teachers College Press.

Bowers, C. A. (1990). How computers contribute to the ecological crisis. *The CPSR Newsletter, 8,* 1–8.

Bowers, C. A. (1993). *Education, cultural myths, and the ecological crisis: Toward deep changes.* Albany: State University of New York Press.

Bowers, C. A., & Flinders, D. J. (1990). *Responsive teaching: An ecological approach to classroom patterns of language, culture, and thought.* New York: Teachers College Press.

Braverman, H. (1974). *Labor and monopoly capital.* New York: Monthly Review Press.

Brown, J. E. (1985). *The spiritual legacy of the American Indian.* New York: Crossroad.

Brown, R. H. (1978). *A poetic for sociology.* Cambridge, England: Cambridge University Press.

Bury, J. B. (1932). *The idea of progress.* New York: Dover.

Campbell, J. (1986). *Winston Churchill's afternoon nap.* New York: Simon & Schuster.

Carroll, J. (1977). *Puritan, paranoid, remissive: A sociology of modern culture.* London: Routledge & Kegan Paul.

Cassirer, E. (1953). *The philosophy of symbolic form* (Vol. 1). New Haven, CT: Yale University Press.

Chapman, L. H. (1985). *Discover art* (Teacher's edition, grade 3). Worcester, MA: Davis.

Cheney, J. (1989, Summer). Postmodern environmental ethics: Ethics as bioregional narrative. *Environmental Ethics,* pp. 117–134.

Clark, W. C. (1989). Managing planet earth [Special issue]. *Scientific American, 261*(3), 47–54.

Club of Rome. (1972). *The limits to growth.* New York: Universe Books.

Davidson, D. (1984). *Inquiries into truth and interpretation.* Oxford, England: Clarendon.

Diamond, S. (1987). *In search of the primitive: A critique of civilization.* New Brunswick, NJ: Transaction Books.

Dissanayake, E. (1988). *What is art for?* Seattle: University of Washington Press.

Douglas, M. (1975). *Implicit meanings: Essays in anthropology.* London: Routledge & Kegan Paul.

Dreyfus, H. L. (1981). Knowledge and human values: A genealogy of nihilism. *Teachers College Record, 82,* 507–520.

Dreyfus, H. L., & Dreyfus, S. E. (1986). *Mind over machine: The power of human intuition and expertise in the era of the computer.* New York: Free Press.

Dupre, L. (1988, Spring/Fall). The broken mirror: The fragmentation of the symbolic world. *Stanford Literature Review,* pp. 7–25.

Education Research Council of America. (1972). *Technology: Promises and problems.* Boston: Allyn & Bacon.

Foucault, M. (1973). *The order of things: An archaeology of the human sciences.* New York: Vintage.

Foucault, M. (1982). The subject and power. In H. L. Dreyfus & P. Rabinow (Eds.), *Foucault: Beyond structuralism and hermeneutics* (pp. 208–226). Chicago: University of Chicago Press.

Freire, P. (1971). *Cultural Action for Freedom (Harvard Educational Review* Monograph No. 1). Cambridge, MA: Center for the Study of Development and Social Change.

Freire, P. (1973). *Education for critical consciousness.* New York: Seabury.

Freire, P. (1974). *Pedagogy of the oppressed.* New York: Seabury.

Freire, P. (1978). *Pedagogy in process: The letters to Guinea-Bissau.* New York: Seabury.

Freire, P. (1981). The people speak their word: Learning to read and write in Sao Tome and Principe. *Harvard Educational Review, 51,* 27–30.

Freire, P. (1985). *The politics of education.* South Hadley, MA: Bergin & Garvey.

Freire, P., & Faundez, A. (1989). *Learning to question: A pedagogy of liberation.* New York: Continuum.

Gadamer, H.-G. (1976). *Philosophical hermeneutics.* Berkeley: University of California Press.

Garson, B. (1988). *The electronic sweatshop: How computers are transforming the office of the future into the factory of the past.* New York: Penguin.

Geertz, C. (1971). Deep play: Notes on a Balinese cockfight. In C. Geertz (Ed.), *Myth, symbol, and culture* (pp. 1–37). New York: Norton.

Geertz, C. (1973). *The interpretation of cultures.* New York: Basic Books.

Giddens, A. (1975). *The class structure of advanced societies.* New York: Harper & Row.

Gilligan, C. (1982). *In a different voice: Psychological theory and women's development.* Cambridge, MA: Harvard University Press.

Giroux, H. A. (1981). *Ideology, culture and the process of schooling.* Philadelphia: Temple University Press.

Giroux, H. A. (1988). *Teachers as intellectuals: Toward a critical pedagogy of learning.* South Hadley, MA: Bergin & Garvey.

Goodenough, W. H. (1981). *Culture, language, and society* (2nd ed.). Menlo Park, CA: Benjamin/Cummings.

Goody, J. (1977). *The domestication of the savage mind.* Cambridge, England: Cambridge University Press.

Goudsblom, J. (1980). *Nihilism and culture.* Totowa, NJ: Rowan & Littlefield.

Gouldner, A. W. (1976). *The dialectic of ideology and technology.* New York: Seabury.

Gouldner, A. W. (1979). *The future of intellectuals and the rise of the new class.* New York: Seabury.

Greene, M. (1988). *The dialectic of freedom*. New York: Teachers College Press.

Habermas, J. (1975). *Legitimation crisis*. Boston: Beacon.

Hamblen, K. (1988). Approaches to aesthetics in art education: A critical theory perspective. *Studies in Art Education, 29*(2), 81–90.

Hanna, P., Kohn, C. F., Lee, J. R., & Ver Steeg, C. L. (1970). *Investigating man's world*. Glenview, IL: Scott, Foresman.

Hansen, C. (1985). Individualism in Chinese thought. In D. J. Munro (Ed.), *Individualism and holism: Studies in Confucian and Taoist values* (pp. 35–55). Ann Arbor, MI: Center for Chinese Studies.

Havelock, E. (1986). *The muse learns to write: Reflections on orality and literacy from antiquity to the present*. New Haven, CT: Yale University Press.

Heidegger, M. (1962). *Being and time*. New York: Harper & Row.

Heidegger, M. (1977). *The question concerning technology and other essays*. New York: Harper Colophon.

Heilbroner, R. L. (1972). A radical view of socialism. *Social Research, 39*, 1–15.

Highwater, J. (1981). *The primal mind: Vision and reality in Indian America*. New York: New American Library.

Hirsch, E. D., Jr. (1987). *Cultural literacy: What every American needs to know*. Boston: Houghton Mifflin.

Horton, R. (1982). Tradition and modernity revisited. In M. Hollis & S. Lukes (Eds.), *Rationality and relativism* (pp. 201–250). Cambridge, MA: MIT Books.

Howe, I. (Ed.). (1967). *The idea of the modern in literature and the arts*. New York: Horizon.

Ihde, D. (1979). *Technics and praxis*. Dordrecht, Holland: R. Reidel Publishing.

Illich, I. (1981). *Shadow work*. Boston: Marion Boyers.

Johnson, M. (1987). *The body in the mind: The bodily basis of meaning, imagination, and reason*. Chicago: University of Chicago Press.

Kay, A. C. (1991, September). Computers, networks and education. *Scientific American*, pp. 138–148.

Kidder, R. M. (1989, November 13). Drawing the human blueprint. *The Christian Science Monitor*, p. 14.

Lakoff, G. (1987). *Women, fire, and dangerous things: What categories reveal about the mind*. Chicago: University of Chicago Press.

Langer, S. K. (1960). *Philosophy in a new key*. Cambridge, MA: Harvard University Press.

Lansing, S. J. (1991). *Priests and programmers: Technologies of power in the engineered landscape of Bali*. Princeton, NJ: Princeton University Press.

Lee, D. (1959). *Freedom and culture*. New York: Prentice-Hall.

Leopold, A. (1970). *A Sand County almanac*. San Francisco: Ballantine.

Lotman, J. M. (1988). Problems in the typology of culture. In D. P. Lucid (Ed.), *Soviet semiotics* (pp. 213–222). Baltimore: Johns Hopkins University Press.

Luckmann, T. (1967). *The invisible religion*. New York: Macmillan.

MacIntyre, A. (1984). *After virtue: A study in moral theory*. Notre Dame, IN: University of Notre Dame Press.

MacIntyre, A. (1988). *Whose justice? Which rationality?* Notre Dame, IN: University of Notre Dame Press.

McClintock, R. (1988). Marking the second frontier. *Teachers College Record, 89*, 345–351.

Merchant, C. (1980). *The death of nature.* New York: Harper & Row

Merleau-Ponty, M. (1973). *Adventures of the dialectic.* Evanston, IL: Northwestern University Press.

Momaday, N. S. (1987). Personal reflections. In C. Martin (Ed.), *The Indian and the problem of history* (pp. 156–161). New York: Oxford University Press.

Mueller, C. (1973). *The politics of communication.* London: Oxford University Press.

Mukarovsky, J. (1976). Art as semiotic fact. In L. Matejka & I. R. Titunik (Eds.), *Semiotic of art: Prague School contributions* (pp. 45–61). Cambridge, MA: MIT Press.

Nelson, R. K. (1983). *Make prayers to the raven: A Koyukon view of the northern forest.* Chicago: University of Chicago Press.

NewsWorks: The teacher's guide. (1985). New York: Newsweek Publishing.

Nietzsche, F. (1968). *The will to power* (W. Kaufmann, Trans.). New York: Vintage.

Numbers Crunch'In. (1987, February 26). *The Oregonian*, p. E-1.

Oakeshott, M. (1962). *Rationalism in politics.* New York: Basic Books.

Ong, W. J. (1982). *Orality and literacy: The technologizing of the word.* New York: Methuen.

Orr, D. (1992). *Ecological literacy: Education and the transition to a postmodern world.* Albany: State University of New York Press.

Ortner, S. B. (1978). *Sherpas through their rituals.* Cambridge, England: Cambridge University Press.

Papert, S. (1980). *Mind storms: Children, computers, and powerful ideas.* New York: Basic Books.

Provenzo, E., Jr. (1991). *Video kids: Making sense of Nintendo.* Cambridge, MA: Harvard University Press.

Radin, P. (1953). *The world of primitive man.* New York: Abelard-Schuman.

Rogers, C. (1983). *The freedom to learn for the '80s.* Columbus, OH: Merrill.

Rorty, R. (1989). *Contingency, irony, and solidarity.* Cambridge, England: Cambridge University Press.

Rossiter, C. (1962). *Conservatism in America: The thankless persuasion* (2nd ed.). New York: Vintage.

Roszak, T. (1986). *The cult of information: The folklore of computers and the fine art of thinking.* New York: Pantheon Books.

Runkel, P. J., Schmuck, R. A., Arends, J. H., & Francisco, R. P. (1978). *Transforming problems in urban schools into a capacity for solving problems.* Eugene, OR: Center for Educational Policy and Management, University of Oregon.

Sahlins, M. (1972). *Stone age economics.* Chicago: Aldine-Atherton.

Sale, K. (1985). *Dwellers in the land: The bioregional vision.* San Francisco: Sierra Club Books.

Schneidau, H. N. (1976). *Sacred discontent: The Bible and Western tradition.* Baton Rouge: Louisiana State University Press.

Schön, D. (1979). Generative metaphor: A perspective on problem-setting in social policy. In A. Ortony (Ed.), *Metaphor and thought* (pp. 255–283). London: Cambridge University Press.

Schutz, A. (1967). *The phenomenology of the social world.* Evanston, IL: Northwestern University Press.

Scollon, R., & Scollon, S. B. K. (1979). *Linguistic convergence: An ethnology of speaking at Fort Chipewyan, Alberta.* New York: Academic.

Scollon, R., & Scollon, S. (1985). *The problem of power.* Unpublished manuscript.

Scollon, R., & Wong-Scollon, S. (1991). *Working papers on China, literacy, and American/East-Asian intercultural communication.* Unpublished manuscript.

Shils, E. (1981). *Tradition.* Chicago: University of Chicago Press.

Silver, C. S., & DeFries, R. S. (1990). *One earth, one future: Our changing global environment.* Washington, DC: National Academy Press.

Skinner, B. F. (1972). *Beyond freedom and dignity.* New York: Bantam.

Snyder, G. (1974). *Turtle island.* New York: New Directions.

Snyder, G. (1980). *The real work: Interviews and talks—1964–1979.* New York: New Directions.

Snyder, G. (1990). *The practice of the wild.* San Francisco: North Point Press.

Sohn-Rethel, A. (1978). *Intellectual and manual labour: A critique of epistemology.* London: Macmillan.

Solzhenitsyn, A. (1975). Repentence and self-limitation in the life of nations. In A. Solzhenitsyn, M. Argusky, E. Barabanov, V. Borisov, F. Korsakov, & I. Shafarevich (Eds.), *From under the rubble* (pp. 105–142). Boston: Little, Brown.

Stanley, M. (1972). Technicism, liberalism, and development: A study in irony as social theory. In M. Stanley (Ed.), *Social development* (pp. 38–52). New York: Basic Books.

Stanner, W. E. H. (1979). *White man got no dreaming: Essays 1938–1973.* Canberra: Australian National University Press.

Stojanovic, S. (1973). *Between ideals and reality.* New York: Oxford University Press.

Strong, T. B. (1975). *Friedrich Nietzsche and the politics of transfiguration.* Berkeley: University of California Press.

Thompson, R. F. (1974). *African art in motion.* Los Angeles: University of California Press.

Turner, F. (1986). *Beyond geography: The Western spirit against the wilderness.* New Brunswick, NJ: Rutgers University Press.

Tussman, J. (1960). *Obligation and the body politic.* New York: Oxford University Press.

Visual Education Corporation. (1985). *Creative living: Basic concepts in home economics.* Peoria, IL: Bennet & McKnight Publishing.

Walens, S. (1981). *Feasting with cannibals: An essay on Kwakiutl cosmology.* Princeton, NJ: Princeton University Press.

White, L., Jr. (1968). *Machina ex deo: Essays in the dynamism of Western culture.* Cambridge, MA: MIT Press.

Whorf, B. L. (1968). Science and linguistics. In A. Dundes (Ed.), *Everyman his own way: Readings in cultural anthropology* (pp. 318–328). Englewood Cliffs, NJ: Prentice-Hall.

Winner, L. (1977). *Autonomous technology.* Cambridge, MA: MIT Press.

Winograd, T., & Flores, F. (1986). *Understanding computers and cognition.* Norwood, NJ: Ablex.

Index

About the Author

C. A. Bowers is Professor of Education at the School of Education, Portland State University. His previous publications include The Progressive Educator and the Depression: The Radical Years (1969), Cultural Literacy for Freedom (1974), The Promise of Theory: Education and the Politics of Cultural Change (1984), Elements of a Post-Liberal Theory of Education (1987), The Cultural Dimensions of Educational Computing: Understanding the Non-Neutrality of Technology (1988), and Education, Cultural Myths, and the Ecological Crisis: Toward Deep Changes (1993). His current interests concern the interconnections among education, belief systems, and the ecological crisis. He received his Ph.D. from the University of California, Berkeley.

221